ALL THE WILD THAT REMAINS

ALL THE WILD THAT REMAINS

EDWARD ABBEY, WALLACE STEGNER,
AND THE AMERICAN WEST

DAVID GESSNER

W. W. NORTON & COMPANY

New York | London

For information about special discounts for bulk purchases, please contact
W. W. Norton Special Sales at specialsales@wwnorton.com or 800-233-4830

Manufacturing by Courier Westford
Book design by Chris Welch
Production manager: Anna Oler

ISBN 978-0-393-08999-8

W. W. Norton & Company, Inc., 500 Fifth Avenue, New York, NY 10110
www.wwnorton.com

W. W. Norton & Company Ltd., Castle House,
75/76 Wells Street, London W1T 3QT

2 3 4 5 6 7 8 9 0

FOR REG SANER,

Teacher and Friend

We simply need that wild country available to us, even if we never do more than drive to its edge and look in. For it can be a means of reassuring ourselves of our sanity as creatures, a part of the geography of hope.

—WALLACE STEGNER, "Wilderness Letter"

Most of the formerly primitive road from Blanding west has been improved beyond recognition. All of this, the engineers and politicians and bankers will tell you, makes the region easily accessible to everybody, no matter how fat, feeble or flaccid. That is a lie.

It is a lie. For those who go there now, smooth, comfortable, quick and easy, sliding through slick as grease, will never be able to see what we saw. They will never feel what we felt. They will never know what we knew, or understand what we cannot forget.

—EDWARD ABBEY, "How It Was"

CONTENTS

ALL THE WILD THAT REMAINS

GOING WEST

It was a summer of fires and fracking. The hottest summer on record, they said, with Midwest cornfields burnt crisp and the whole West aflame, a summer when the last thing a card-carrying environmentalist would want to be caught dead doing was going on a nine-thousand-mile road trip through those parched lands.

I was going anyway. For almost a decade I had dreamed of getting back out west, where I had lived during my early and mid-thirties, and as it happened the summer I picked was the one when the region caught fire. Drought was the word on everyone's dry lips, and there was another phrase too—"the new normal"—that scientists applied to what was happening, the implication being that this sort of weather would be sticking around for a while. Though I hadn't planned it that way, I would be driving out of the frying pan of my new home in North Carolina and into the fire of the American West. In Carolina, I had been studying the way hurricanes wracked the coast, but now I would be studying something different. Though my hometown's problem was too much water, not too little, I had the sense these things were connected.

I loved the West when I lived there, finding it beautiful and inspiring in the way so many others have before me, and at the time I thought I might live there for the rest of my life. But circumstances, and jobs, led me elsewhere. It nagged me that the years were passing and I was spending them on the wrong side of the Mississippi. But I followed the region from afar, the way you might your hometown football team, and the news I heard was not good. A unique land had become less so, due to an influx of people that surpassed even the Sunbelt's. The cries of "Drill, Baby, Drill!" might be loudest in the Dakotas, but they echoed throughout the West. The country's great release valve suddenly seemed a place one might long to be released *from*. And now the fires, biblical fires, wild and unchecked, were swallowing up acreage comparable to whole eastern states.

The plan was to leave sometime in early summer and aim my Toyota Scion for Eldorado Springs, Colorado, the place that had served as my first western home and a place that at the moment just happened to be around the midpoint between the historic fires to the north in Fort Collins and the historic fires to the south in Colorado Springs. Though there would be no one else in the car, I would not be traveling alone. Along with my atlases and gazetteers, I would carry a box filled with a couple dozen books. Over the previous year, knowing I would be returning to the West, I had also returned to the two writers who had helped me make sense of the region. When I mentioned the names of these writers in the East, I sometimes got befuddled looks. More than once I had been asked: "Wallace Stevens? Edward Albee?" No, I would patiently explain. Wallace *Stegner* and Edward *Abbey*.

It was kind of funny, really. Stegner and Abbey were both so firmly entrenched in the pantheon of writers of the American West that if the region had a literary Mount Rushmore their faces would be chiseled on it. But back east their names, as often as not, elicited puzzlement. When this happened, I would always rush to their defense. Wallace Stegner, I would explain, won the Pulitzer Prize for a novel one year and the National Book Award for another the next, and singlehandedly corrected many of the facile myths about the American West, earning him the role of intellectual godfather, not just of the region but of generations of environmental writers. As for Ed Abbey, I would say, he wrote a novel that sparked an entire environmental movement—have you heard of monkey-wrenching or Earth First!?—and a work of nonfiction that some consider the closest thing to a modern *Walden*, a book that many describe as life-changing.

But for all that, I wasn't sure at first how relevant Abbey and Stegner would be to my current life when I returned to their work a year ago. My goal was to read everything the two men had written, and I came pretty close. I did my reading in the small writing shack behind my house, a place that I'd nailed together out of plywood and two-by-fours. The shack sat on a marsh, hidden by trees and sometimes flooded during moon tides, and it was as close as I got to daily wildness. During my ordinary life I would head down there in the evening, maybe drink a beer or three, read a little, watch birds. But during the year before my trip, I was all but camped out there. I sat amid a growing pile of Abbey's and Stegner's books, biographies of the men, their letters, journals, photographs, and a gerbil's nest of my own notes.

What I came to believe over the course of the year, and what I suspected all along if I am honest, is that Wallace Stegner and Edward Abbey, far from being regional or outdated, have never been more relevant. What I came to believe is that, in this overheated and over-crowded world, their books can serve as guides, as surely as any gazetteer, and as maps, as surely as any atlas. It was thrilling, really, if you are allowed to use that word for reading. To see that as far back as fifty years ago Stegner and Abbey were predicting, facing, digesting, and wrestling with the problems that we now think uniquely our own. And that wasn't all. If the two men had just tackled problems and laid out plans, they might as well have been politicians. In fact, they were a lot more than that: artists who labored to make something great, and human beings who lived vibrant, rich, and often contradictory lives.

As i read my way through the year, I noticed a fundamental difference in the pleasure of reading Edward Abbey and that of reading Wallace Stegner. With Abbey it was the pleasure of being in the
company of a man who accepted himself as he was (with the hidden
invitation to do the same ourselves). With Stegner, for all his honesty
about the way we can't shake our own pasts, there was a vigorous
sense of trying to be more.

Reading multiple biographies of Stegner, you got the sense that
he charged, or at least marched briskly, through his life. Of the two

WALLACE STEGNER.

writers, his career was the more monumental, stretching from his first book in 1937 to his last in 1992, his reputation built by accretion over the decades through essays and biographies and short stories and novels, including the brilliant Pulitzer Prize–winning *Angle of Repose*, written at the age of sixty-two and kicking off the sort of late-life burst we have recently seen from Philip Roth. But while Roth's turf was the Weequahic neighborhood of Newark, Stegner's was the whole Wild West, and his considerable energy was directed toward both making art and trying to protect the land he loved. He did this in a style that was both inspired and no-nonsense. In *The Uneasy Chair*, his biography of his friend and fellow western writer Bernard DeVoto, Stegner wrote of DeVoto: "He marshaled facts with great swiftness and made them into generalizations, and he discriminated among ideas with the positiveness of one discriminating between sound and rotten oranges." There was something of the same briskness, the same intellectual vigor and sweeping aside of the inessential, about Stegner. He was an unrepentant workaholic, and delighted in crossing items off his lists, always working at the multiple tasks of writing, teaching, and environmental advocacy.

He saw the West as clearly distinct from the East due to its aridity and vulnerability to human incursion, but also because the land could be so hostile to those who tried to settle it. Many of his ideas grew directly out of his own childhood, a childhood spent migrating from the Dakotas to Washington State to a frontier homestead in Saskatchewan and then down through Montana before landing in Utah. The man driving the Stegner family's constant movement was his father, George, whose motivation was one well known in the West: he was looking to strike it rich. His father embodied a type of western character that Stegner would write about all his life, the "boomer" who searched for the quick strike whether in oil, gold, land, or tourism. In contrast to the boomer, Stegner idealized his mother as a "sticker," one who tried to settle, learn a place, and commit to it.

From these latter qualities the writer built the platform from which he both wrote and preached: commitment to place, respect for wild and human communities, responsibility for and to the land. Having grown up with a man who was the classic western "rugged individualist," Stegner spent a lifetime debunking that myth. And having spent a good deal of his youth in Utah, he was one of the few to see in Mormon culture an overlooked quality that made them one of the only communities to thrive in the West. That quality, surprisingly, was *sharing*. It's easy to laugh and note that this notion can get a little twisted when applied to, say, marriage, but it turned out that it worked quite well when it came to sustaining agriculture in what was, despite the insistence of many boomers, a desert. Stegner understood, and put forcefully, the fact that the West's greatest resource wasn't gold or oil or uranium or even land, but water. In 1920 drought drove his family from Saskatchewan, the place where the young Wally felt most at home, and he saw in his own past his region's future. He would have been saddened, but not surprised, by this summer's conflagrations. Nor would he be surprised that a dry place has become drier.

If there is a sense that Stegner's career was one vigorous upward march, Abbey's was, at first, more tentative. As a young man, Abbey read aggressively and compulsively kept journals, mostly morose things through which great streaks of light occasionally flashed. His temperament was depressive, though he preferred the old-fashioned term "melancholic." In the end he both blazed and stumbled through his career, exciting a cult following with books like *Desert Solitaire* and *The Monkey Wrench Gang* before dying at the young (some would say immature) age of sixty-two in 1989, and being buried illegally in the desert wilderness that he celebrated. While one always had the feeling that the writer behind Stegner's work had good manners, this could not be said of Abbey. Once, after trying to adhere to the more proper standards of *National Geographic*, he complained that writing for the magazine was "like trying to jerk off while wearing

EDWARD ABBEY.

ski mitts." And here he is after waking and climbing out of his sleeping bag in the essay "A Walk in the Desert Hills":

> Cocky as a rooster I told myself: you are an artist. An adventurer. A human man. Not some shoe store clerk, kneejerk liberal or kneepad Tory, insurance adjuster or group-encounter therapist or assistant professor of data processing at your Vocational Tech. No androgyne with retracted balls and frightened pizzle. So I told myself; and so I believe right now, and so it has to be.
>
> Arise. Piss. Pull on pants and boots. Build a fire.

Though often poetic and high-minded, Abbey seemed always ready to embrace his own id: his persona was lecherous, combative, unpredictable, contradictory. He was free with insults, too, and with boasts and challenges. All who knew him said he was actually quiet and reserved in person. Not on the page, where he could sometimes be as subtle as a whoopee cushion.

But he could describe nature like no one else. If he was often tagged with that much-overused encomium "a modern Thoreau," there was some truth to it. Thoreau said he spoke loudly because those he addressed were hard of hearing; if he crowed like a chanticleer, it was to rouse the sleeping. What stirs people? What wakes them up? These were questions that concerned Thoreau, and that concerned Abbey, too. Perhaps the greatest resemblance is between the shapely shapelessness of each man's greatest books. Abbey's *Desert Solitaire* tells the story of a year in the wild in the tradition of *Walden*, recounting the time Abbey spent as a ranger at Arches National Monument in Utah. There were many of these types of pastoral books before Abbey's and have been many, many since. But there was something different about this one. For one thing it was full of bliss and rage, evoking visceral responses in its readers. It had the ability, as the writer David Quammen put it in his appreciation after Abbey's death, to "change lives." It could make a salesman in Ohio buy hiking boots and head west. It was a book about spending a year alone in a government trailer out in a place full of giant twisting red rocks, a book about the rawness of the desert, a book about paradise found and paradise threatened, a book about wedging downward through the bullshit of modern, industrial life in an attempt to find the hard rock of reality. And it was a book largely about Abbey, or the Abbey character, through whom the reader vicariously luxuriates, lounges, rages, and delights. Built in part out of his journals, the Abbey on the pages of the book excited the imaginations of thousands of readers.

Abbey, like Stegner, defined himself as a novelist, and he dismissed *Desert Solitaire* as mere "journalism." But as the writer Wendell Berry once said of him, his finest invented character was his nonfiction self, and that self, like Thoreau's, was a "man with the bark on him." It is the fun of seeing this contradiction-filled self play out on the page that for most readers overwhelms that self's occasional idiocies (though quite honestly the idiocy was part of the fun). Abbey claimed the only journalist he admired was Hunter S. Thompson, and it showed. Like Thompson, he attracted groupies and wannabes, and like Thompson he sometimes devolved into shtick. Come see the hairy barbarian and watch what he does next. Too often his jokes came off like bumper stickers (which he admitted a fondness for) and too often his later essay collections seem slapdash, as if to cash in on his fame. But those who neglect Abbey's brains, or art, do so at their own risk.

Even at its silliest, Abbey's work, like Stegner's, never neglected that element that had gone missing in the writing of so many of their East Coast contemporaries: wilderness. And during the '70s, when plotlessness and metafiction ran amok, the work of both Stegner and Abbey was political in the broadest sense of the word. Here is what Secretary of the Interior Bruce Babbitt said about Stegner's biography of John Wesley Powell:

> When I first read *Beyond the Hundredth Meridian*, shortly after it was published in 1954, it was as though someone had thrown a rock through the window. Stegner showed us the limitations of aridity and the need for human institutions to respond in a cooperative way. He provided me in that moment with a way of thinking about the American West, the importance of finding true partnership between human beings and the land.

Both Stegner and Abbey would eventually be described by their biographers as "reluctant environmentalists," the reluctant part due mostly to their commitment to writing, but reluctant or not, they would become in very distinct ways two of the most effective environmental fighters of the twentieth century. And in their passion for the fight they showed their core kinship, even as their manner of fighting revealed wide personal and stylistic differences. While Stegner's political thinking was more sophisticated and restrained, Abbey's words had a rare attribute: they made people act. Monkey-wrenching, or environmental sabotage, has recently been lumped together with terrorism, but Abbey could make it seem glorious. After finishing a chapter or two, readers would want to join his band of merry men, fighting the despoiling of the West by cutting down billboards and pulling up surveyors' stakes and pouring sugar into the gas tanks of bulldozers, all of this providing a rare example of true literary influence at work.

It is worth noting that both famously western men were secret easterners. Stegner, well connected through his stint in the '30s at the Bread Loaf Writers' Conference, was among the first Briggs-Copeland lecturers at Harvard, and later spent almost all of his summers in Vermont. Abbey, the prototypical western wild man, was born in the East, near the town of Home, Pennsylvania, and didn't see the West until after high school when he hitchhiked cross-country. Both men were understandably unhappy about the career-deflating tag of "regional writer," but the tags have stuck to some extent. Like a few of the easterners I've talked to, Abbey once jokingly referred to himself as Edward Albee. "Never make the New Yorker's mistake of taking New York for America," Stegner warned. Abbey, as usual, was more confrontational about his geographic inferiority complex. He railed against being ignored in print and person. When a friend from New York City suggested that the problem was that Abbey was a big fish in a small pond while he, the New York friend, was a small fish in a big pond, Abbey wrote in his journal: "Perfect. This guy thinks New York is the big pond and the American West the small one."

The only confluence of the lives of the two men came in California at Stanford's Creative Writing Program, which Wallace Stegner returned from the East to found in 1946. Too busy teaching writing to involve himself in the even-then stale debate over whether or not writing could be taught, Stegner brought his usual level of commitment to the job. "It was like playing football under Vince Lombardi," said Ken Kesey, who began *One Flew Over the Cuckoo's Nest* while at Stanford. Among Stegner's other students were Wendell Berry,

Larry McMurtry, Tillie Olsen, Ernest Gaines, Nancy Parker, Robert Stone, William Kittredge, and a scraggly hillbilly with a master's in philosophy named Edward Abbey.

Abbey attended Stanford briefly, for just two semesters, starting in 1957, driving over the hills from Half-Moon Bay to attend classes. Stegner, a year before he died in 1992, had this to say about Abbey's time at Stanford: "He lived over in Half Moon Bay, so that we saw him only at class time twice a week. He attended faithfully, made great sense in class, had all his later attitudes well in place but did not express them quite so forcibly as he did later. . . . I don't think he was particularly happy at Stanford—indeed he barely broke the surface—and the reason was the reason for his later great success: he yearned to be back in the sagebrush and not hanging around in classrooms. I respected him greatly, both for his environmental views and for his often manic writing ability, and I think he respected me; but the circumstances were not the kind that permitted the growth of real acquaintance."

Stegner added that one of Abbey's responsibilities was to help in reading the materials of applicants for the next year, and that in that role he had come upon a novel focused on football by an applicant named Ken Kesey. Though not required to comment on the manuscript, only to rank it, Abbey couldn't help himself and wrote: "Football has found its James Jones."

Stegner ended his letter: "I never saw Ed Abbey after he left here, though I read his books with pleasure and we had some correspondence, reviewed each other, wrote blurbs for each other's books. I couldn't attend his funeral service in Moab; all I could do was send a letter that Wendell Berry read for me at the 'ceremony.' "

This was written well after the fact, however, when Abbey was already well established as an environmental icon. The truth is that for two writers who shared so many of the same loves and so much of the same subject matter, the two men didn't seem to make much of an impression on each other. "He has the most distinguished-looking bags under his eyes," was the only mention Abbey made of his professor in his journal. Later, in a book review in the *New York Times*, Abbey would say that Stegner suffered from "an excess of moderation," and that perhaps begins to get at the differences between the two. Stegner, born on a cultureless frontier, spent a lifetime making himself into a person of culture, and valued restraint and reason as virtues. Abbey valued something else.

Stegner remained generous about his ex-student throughout the rest of their lives, publicly praising his books and regretting that he had not offered more financial aid to help Abbey stay at Stanford longer. But one has to wonder if privately Stegner didn't find in Abbey that excess of excess that marked the '60s, which Stegner called "that mangled decade." The split between the two men was right there in their haircuts: the one sporting a neat, coifed, ever-whitening mane, not a hair out of place, while the other's hair grew ever longer, his shaggy beard ever shaggier. As the '60s began, the older writer found himself at odds with some of the young mavericks in the Creative Writing Program, notably with Kesey, who said of their split: "I took LSD and he stayed with Jack Daniel's." But it wasn't the superficial differences that increasingly irritated Stegner. He believed that the hippie philosophy was essentially phony, a false and easy view of life that ignored its hard realities and responsibilities, and when he sorted through the fruit he knew it to be a particularly rotten orange.

At core one man believed in culture while the other, in a very deep and ingrained sense, was countercultural. But for all their differences they shared common ground. While neither liked to be considered regional, their region deeply concerned them. "The geography of hope" was how Stegner described the western landscape, but as the years passed he felt a growing sense of hopelessness. Abbey also grew more frustrated, and angrier, as he saw the place he loved being despoiled. He came to believe that the proponents of growth were insane men who thought themselves normal but who didn't understand that growth for growth's sake was really the rapacious "ideology of the cancer cell." He wrote: "They would never understand that an economic system that can only expand or expire must be false to all that is human." Both men fought until the end of their lives to preserve the land they loved, but for both it was an increasingly desperate fight.

Would they be surprised at what the West has become? I doubt it. The region was already heading the way it has gone and they were among the first to point this out. True, they couldn't have known the full extent of man's capacity to alter climate and make the region an even hotter and drier place. But today's West is a kind of fulfillment of their darker prophecies, and if they died too soon to know the role that climate change would play, they were acutely aware of the way that the West's aridity made it more vulnerable than the rest of the country. Indeed, drought has helped aid massive fires and bark-beetle infestations that have already destroyed close to 20 percent of the region's trees. As for the boom in fracking and other mining, it would not have surprised them one whit. The West had always been a resource colony, there to be exploited.

That is the West I was headed toward. A place of startling beauty and jaw-dropping sights. But also a place in a world of trouble. It seems to me that anyone who cares to really think about the planet today has to hold both of these things in mind, to remember to see the beauty, and to still take joy in that beauty but not shy away from the hard and often ugly reality. And it seems to me that Stegner and Abbey, who after all walked this same path before us, are well suited to help guide us in this difficult task.

Robert Frost, whom Stegner got to know at Bread Loaf, wrote in "The Oven Bird": "The question that he frames in all but words / is what to make of a diminished thing?"

That is my question too.

In late spring I began to spend even more time out in my writing shack, surrounded by books, mostly reading but also checking in with the abandoned wren's nest above my window and staring out at the marsh where the secretive birds called clapper rails hid and let loose their sporadic, riotous songs. Samuel Johnson once said that the most important element of biography is that which we can "put to use" in our own lives. I agree. I have always been a selfish reader, and as the year went on I read more and more selfishly. As it happened, I too was a writer, a teacher, a father, an environmentalist, and so was greedy for what Abbey and Stegner could offer.

In late May I bought several maps, maps of the West in general and of the Colorado Plateau in particular. I daydreamed and doodled over the maps, planning out routes, circling places I had to see. And

THE VIEW WEST FROM THE WRITING SHACK.

then in June, before launching my larger journey, I took a couple of preliminary trips. In Vermont, I visited Wallace's only child, Page Stegner, on the lush green land where his father once summered and where *Crossing to Safety*, his final novel, takes place. In Pennsylvania, I was given a tour of Abbey's childhood haunts by Jim Cahalan, Abbey's biographer.

These trips were nice, but by summer solstice I was growing restless. There was an obvious missing ingredient in what I was learning about the two writers. "I may not know who I am but I know where I am from," wrote Stegner. Exactly. If any two people grew directly out of the places they loved it was these two. Vermont and Pennsylvania were fine, helpful. But neither of these were the landscapes that truly defined the men.

It is westward, of course, that you go to find Edward Abbey and Wallace Stegner.

And so in early July, I finally packed up my books and maps and headed west.

FIRST SIGHT

The land buckles and rises.

For a thousand miles it rolls out, sometimes up and down and sometimes flat like a carpet, all the way from the old crumbling eastern mountains. But then comes a kink in the carpet. A big kink. The continent lifts itself up, its back rising, and most *Homo sapiens* who are seeing that lift for the first or second or even the fifty-third time feel a corresponding lift in their chests. A feeling of possibility, of risk, of excitement.

That was what I felt, at least, as the West announced itself. What had been a sometimes imperceptible rise for the last few hundred miles suddenly became an undeniable one. The continent convulsed and lifted, mountains thrusting into the sky.

It is an inherently American moment. The same moment that trappers and early pioneers wrote about in their diaries. That mystical moment when East becomes West. The place where the country finally gets bored with itself and reaches for the sky.

Here is the seventeen-year-old Ed Abbey's reaction upon first seeing the sight he had dreamed of: "There on the western horizon, under a hot, clear sky, sixty miles away, crowned with snow (in July), was a magical vision, a legend come true: the front range of the Rocky Mountains. An impossible beauty, like a boy's first sight of an undressed girl, the image of those mountains struck a fundamental chord in my imagination that has sounded ever since."

My first sight came at about 130 miles out. A hazy blue outline like a whale half submerged. I would hate to argue with Abbey, but the mountains I was seeing were not really the front range, or at least not the front line of the front range, but the mountains behind them, mountains that, as I got closer, would be foreshortened out of sight by the view of those in front. These farther mountains loomed, bald for the most part after the weak winter but a few tiger-striped with snow. For someone coming toward them from the plains they stood as a clear statement of change, serving notice you were entering a different realm. They shimmered like a mirage but they were not a mirage. Ledge after ledge, ridge after ridge.

I rolled down the window and it was cool. A godshaft of dying light slanted toward me, coming from behind Longs Peak. The weather had broken, but all summer the mountains had been on fire, and those fires, the most destructive in the state's history, had scarred the hills both to the north and south of Denver. In June the mountains had been hidden behind a veil of smoke. And yet there they were, and, despite the fires, despite the drought, despite myself, I was feeling that old feeling and getting excited.

Most of us who were born in the East have stories about our first time seeing the western mountains. My initial sighting came when I drove out here after college with two good friends, and from the far back of a Toyota Tercel, where I had been banished after falling asleep behind the wheel in Alabama, felt my jaw drop upon seeing the hazy, trippy mountains of New Mexico. The next time I visited the interior West I came from San Francisco and the next on a train trip from Massachusetts to Denver, where I pulled in at night. But it was the fourth trip, my third from east to west, that stands out and retains something of personal myth. I was thirty years old and had spent the previous year back in my depressed and depressing hometown of Worcester, Massachusetts. I was there because my girlfriend of seven years had, with my support, chosen to attend medical school in Worcester, and I'd thought myself mentally strong enough to withstand a return to that dying place. I was wrong. The first few months I sunk into a morass of depression and unemployment, and that was *before* I found out I had testicular cancer. My operation occurred the week of my thirtieth birthday, followed by a month of radiation treatment, which sapped me of energy and hope. But it was in the midst of radiation that I was delivered from Worcester through a kind of deus ex machina. The December before I'd applied to graduate schools, but in keeping with the overall failure of that year I had been rejected by all of them. All except one. That one was in Boulder, Colorado, and by the following August, recovering now from radiation and growing stronger, I found myself heading there.

Declared clean from cancer, I was so excited that I drove across the country in little more than two days. My car, a Buick Electra, was overdue for inspection, but it seemed to make no sense to register it in Massachusetts when I would soon be living in a whole new state. The unregistered car lent a western outlaw element to the trip, as did the fact that each day, after my coffee buzz wore off, I turned to sipping beer. I drove through almost the entire second night in that manner, grabbing a hotel for a few hours near the Colorado line. Seeing the Rockies the next morning at dawn—the peaks white and full and completely unexpected—was one of the most elevated moments I have ever experienced. It hit me with a jolt: my new life! Had John Denver himself come on the radio I would have started weeping, and whatever did come on I assure you I warbled along. I felt real joy then, and hope. It was a feeling of coming back from the dead, a feeling of renewal, and it is a feeling that I will forever associate with going west.

WALLACE STEGNER SPENT his formative years in the West on what he called "the bald-assed prairie." Not so Ed Abbey, who grew up in the green skunky hills of western Pennsylvania, a lopsided land of hollers and thick vegetation. If our childhood homes imprint on us, then the place that first formed Abbey couldn't have been more different from the one that formed Stegner. One was closed-in enough to leave you feeling claustrophobic, the other open enough to make you feel both small and singular. One hunched up its shoulders and blocked the view of neighbors, the other laid the land open. One was, for all intents and purposes, a rain forest while on the other drought always threatened.

I knew Abbey's hills a little thanks to his biographer, Jim Cahalan. A month before my trip west, in early June, I'd visited him in the town of Home, where Abbey spent what he considered the best years of his childhood. I was immediately struck by the slant of the place, the sheer green, the lushness, the shade of the hills. Up that far north, the word *Appalachia* is not used much, but Appalachia it is.

This was the landscape that Abbey knew as a child, the place where he grew up without running water or electricity. Abbey would gain fame for celebrating a southwestern landscape that was sere, strange, red, and haunting, but he would not see that landscape until he was seventeen. The landscape he first knew was verdant, overgrown, and hilly, a place where farms always seemed ready to slide sideways off of the hills.

As we drove toward the old Abbey farm, Jim pointed out that while Abbey liked to claim he was born in Home, he was in fact born in the larger nearby town of Indiana, Pennsylvania, and his early years had been almost as migratory as Wallace Stegner's, his family moving constantly as his parents tried to make ends meet.

Abbey would remain close to his parents his whole life. Paul Revere Abbey, his iconoclastic father, was an unrepentant Socialist who cried when the Soviet Union fell and fearlessly spouted his political opinions, which imprinted themselves on young Ned Abbey as surely as the landscape. His mother was better educated and more refined, but equally tough. He would always think of her as "saintly," and Mildred Abbey didn't fall too short of that mark: a tiny ball of energy, she taught first grade, raised five children, and essentially ran the Presbyterian church down the road. In her spare time she took walks over hill and dale, played Chopin on the family piano after the kids were tucked in, and studied at the local college until she was eighty. Her own father looked down on the family of her husband. Paul, with little education, was an immensely capable Jack-of-all-trades, though the job he liked best was the solitary one of cutting down trees in the forest. His early years had been spent working in mines, where he picked up the politics of populist fever, and he later worked selling real estate, hawking magazine subscriptions, logging, farming, and driving a school bus on the side.

"Actually, he did pretty much everything on the side," Jim said as we pulled up to the old homestead.

Money was always short and the Abbeys were rootless. Until they moved to this farm when Abbey was fourteen. Wallace Steg-

ABBEY WITH HIS PARENTS, PAUL AND MILDRED.

ner would frequently romanticize his home in Saskatchewan, seeing it as his great childhood idyll, and Abbey romanticized this place, which he called the Old Lonesome Briar Patch. Here Abbey grew up without flush toilets, with a gun sometimes in hand, and with an intimacy with animals both wild and tame. He loved roaming the nearby Big Woods, where the boys trapped and hunted, and he loved books, reading hundreds of them, and baseball, setting up games against nearby neighborhoods. At home he did his best to avoid chores, showing an early gift for indolence. At school he was quiet, something of a loner, but people always suspected he was smart, and he had a gift for words right off the bat.

Jim and I didn't actually get to look inside the house that Abbey loved so, since it had burned down in the early '70s, but the old pump house remained, and looming above it was a huge gnarled, crooked evergreen, one I remembered seeing a sketch of somewhere in Abbey's journals. A horse chomped grains in the open cellar below the pump house. While we explored the place, a neighbor strolled down the hill to say hello. Her name was Cathy, and it turned out that hers was the family that had bought the house from the Abbeys in 1967.

"I remember that Paul was a very smart man," she said. "Mildred, too, but that was more obvious. Paul hadn't had much school but he read a lot. In fact they left a bunch of books behind when they moved out. When we first moved in we used their old washtub as our dining-room table for a while and stacked up piles of books as our chairs."

I asked her if she remembered anything else.

"I remember his hands. They were big hands. They could fit over a can of paint."

Paul and Mildred had five children, all boys except for Nancy. The boys were thin, rangy, tall, laconic like their dad.

Jim and I climbed into the car and drove about a mile down the road to the Washington Presbyterian Church. The minister there had once admitted to Jim that Mildred was the most important member of the church, himself included. While Mildred attended church every week, Paul Abbey never went. An atheist as well as a Socialist, Paul enjoyed boldly stating his opinions no matter the company. In other words, Ed Abbey's instinct to offend, to tweak, to go against the grain, and to state the bold and controversial was learned at his father's knee.

"But not only his father," Jim said when I suggested this. "In the 1960s, Mildred came out in favor of having gay and lesbian ministers. In the 1960s! Around here! At the time it was like coming out and suggesting that space aliens could be ministers."

We walked up to the old cemetery. Like everything else there, it existed on a slant; even the gravestones were propped up below with rocks against the slope of the hill. I imagined farming that tilted land, how having one leg shorter than the other might come in handy. The gravestone nearest to the Abbey plot had the name "Lightcap" on it, the same surname that Abbey gave to the title character in his autobiographical novel, *The Fool's Progress*. On the way to the cemetery we had driven under a train trestle, and I remembered a scene from that novel in which the young Henry Lightcap, Abbey's fictional stand-in, was instructed by his father on how to steal coal from the train. It was on that same train that Henry hitched his very first ride west, making it all of seven miles to the town of Sawmill.

This was just a warm-up for the epic western trip to come. Throughout his childhood, the West beckoned Abbey, and if Wallace Stegner lived the western reality, Abbey dreamed the western dream. He watched countless cowboy movies, read Zane Grey, and listened to his father tell stories of his own hitchhiking trip west, stories that glowed like legend. These stories also sparked a family tradition, a rite of passage that Ed and his brothers would all follow. Ed's first attempt came in July of 1943, when he was sixteen, the same month American boys not much older than he was were landing in Sicily. On that attempt he didn't get very far before running out of money and returning home to Pennsylvania. Then, the next summer, Edward Abbey finally broke free of the East, traveling for three months across the Rockies and to the Pacific, then back through the Southwest. It is not going too far to say that for Abbey that trip changed everything.

That trip west gave hints of the type of westerner Abbey would become. In the Pacific Northwest he got a ride with a Gary Cooper look-alike named Fern. Fern taught the boy how to siphon gas, let him fire his revolver, gave him his first taste of hard liquor, and then, finally, drove off with his wallet and all of his belongings. Undeterred, Abbey got a job canning peaches, saved up forty dollars, and this time was smart enough to stow his money in his shoe. In Arizona he found "a land that filled me with strange excitement: crags and pinnacles of naked rock, the dark cores of ancient volcanoes, a vast and silent emptiness smoldering with heat, color, and indecipherable significance, above which floated a small number of pure, clear, hard-edged clouds." He felt he was "close to the West of my deepest imaginings—the place where the tangible and mythical become the same."

At the Grand Canyon he walked to the edge where the land fell off and stared down, then celebrated his arrival by urinating over the rim onto a juniper protruding from the cliffside. Roaming the streets of Flagstaff, he was picked up and arrested for vagrancy and spent the night in jail. The next morning he was released after paying a one-dollar fine. That day the view through the open door of a Pullman car on the freight he'd hopped was dazzling. He saw for the first time "the high rangelands of the Navajos, the fringes of the Painted Desert, the faraway mesas and buttes of Hopi country." And then came New Mexico. He "stared, like a starving man, at the burnt, barren, bold bright landscape," a land that seemed to him "full of a powerful, mysterious promise."

For Ed Abbey, that first sight of the mountains was something he could never forget. He would write about it during his senior year of high school, prompted by his English teacher, and publish it in serial fashion in the school paper. And he would hold on to the dream of that landscape after graduating and enlisting in the Army, and hold on to it still while in Europe on mop-up duty after the war, serving as an MP in occupied Italy. Those dreams would continue upon his return home, where he passed a year at the local college, until they would finally be realized when he headed out to enroll, with the help of the GI Bill, at the University of New Mexico in Albuquerque in 1948.

Abbey's education would far exceed that of his parents. But he wasn't in New Mexico for school, not really. He was there to fall in love, which he did with great frequency, marrying twice in six years. Of course the place itself was the real reason he'd come, and, you could argue, his truer love. He roamed the red rocks and deserts in his old Chevy, living out his dream of exploring a still-wild West. These adventures culminated in 1949, with his five-week solo trip into Havasu Canyon in the Grand Canyon, where he slept next to a turquoise waterfall and wandered naked, and where he almost lost his life high up on the canyon walls.

It was love at first sight. And this became his topic in the main: the falling in love with the place and the fight to protect the threatened loved one.

His journal notes from this time reflect an expansiveness and intoxication.

"Love flowers best in openness and freedom," he wrote, a line that would later make its way into *Desert Solitaire*.

Clearly he had discovered his subject and, in his journal at least, the beginnings of his mature voice. Though it would take a few years for that voice to make its way onto the published page, and though there were battles ahead with depression, divorce, and the publishing world, it could at least be said that he had found his place.

———

Edward abbey's first trip west was about romance, novelty, surprise. Wallace Stegner's first trip from east to west as a young man was different. He was twenty-one and driving back after a year of graduate school in Iowa, so that, unlike Abbey, he was not heading into novelty but heading home.

Stegner spent almost his entire childhood wandering the West. Born during a visit to his mother's parents in Lake Mills, Iowa, he soon moved to North Dakota, where his father managed a hotel in Grand Forks, and then on to Seattle when he was three. Stegner's childhood was filled with rough years, but Seattle was a low point: Wally and his older brother Cecil were deposited in an orphanage so that their mother, Hilda, could work. The reason Hilda needed to work was that George Stegner had ditched the family, off as always in pursuit of the big strike.

By that relatively late date the frontier had been proclaimed dead, but George didn't buy it. He was determined to find the frontier, or what was left of it, hungry equally for its wildness and the riches it promised. The search to find the Big Rock Candy Mountain defined him, in his son's eyes at least. But while he fantasized about the big strike, Hilda Stegner hoped to find a place and make a living—as opposed to a killing—and settle.

The closest she would come was Eastend, Saskatchewan. In a way it was the closest they both would come. It was to Eastend that the Stegners, after reuniting and rescuing the boys from the orphanage, moved in 1914. Wally was five and they would stay there until 1920, when he was eleven. George went up first to stake their claim and then the boys came later with their mother. They arrived on a stagecoach driven by a man named Buck Murphy, who, as Stegner would never forget, wore a gun in a holster.

Eastend itself was still barely a town, born the same year Wallace was, and the Stegners at first lived in a derailed dining car. It was a place full of immigrants, of cowboys who had migrated up from the States, and of French-Indian half-breeds. There was still possibility in a place like that, and George smelled it. The early results were good. From their dining car the family moved into a rented shack and from there into a "four-gabled, two-story" house in the center of the growing town. While George Stegner would come to represent the antithesis of home in his son's writing, the house that he built with his own hands still stands and is one of the finest in Eastend.

Living there was a paradise of sorts for young Wally and his brother. The Frenchman River curled right behind their backyard, an easy stone's throw away, and they swam in it in spring and skated on it in winter. They also roamed unsupervised with a pack of boys, built forts, had "shit fights" with cow manure, put blasting caps on the railway tracks, and generally behaved in ways that would send today's parents into shock.

When the school year ended, the Stegner family would take the daylong trek south to their farmland, snuggled right up against the unmarked American border, where for three months they would live in a shack, sleep on the shack's screened-in porch, and attempt to bring in a wheat crop. Stegner later remembered those summers as a time of "savage innocence" and his and Cecil's lives were as "isolated, lonely, wild, and free as the life of hawks." The first couple of years the wheat crops were good ones, with Hilda's hopes rising that they had really found a home. Stegner remembered experiencing an "incomparable intimacy with the earth, for the ferrets and burrowing owls and magpies and coyote pups that we captured and tamed, or rather kept prisoner, and for the sunstruck afternoons when we lay in the sleeping porch listening to the lonesome wind in the screens, and dreamed of buying all the marvels pictured in the Sears Roebuck catalog." That life "had a wild freedom, a closeness to earth and weather, a familiarity with both tame and wild animals."

As it turned out, the young Wally had a gift for killing. By the age of eight he owned a gun, but poison and drowning were his preferred means and he would soon win the county award for most gophers exterminated. He killed prairie dogs and ferrets, too. Tiny compared to his burly, athletic brother, Wally would at a young age display a thoroughness and determination that would never leave him. He was driven in part by a desire to impress his hard-to-impress father, who, though happier in Eastend, was still restless and prone to bursts of violence. Stegner later bemoaned the fact that experiencing the remnant frontier had given him not just an intimacy with wild animals and a wild place, but guilt for his role in taming the place. On a larger scale this was being acted out by his father and their neighbors: they were farming untenable land and unknowingly creating a dustbowl. After two wet crops, the Stegners faced three years of hot winds and drought. But George kept putting in more acreage. As his son later wrote: "It was a gambler's system—double your bets when you lose."

When his final crop was burnt to a crisp by the rainless summer of 1920, George Stegner gave up and moved the family south of the border to Great Falls, Montana. Great Falls was remarkable to Wally Stegner for having previously unheard-of things like lawns and sidewalks and, even more remarkable, flush toilets. There Wally was ridiculed for his half-Canadian manners and clothes. It didn't help that he skipped two grades ahead, or that he was a self-described "runt." Books became a solace, and he memorized passages that he could still quote fifty years later. Despite finding some peace when lost in a book's pages, he would continue to feel intensely out of place until the family left Great Falls and settled in Salt Lake City during his teenage years. "Settled" might be something of an overstatement, since they moved more than twenty times from house to house within the city, as George, now running illegal drinking parlors in the various houses, tried to stay one step ahead of the law. Still, Wally felt that Salt Lake was his real hometown: it was there he began to excel in school, and there that he for the first time made

WALLACE STEGNER ON THE TENNIS
TEAM AT THE UNIVERSITY OF UTAH.

lifelong friends. In his senior year of high school the runt suddenly
shot up, growing six inches. Finally having found a place where he
fit in, he had no interest in going anywhere else, and for college he
attended the University of Utah. Belonging to a place, after a life of
movement, was something to covet.

Wallace Stegner later wrote that he would have been quite content staying in Salt Lake for the rest of his life, rising up through the
ranks of the linoleum and floor-covering's store where he worked
and marrying his local sweetheart. Perhaps he would have. Instead
a generous professor saw promise in him and finagled a teaching
assistantship in the English Department at the University of Iowa.
It was that move eastward that let Stegner begin to understand how

much the West defined him. His first fall in Iowa was a rainy one, and there, in that green, wet place he began to miss "earth colors—tan, rusty, red, toned white . . ." Away from the region he grew up in, he saw that it had created him. He might not yet know who he was, but he knew where he was from. Furthermore, as a budding writer, he began to recognize the West as his subject.

It was on the drive back from Iowa that his eyes began to open. The fictional portrayal of that return home is one of the climactic scenes of his novel *The Big Rock Candy Mountain*. As he leaves Iowa behind, the young Bruce Mason, modeled on the young Wallace Stegner, finds himself questioning the whole idea of home. He curses his father's vagabond instincts and wishes he was "going home to a place where the associations of twenty-two years were collected together." Bruce envies those who have lived in only one place, and as he drives he ties himself into knots, all but convincing himself that the notion of home doesn't really exist. But then, suddenly, the land rises and starts to take on a familiar look. The air grows drier, the towns farther apart, the colors more sere and less green. It is then that it occurs to Stegner that for him home is not a particular house or town but an entire region. He settles on a new definition of himself: "He was a westerner, whatever that was."

What did that mean, exactly? Different things to different people, of course. But it would fall to Stegner, and in many ways was his life's work, to clarify what it meant to most. "Scale is the first and easiest of the West's lessons," he would write, and by that he meant getting used to the larger, less cozy, "inhuman" scale of the natural world in the West. Similar to this idea, but slightly different, is the concept of space: "In the West it is impossible to be unconscious of or indifferent to space," he wrote. Space "continues to suggest unrestricted freedom, unlimited opportunity for testings and heroism, a continuing need for self-reliance and physical competence." By space he meant the distance between things: people, buildings, towns. Space lent people "the dignity of rareness."

Then there was the look of the place, a look that could take a while for a non-westerner to appreciate. "Colors and form are harder," he said, and they are for those raised to see comfort in green. Of course, the reason things aren't green is because they are dry, and dryness was a note Stegner played over and over in defining his home region.

He also realized something else about the West: a lot of the living took place outdoors. The home he was returning to was a place of constant physical challenge, of hardship. It rose up, Stegner often said, like a dare.

D ROUGHT HAD BEEN one of Wallace Stegner's great themes, and that theme was playing out over much of the country in the summer of 2012. I had seen evidence of it in the burnt Midwestern cornfields, and more when I arrived in St. Louis. There I stayed at the home of my friend Tom, and he took me out to a park near his house where we walked through the woods down to a spur of the Missouri River. Or rather what was left of the spur: it looked more riverbed than river. In fact the Missouri, the waterway that had been the gateway to the West, that had been the path that Lewis and Clark traveled on, was, as it neared St. Louis, at a historic low.

The next morning I got up at dawn and drove through the long, interminable flat to the west of St. Louis, a flat that is in reality a barely noticeable rise. I breathed the slaughterhouse stink and passed the miles of wind turbines that weren't there when I'd last made this trip and looked up at a looming billboard that hollered down: IF YOU DIE TODAY WHERE WILL YOU SPEND ETERNITY? ("In the ground," I answered out loud.) In the middle of Kansas, I was pulled over for speeding (which didn't stop me from speeding again as I raced toward the mountains after hitting the Colorado line). After my drive from St. Louis, I spent the night at my friend Randy's house in Denver, but I was out of the house before he woke, beating the morning traffic north, eager to get back to the small mountain town of Eldorado Springs, ten miles south of Boulder. This was the town where I had settled in a blue gingerbread cabin after my escape from Worcester. For me it was a necessary first stop in the West.

I can't claim that I felt quite Abbey's level of intoxication as I drove back into Eldorado Springs on my first morning. But some of the old sensations came back from that distant fall when I'd moved there, over twenty years before, a time that was in many ways the most exciting—the most *alive*—of my life.

The canyons and mountains loomed above me. *Eldorado.* I used to laugh about the name. It was perfect. The anti-Worcester. I had spent my twenties trying to be a writer but before that fall my writing had come in fits and starts. Then suddenly, living below those canyon walls, I wrote a draft of a book straight through. As it poured off my pen I was half-convinced that it was the place itself that had done it.

It had been a glorious fall. When I was done with those long writing sessions at my desk, I would hike into the great cleaved canyon of the park, not a hundred yards from my front door, and study the trees and birds and rocks. I wanted to know everything about my new home. I watched swifts carve the air above the mountain meadows and water ouzels, called dippers, do deep knee bends in the creek, and once I saw a ringtail scramble up a scree pile. I hiked the squiggly red trail that led almost from my door up into the mountains, gasping for air from the altitude at first but with each day getting stronger and more acclimated. Before long I was running the trails instead of walking them. In the afternoons I took baptismal baths in South Boulder Creek, stripping down to my boxers, parting two tamarisk bushes like a curtain, and dipping into my tub behind a pink-purple rock. When I climbed out of the water I trembled with cold.

All in all, it would be hard to exaggerate how *transformed* I felt. It was not just being healthy again or the new life I found there. I felt, rather, like I had become a new person. A kind of giddiness about where I lived came over me, a definite sense of liberation. Edward Abbey spoke of a chord being rung, as if he'd found a match for something inside him in his new landscape. It would not be going too far to say that I knew a little of how he felt. I was coming back from the dead after all, and playing out an essential American trope: heading west to remake myself.

Now, returning to Eldorado Springs, I felt memories flood back in, the memories aided by the weather. We were in the midst of the hottest summer on record, and just a week before the residents of Denver had experienced an unheard-of five consecutive 100-degree days. But a cold front had preceded my arrival, sweeping out the heat, and for one day at least it felt just like that long-ago fall, cool almost cold air blowing down the canyon. The smells and the nap of the air were familiar: the lack of humidity, the dryness, the smell of sage, the crumbly plants all around. Everything so clear in the dry air. I do not pretend to Stegner's perspicacity, and I can't claim that I had any immediate revelations about the landscapes of the East and West when I arrived two decades before. But I did notice that something was different about my new home. The air, for one. My nose had never been so dry, my hair so flat, and my heart, not accustomed to the altitude, never so ready to trill off into palpitation.

Eldorado Springs is a town of dirt roads and maybe a hundred cottages. It is also home to a state park, which I now pulled into. The dirt road—and the roaring creek—run down through a canyon of salmon-streaked rock, and when I climbed out of the car the rocks rose so high above me that I had to bend my head all the way back to see their tops. I took a short walk, stopping on the shaky wooden bridge that spanned the water. Because dryness so defines the West, so does the water that flows through that dryness like lifeblood. Tree swallows shot out over the creek, feasting on insects and exposing their white bellies. This was the same creek where I saw the water ouzels dip, the creek where I took my daily baths that long-ago fall.

Swollen by the recent rains, it spilled over the sides, cold and clear. I had the park to myself except for the rock climbers, two hundred feet up, doing their insane death-defying thing, wedging fingers into cracks before hefting their bodies upward.

I pulled my bike off the back of the car and pedaled out of the park to the middle of the tiny town. Eldorado's famous spring water used to come straight out of a hose in the side of the wall of an old building in the town center. Now it had been rigged up as a kind of self-service device where you needed to pay twenty-five cents. I dropped in my quarter and filled my water bottle and then started the climb back into the park. The road headed up, parallel to the creek, and I climbed with it, breathing heavily. *Up* is where everything seems to head in this landscape, unless of course it is heading down. So many of my memories of this place were of climbing, of sweating to gain elevation. I was not a father yet, nor a teacher, was barely a writer, really. But I was after something and I think I knew, even then, what that something was.

"Transcendence," Abbey wrote in his journal. "It is this which haunts me night and day. The desire to transcend my own limits, to exceed myself, to become more than I am. Why? I don't know. To transcend this job, this work, this place, this kind of life—for the sake of something superlative, supreme, exalting."

I stared up at the purple rock faces streaked yellow with lichen from bird dung. A small ponderosa pine clung to the steep wall, growing almost horizontally out of the sheer fountain sandstone. Near the top of the road the creek flattened out and the water, no longer descending and gushing over rock, turned a copper color. I leaned my bike against the visitor center and watched two ruby-throated hummingbirds chase each other: the green backs, the zigzag speed, the blur of the wings. One stopped to drink and hovered, entirely still except for the wings, leaning its head back like a kingfisher. I went inside and soon was talking to a woman behind the desk, a ranger named Chelsea, about the recent fires and record heat, and then, abruptly, found myself laughing out loud when I saw the book behind her on her desk. It was, of course, *Desert Solitaire*.

Upon first spotting the book it seemed like a great coincidence, a talisman of sorts. But back outside, biking down not up, I understood that it really wasn't such a big deal. It sometimes seems that it's required by law for every western ranger to keep *Desert Solitaire* close by, like having a handy fire extinguisher. It's a book that has created more than its share of rangers, and certainly has created plenty of nouveau westerners.

When I'd lived here last I was full, maybe stuffed, with the romance of the place. We've all heard the songs and stories of the mythic pull of the American West, and the oft-repeated narratives of the easterners who go west to re-create themselves. It's there in the histories and the Westerns, in both high culture and low, from Teddy Roosevelt leaving behind what he called "the taint of Eastern effeminacy" to become the most manly of manly men, to John Denver warbling, "He was born in the summer of his twenty-seventh year, coming home to a place he'd never been before." In all of these accounts there's a sense of the almost religious conversion that infects so many of those who leave behind their old places and head west to find home.

I felt it too, though with a particular twist. While those who redefine themselves in the West have been much chronicled by pop singers, historians, moviemakers, and artists, I was part of a less-noted group of migrants. This smaller group finds not just their geographical home in the West, but their literary one. Back then I thought my brand of western awakening unusual, but I now recognize myself as a type. The type I was, the apprentice literary westerner, was as common as sagebrush, and if you were to examine the bedside table of that type, over the last thirty years, you would find, depending on the exact date, reading material like that which soon started piling up on mine: Marc Reisner's *Cadillac Desert*, Rick Bass's *The Watch*, Terry Tempest Williams's *Refuge*, Charles Bowden's *Red Line*, Leslie

Marmon Silko's *Ceremony*, Doug Peacock's *Grizzly Years*, and Pam Houston's *Cowboys Are My Weakness*.

At the time of my arrival in the West, in August of 1991, I hadn't yet read any of those books, nor had I read a word of Stegner. But I did already have one such book packed in my luggage in the trunk of the Buick Electra. It was a battered and dog-eared copy of Abbey's *Desert Solitaire*, an old mass-market paperback with its spine held together by duct tape, and it would prove a fine guide to my new landscape. I had picked it up a couple of years before during an earlier trip west, and its effect was immediate. While car camping in Lassen Volcanic National Park in California, I read *Desert Solitaire* almost straight through, and when the book's author suggested that car camping was not really camping at all, I took his challenge and headed, for the first time in my life, alone into the backcountry. I spent that uneasy night wide-awake, hearing grizzlies in the footfall of every deer that grazed near my campsite by the lake.

I came to Ed Abbey relatively late, already twenty-eight when I made that camping trip. In this way I was spared the worst of the cultish emulation that tends to strike first-time Abbey readers: the buying of an old pickup, the entry-level monkeywrenching, the constant over-the-top exhortations about fighting the man. It is true that I began to eat refried beans from a can during my year in Eldorado Springs, a dietary choice directly influenced by reading Abbey. But what attracted me to the man were not the externals but lines like this: "On this bedrock of animal faith I take my stand."

And this: "I am here not only to evade for a while the clamor and filth and confusion of the cultural apparatus but also to confront, immediately and directly if possible, the bare bones of existence, the elemental and fundamental, the bedrock which sustains us."

And: "Simply breathing, in a place like this, arouses the appetite."

I liked the way the sentences rang out, an anthem, or so it seemed to me at the time, of my own return to animal health.

———

To see the romance of the West isn't difficult. Most Americans grow up steeped in it. Indeed, thanks to Hollywood, most humans do.

To see the reality of the West takes somewhat sharper eyes.

Wallace Stegner spent a lifetime ripping aside the veils of western myths and rationalizations, starting with the ugly first facts of extinction: "No one who has ever studied western history can cling to the belief that the Nazis invented genocide." Stegner knew that the same impulse to conquest remained very much alive. "The West does not need to explore its myths much further," he wrote, "it has already relied on them too long."

Behind this sometimes cutting criticism of his home region there lurked a question. The question stayed with Wallace Stegner his whole life: how could human beings best inhabit the massive, challenging, and unique landscape west of the 100th meridian?

For starters, he knew how we *shouldn't* inhabit it. He knew this instinctively, from childhood, but he also knew it from long study and thought. We shouldn't inhabit it like a bunch of drunken raiders. We shouldn't come to a place, core it out, and leave behind the husk. Both his experience and his studies had taught him that this had historically been the most common relationship of man to western land, or at least of post-aboriginal man. Men came to the West to get something and get out. At that they had done a fine job, masters of extraction. One of the first things they extracted from the West, for instance, had been beavers, and they had done so at such a startling clip that the trade went from boom to nonexistent in less than a decade. Ditto buffalo, trees, gold, silver, you name it. They approached the new land with a kind of chronic rapacity, a gnawing hunger.

That was how it was: humans went to a place, took from it, left the place behind. Even western agriculture, to Stegner's mind, most often fit this bill. He had learned this firsthand from the wheat fields of Saskatchewan. His family had tilled the dry land without any deeper understanding of its ecology, destroying the topsoil and leaving behind their very own dustbowl, just as thousands of other families were creating dustbowls around the West. In his unpublished autobiography, Stegner writes of his own culpability: "While shooting, trapping, drowning out, snaring, and poisoning the gophers, we also did unforgivable damage to the prairie dogs, black footed ferrets, badgers, and other members of the wild community on the prairie, and we helped prepare a future dust bowl by plowing up buffalo grass that should never have been plowed, and that had to be restored to grass, at great provincial expense, in the 1930s."

This was not malicious, but it was not intelligent, either. It was certainly not, in the language of the present, sustainable. Topsoil from denuded farms all over the West flowed sludgelike down western rivers and by the 1930s dust from western lands was announcing its own disaster in the great clouds that blew all the way back to Washington, DC.

This was the West that Stegner knew in his bones, having lived out this essential western drama. He had watched it destroy not just the land but his family. Watched his mother's desperate attempts to root down, to make a home, as his father, beguiled by his own dreams, moved on in hopes of the next strike. Specifically, he had watched the damage that false hope and illusion could bring to human lives. All the pretending and the myths were, to his eye, no more real than the false fronts of the towns in Hollywood westerns.

To combat this, one of Stegner's primary goals was to strip away myth. To see things as they were. The West, Americans had long been told, was the Garden of the World, a kind of American Eden. The West was a Promised Land, a place of new starts and possibilities, a place that may at first seem dry but where, the boosters and their scientist backers told pioneers in the 1800s, "rain follows the plow"—that is, where cultivation of the land would lead naturally to more rainfall. Doozies like this were presented as fact, one of the many dreams sold to entice people. But the reality that settlers found was quite different. They found, with a few exceptions, vast arid and semiarid lands of wildly varying landscapes and violent weather extremes, held together by one thing, what Stegner called "the unity of drouth."

Drouth, or drought, defined the West. Stegner wrote: "With local and minor exceptions, the lands beyond the hundredth meridian received less than twenty inches of rainfall, and twenty inches was the minimum for unaided agriculture." This was the fact, not the myth, but it was a fact that was not acceptable to "the apostles of progress," both in government and business, who pushed for westward expansion. The critical mistake, in Stegner's mind, was taking habits and lessons learned in the wet, green East and transplanting them to the dry West. The most basic of those mistakes, born of illusion, was the Homestead Act, which allotted 160 acres for each settler, treating the United States as if its regions were all of a piece: "It took a man to break and hold a homestead of 160 acres even in the subhumid zone. It took a superman to do it on the arid plains."

Stegner knew all this instinctively, in a way no easterner could, but it was only years of study that allowed him to take this personal, instinctive feeling and transform it into something universal and artistic. He had been thinking overtly about these issues at least as far back as his college years, when he read Clarence Edward Dutton's *Report on the Geology of the High Plateaus of Utah* (1880), a book that would later spark a PhD dissertation on Dutton. Then, while he was teaching at the University of Wisconsin, he discovered the work of Frederick Jackson Turner, one of the first historians who tried to understand the meaning of the frontier for the United States as a whole. But this was all preamble, and it would take meeting Bernard DeVoto at the Bread Loaf Writers' Conference in 1939 to push his thinking to deeper and more universal levels. At that moment Stegner was thirty and DeVoto was forty-two, already famous, opinionated, wildly engaging. They would become good friends and would stay friends as Cambridge neighbors, and, after DeVoto's death, Stegner would write a biography of DeVoto, at least in part to correct what he saw as the misconceptions and underappreciation of his ornery friend. Like Stegner, DeVoto was a born westerner who thought hard about what the West meant. He was also a cantankerous, brilliant, opinionated, often angry, sometimes charming man who pushed the younger Stegner to defend and broaden his ideas. As Stegner developed intellectually the pushing also went the other way, and there are times it is hard to parse where DeVoto ends and Stegner begins.

DeVoto decried "the economy of liquidation" that had prevailed in the West since it was first settled, a philosophy that applied to aquifers and farms as well as mines. In the West "the miner's right to exploit transcends all other rights whatsoever." As for agriculture, it soon became clear that it was impossible without irrigation, and that irrigation itself was impossible without the massive dams that only the federal government could build. Which, combined with the fact that much grazing and mining occurred on public land, made westerners chronically dependent on government help. In fact, contrary to the image of rugged individualism, westerners were more dependent on help and community than any other region. Dams, irrigation, free private use of public land. It all amounted to a rugged, beautiful, and wild welfare state.

For Bernard DeVoto, it was key that for many coming from the East the first sight of the West began with "an illusion and a misconception." Upon first seeing the Rockies many travelers thought they saw clouds, not mountains. This illusion was important to DeVoto, because if the West spoke of hope it also spoke of fear, of vast places where terrible things could happen, and those heading there "traveled toward paradise and frequently arrived at inferno." If the West was a promise, it was a promise often left unfulfilled.

The promise still draws people to the West—in droves, actually. In recent years, the West has boomed like no other area in the country. Those who travel here now come by car and plane, not by stagecoach, and they often forget that the old dangers remain. But computers and cell phones can't hide this more primal reality, and during the summer of my trip the country was relearning the truth of DeVoto's line about the region: "A light winter means a hard summer." It is a truth that had hit particularly hard with last winter's snowpack reaching only 50 percent of its norm, with much of the precipitation falling as rain, which, unlike snow, doesn't stick around. DeVoto also warned that due to the West's dryness it is less resilient than other places, and that the snowpack is the only thing that keeps the West from being as empty as the Sahara.

He wrote: "Catastrophe might destroy half the region."

During the summer of 2012, the hottest on record to that point, that catastrophe was playing out in the form of historic fires.

I SPENT MY SECOND night in the West in a hotel in Boulder, and the next morning got up early to bike up Flagstaff Mountain to see the scars from the recent Bear Peak fire. Joining me for the climb were two old friends, Chris Brooks and Rob Bleiberg. Chris, a lifelong Coloradan, had been an Ultimate Frisbee teammate of mine. Rob had too, and we had become roommates after I moved from Eldorado Springs to Boulder during my second year in Colorado.

In deference to the out-of-shape easterner, Chris and Rob agreed to cheat a little and use the car to get up to the summit parking lot of Flagstaff. Rob was visiting from the western slope, where he directed the Mesa County Land Conservancy in Grand Junction. His main job there was to try to convince western slope ranchers to put their vast acreage into conservation trust, and not to sell out to those who wanted to develop or drill on the land.

"People come to Grand Junction and take stuff out of the ground and then take the money back to Houston," Rob said as we drove to the summit. "It's 2012 and they still regard this place as a resource colony."

Rob is a strong, square-shouldered man who in many ways embodies a certain western myth. Growing up in the suburbs of Washington, DC, Rob came from a family where his grandfather, great-grandfather, and two uncles were all rabbis. He had little interest in the West, or wilderness, until his sophomore year at Wesleyan, when his teacher, Bill "Brutus" Lester, took ten students on a twenty-one-day hiking trip through the high Sierras. They hiked and camped, reading John Muir and Edward Abbey at night. "It was a transformative experience," Rob said. By the next summer he had finagled an internship with the National Park Service working in North Cascade National Park, where he would spend five nights at a time alone in the backcountry collecting bear scat for scientific analysis. A year later he had become a wilderness ranger in Eagles Nest Wilderness in Colorado. After graduation he left the East behind and never looked back.

"The West was nothing to me and then after it was everything," he said.

His reading kept apace with his hiking, and when he moved into my rental cabin in Boulder in 1993 he filled up the living-room bookshelves with the work of Wallace Stegner. For a while I left those books unread, but eventually I picked one up. That was the accidental beginning of a deeper education about my new home.

I had last visited Rob in 2008, when I traveled to Grand Junction to write an article on the latest oil boom. The town was then spilling over with oil workers and I paid $220 for my hotel room. "Exxon rates," the locals called them. Everywhere you looked you saw young men in big trucks, though Rob cautioned me when I said that I was pretty sure I was the only guest in the hotel without a tattoo and a four-by-four.

"What would you do if you had the choice? You're a kid with a high school education. Do you work at Burger King or make a hundred grand a year in the oil fields?"

He shook his head.

"The case for not selling out gets harder and harder. I see it every day. We work with ranchers to keep the land in their families. The tools are complicated and it takes a long time to get things done. It's the opposite of instant gratification."

"We aren't just fighting the lure of money," he added. "We're fighting a society that teaches us we should get what we want and get it right now."

Rob was an old friend and I was therefore allowed to tease him at will. But I decided not to tell him that his Stegner was showing.

We reached the Flagstaff summit and took the bikes off the back of my car. Though it was the summit of that particular mountain, there was plenty of *up* left. We pedaled the steep section above the summit that we used to call Old Bill. Rob seemed to get some slight sadistic pleasure in seeing me gasping for air like a landed fish. I made it to the top, just barely, and only after Chris pedaled up and shouted encouragement, finally pushing my bike from behind during the steepest section.

After we reached the top we rode down the mountain's other side so we could get a good look at the area that had burned. A charred ridgeline greeted us. Chris told me that all June Boulderites had stared up at the smoke, praying that winds wouldn't blow toward town.

"It's so dry that the mountain houses would be like kindling," Rob said.

Of course, what went unsaid is that Boulder had been lucky, at least compared to other front range towns. Less than two weeks before, the Waldo Canyon fire in Colorado Springs had leapt over two lines of containment to torch houses in the city proper. It became the most destructive fire in the state's history, destroying 350 homes, surpassing the record of 259 set only nine days earlier by the High Park fire in Fort Collins (which would be surpassed again the next summer). A decade earlier, when Colorado experienced a similar if less destructive fire season, those in the firefighting community were skeptical of the role that climate change played in the fires. No longer. With record temperatures and light snowpack the fire season now regularly starts almost two months earlier than it did just a decade ago. A century of fire suppression has led to forests unpurged by smaller fires, and therefore packed with deadfall and groundcover that helps light up the drought-dried wood like torches. And with more people building houses in fire-prone areas there is plenty of added fuel. I couldn't help but be reminded of the trophy homes that line the beaches in the Outer Banks in coastal North Carolina, houses that have been set up like bowling pins to be knocked down by the next hurricane. In both places it is most often the wealthy who build homes that are endangered, and frequently these are second homes. I thought of how, back in Carolina, summer is always an anxious time, with people awaiting the beginning of hurricane season. Here they awaited fire. There was also another similarity. The same fervent belief in rebuilding infects both the homeowners who have seen their homes burned down and those who have seen theirs slammed by the sea.

"Rebuild!" they all shout. But there are other voices too, and more than there used to be, voices that suggest that perhaps it would be better not to rebuild. You could argue that, with the embers barely cooled and whole towns engulfed in tragedy, this wasn't the right moment to question the wisdom of rebuilding in the dry Colorado hills. Or maybe it was the exact right moment. In the fervor after a disaster there is always talk first of loss, then of hope and rebuilding. What there is not a lot of is cold-eyed clarity.

Which is where DeVoto and Stegner help. In this burning summer, these two dead writers couldn't be more alive. In a time of drought and fires it is hard not to return to their central contention: that this land that we are treating like the land of any other region is in fact quite different, a near desert, and that its life depends on that not-always-reliable snowpack. Much more reliable are the cycles of drought, which have been a part of the West forever. As it happens we are now in the midst of one of those cycles. It would be wise to acknowledge this and deal accordingly.

What would that mean? For starters, acknowledging that there is a reason that the West has always been relatively unpeopled. Large stretches of it are simply not fit for human habitation. The booster says, "Well, let's make them fit!" The Stegnerian realist says, "Well, maybe we shouldn't live there." Don't move to a place where your houses are likely to serve as kindling. There are some places that are better left alone.

But what's the point of saying this now, when the houses are already built and when those burned will surely be rebuilt, the genie already out of the bottle? Because we are at this moment seeing many of the things that Stegner and DeVoto warned about coming home to roost. And because even if warnings are not heeded, they still must be given.

Stegner understood well the necessity of hope, but in the end knew that cold-eyed clarity was more important. Today cold-eyed clarity tells us this: the world is warming and some of the places that are least ready to adapt to that warming are places that are already, as Stegner called them, "subhumid and arid lands." In a place already on the edge, a slight tip puts you over. In a place where drought is already commonplace, more heat and less rain are killers.

The majority of climatologists believe that, along with low-lying coastal areas, it will be the water-stressed areas of the world that will be most affected by climate change. At first this sounds simple to the point of being a tautology. It isn't. They are not merely saying that the dry places will be hardest hit. They are saying that the driest places, like the American Southwest, will change the most compared with their baseline. And how will they change? The predictions are consistent. Drought is, by definition, an anomalous word, but what we now call drought will become the norm. And with that as a new baseline, the droughts will be of a sort the region hasn't seen since the Middle Ages, when so-called megadroughts drove the Puebloan people from the region.

For Wallace Stegner, real knowledge of a place, and science, trumped myth. And what science is now telling us is straightforward: that a place that historically had little water will have less.

"WE WATCHED THE fire for days," Reg Saner told me an hour later, over lunch.

Rob and Chris had biked home, while I rode back to my car at the Flagstaff summit. There was no time for a shower before racing to meet Reg for lunch in town.

"There was a voluntary evacuation but I wasn't going to leave," he continued. "I'd calculated that there wasn't enough vegetation to burn between the mountains and our house."

Reg is one of the few people who can speak a sentence like that and not sound ridiculous. "Calculated," when he says it, really means something. He is the smartest man I know. At almost eighty years old, he still looks like Marcus Aurelius—noble brow and Roman nose—and sounds like him too, come to think about it.

Reg was my first and best teacher in the West. If reading the books that Rob Bleiberg had left on my shelves proved the accidental beginning of my deeper education, then with Reg the accidental became intentional. During my third year in the West, I began taking classes with him, including an independent study that required that I read one book a week by Wallace Stegner. Most of the professors who taught at the writing school I attended in Boulder seemed like they could have come from anywhere and been writing about anyplace. Not Reg. He'd spent his entire adult life studying the West, its landscape and people.

When I told him about my new project he feigned interest, but I knew he was skeptical. Abbey was not his type, a tad too flamboyant for his refined tastes. As for Stegner, I remembered what Reg said to me back during our independent study: "He was a man who knew a lot. And who *knew* he knew a lot." It's hard to deny this. Some saw Stegner's confidence as *over*confidence or worse. Stegner knew it too. In *Crossing to Safety*, his stand-in character's wife compares his character to their imperious friend Charity, and then says of them both: "Neither of you would win any prizes for self-doubt."

While Reg may be somewhat critical of Stegner, you could make an argument that he has as valid a claim as anyone to being Stegner's heir, at least in terms of large-scale thinking about the West. Both a mountaineer and a philosopher (he would deny the second), he has spent six decades roaming the West, climbing its mountains and talking to its people and exploring the haunts of its ancient indigenous cultures. After these explorations he heads back home to Boulder and takes what he has learned and turns it into poems and essays. To my mind these essays are brilliant—brilliant in the old-fashioned sense: glittering mosaics full of light. But they are also filled with facts that, taken together, provide a geologic and human history of the West. Those facts do not make for a pretty picture.

When I brought this up, Reg shook his head.

"I'm afraid I don't see too much reason for optimism," he said. "The problem is simple enough: too many humans."

I nodded. In just the time since I'd lived here, the western population had boomed. The 2010 census revealed that four of the five fastest-growing states were all in the West (with Texas, its own country, the fifth), and that for the first time in United States history, the population of the West exceeded that of the Midwest.

Twenty years ago, when I was his student, Reg was already fairly pessimistic about the fate of the region. But in the time since, new reasons for pessimism have arisen, with climate joining population as a central, seemingly ineradicable factor of the western crisis. While I didn't know it at the time, the years I was here were wet ones, full of false promise, but the years since have been ones of historic dryness and temperature rise. While most scientists agree that this is due to anthropogenic, or human-caused, factors, in some ways it doesn't really matter what is causing the change. The point is that it is here. The moisture, always precious, has been sucked out of the region.

If climate ends up having a radical effect on human culture, and it's pretty hard to see how it won't, then Reg for one can say that the West has seen it all before. He is a man who thinks big, and both the cosmos and geological time weave through his mediations, day-dreams, and resultant writings. In particular, he has spent many years exploring the ancient ruins of the Anasazi and other Pueblo cultures, and like anyone else who has thought deeply about those southwestern cultures he has ended up considering a central question: why did these people, who had so long and so well inhabited the dry lands, suddenly leave? To ask this question among sophisticated westerners is to open an interesting and of course speculative can of worms. But no discussion can avoid certain facts. These facts, revealed to scientists by the rings of trees, tell us that in the year 1130 a great drought began, and that it is around this time that we see a desertion of flourishing communities like those at Chaco Canyon. That drought paled when compared to the Great Drought of 1276 to 1299, which seems to have driven the last of the Puebloans out of the region. In other words, climate had its way.

But while the people left, their homes remained, preserved and mummified by the dryness of the desert. In the region where I now live, we have myths of Atlantis, myths that are becoming more relevant as the sea rises. But here you can see and walk through an arid Atlantis. In fact, many of the sites are unmarked and I can't think of many better moments on Earth than when, after a long desert hike, you see a dwelling that at first seems a part of the stone cliff you are staring up at, like a swallow's tunnel, and then clarifies itself into the most organic of human homes, made of the stone it grows out of. In his essay "The Pleasure of Ruin," Reg writes: "When it comes to proto-Pueblos like the Anasazi, the who without the where becomes unimaginable, so fused with their culture were the high deserts they lived in and by means of."

That such a placed people could be displaced is remarkable, and that climate had a hand in the displacing undeniable. Theirs was a climate change that had nothing to do with the fact that they drove their cars too much. But it was a change that demonstrated climate's power. And today in thinking about the desertion of Chaco or Mesa Verde, is it such a long jump to thinking about Phoenix or Las Vegas?

I won't pretend, however, that Reg and I spent our entire forty-five-minute lunch, between bites of our burgers, discussing high matters of the cosmos, climate, and distant culture. Much of it was actually spent talking about how his family was doing, and how, in turn, my wife, Nina, and my daughter, Hadley, were. Geological time was important to Reg, but the present mattered too. He had particular fun with the fact that since leaving Boulder in 1997 I had stored a trunk filled with old manuscripts in his basement.

"The Smithsonian called the other day inquiring about the Gessner papers," he said.

Reg paid the bill, as always. It occurred to me, not for the first time, that he had appeared in my life at almost the exact moment my father died, the universe providing.

Before I hit the road, I promised I would visit again when Nina and Hadley arrived in a few weeks. For today my goal was to get up over the Continental Divide and into the real mountains by late afternoon. I knew that Reg, for his part, didn't like good-byes and used to have the habit of paying the bill and ducking out when I went to the bathroom. Now we saw each other so infrequently that saying good-bye was particularly hard, and he told me that he worried that this time would be the last.

Reg knew the western land as well as anyone, but he, like Edward Abbey, wasn't born here. He grew up in the flatlands of Illinois and first saw real mountains when he was sent to Alaska for officer training for the Korean War. There he learned to cross-country ski, a sport that became a lifelong love. When he returned from the war, he knew he wanted to be close to big mountains, and the job he took as an English professor at the University of Colorado gave him that, as well as a jumping-off point to explore the rest of the West.

In many ways Reg's first taste of the West, followed by his permanent move to the region, is archetypal. It is Abbey's migration, Rob Bleiberg's migration, the migration of so many who fall for the place and leave the East behind.

The move opened up his world. *Lifted* him. Abbey talked of first seeing the West as being like seeing a naked girl. But there is another way of describing what the West eventually does to some people.

Reg Saner fancies himself a realist, not a romantic, and he is just about the most openly atheistic person I know. For instance, he once wrote in an essay: "God is the single worst idea human beings ever had."

Which makes how he described what it was like to move west even more powerful.

He said it was as if he had been "born again."

LIGHTING THE WAY

There were plenty of ways I could follow—and learn from—Ed Abbey and Wallace Stegner as I drove through the West. I could go to the places that had been important to them, talk to people who knew them, and, of course, continue to read their sentences. I could even, courtesy of YouTube, listen as the men spoke to me from beyond the grave, and, in fact, I got to know the tone and timbre of their voices in this way. I learned that Abbey seemed to talk without moving his lips—a low, garbled baritone that sounded as if he had a mouthful of pebbles. And that Stegner, meanwhile, had not a trace of the frontier in his voice, self-trained out of him no doubt, until he ended up sounding a little like William F. Buckley Jr.

In other words, I could learn a lot about the men, but only to a certain point. What I could not do was what I would have most liked to. I could not *talk* to Edward Abbey or Wallace Stegner. I could not meet them one on one, man to man.

But there was something else I could still do, and something I had already done on the first stop of my trip. I could talk to writers who had known the men, and who in many ways had inherited their ideas and continued their work.

My trip had begun on a Sunday morning, July 8, in the thick, green humid East. Driving out from the coast on Route 40 before dawn, I saw the headlights of early beach traffic coming the other way. And then a sign: BARSTOW, CALIFORNIA—2,554 MILES. I headed west toward the Carolina mountains that Thomas Wolfe couldn't go home to, and then drove out of North Carolina and up through Virginia and West Virginia, entering the Appalachian hills like those where Abbey was raised.

My destination was the home of Wendell Berry, a writer whom I deeply admired. Berry had written the most insightful essay I had read on Ed Abbey, and had been a student and friend of Wallace Stegner's. I stopped at the small store just short of Berry's home in Port Royal, Kentucky, where the thermostat outside read 104 degrees. We'd had more rain than the West, but the summer heat had been pressing down on us. I slurped from a bottle of water as I wound along River Road, which followed the twists and turns of the Kentucky River. I arrived early at the address Berry had given me— by letter of course, since he did not use e-mail—and not wanting to bother the Berrys I took a small detour to explore the nearly empty streets of Port Royal, a small town seemingly preserved in a time capsule. I drove past the Port Royal United Methodist Church— "Scripture/Study/Service" were the three words below the church's name—and Rick's Farm Center Service Restaurant, and then, having killed enough time, circled back along the river to the white house on the hill.

Wendell Berry greeted me at the door, wearing khakis, a long-sleeved blue-and-white striped shirt (despite the heat), and a wide smile. He introduced me to Tanya, his wife, and to his guests, a minister from Texas and his wife, who had dropped in for a visit. Sunday, I had been told in the letter he'd sent, was visiting day. A necessary day of rest, or at least of variety, for a man who had produced more than thirty works of nonfiction, twenty books of poetry, and a dozen novels over the past fifty years. I presented him with a bottle of Maker's Mark, which I'd heard he favored, and he thanked me.

WENDELL AND TANYA BERRY AT THEIR HOME.

We sat at the dining-room table and talked. For hours. Wendell Berry is many things on the pages of his books—prophetic, confident, lyric, meditative—but one thing he isn't very often, at least in the nonfiction, is funny. In person it was different. Berry's loud and infectious laughter punctuated the conversation.

The first story he told was about attending a conference of the Modern Language Association. He came upon two janitors, one leaning on the mop in his bucket, who were looking up at a TV monitor that displayed the titles of the different sessions that the conference offered. The titles were typical for that sort of conference, with names like "The Linguistic Construction of Narrative Space" and "Post-Colonial Structuralist Theory."

"The janitors were just staring up as the titles streamed by," he said. "And they were pointing and saying the names out loud and laughing their heads off."

Though I was there to talk about Abbey and Stegner, we spent the better part of the first hour discussing Ken Kesey, who was both Stegner's student and Wendell's friend. Wendell, as he insisted I call him, told me a story about arriving at Kesey's house, exhausted after a cross-country trip, to find everyone sitting in a circle passing a joint around. What impressed Wendell was how solicitous Kesey had been, understanding his exhaustion and his desire not to join in, and so ushering him off to a well-made bed in a guest room.

Wendell Berry pointed out a similarity between Kesey and his old teacher.

"Ken stayed married to the same woman his whole life," he said. "He was a curiously devoted man."

I asked what it was like having Wallace Stegner as a teacher.

"I never felt comfortable calling him anything but Mr. Stegner," Wendell said. "It took many, many years for me to address him as Wally."

Then Wendell used another term to describe the individual he had for so long called Mr. Stegner.

"He was a *decided* man," he said.

Wendell told me that he shared with Wallace Stegner the belief that writers are part of a "great community of recorded human experience," and that no writer, no man or woman, ever accomplishes very much on their own. Stegner was a great teacher, and he had, as Wendell put it, lighted the way for him.

"I never felt anxiety of influence," he said. "I always knew how much I owed to other people. You need the way lighted."

And, he added, we don't always know who is lighting our way.

"It is your personal ecosystem," Wendell said. "An ecosystem is full of dependencies, and nothing in it knows what it is dependent on."

"Ed Abbey," he added, "also lighted my way."

I pointed out that Abbey had not always been virtuous, in the traditional sense.

"But you can't argue with the end product," Wendell said. "He wrote books that will last."

He meant, first and foremost, *Desert Solitaire*. It was Wendell who, in his essay "A Few Words in Defense of Ed Abbey," most clearly defined what it was that Abbey was doing in that book, what he was really best at. "He is, I think, at least in the essays, an autobiographer," Wendell wrote. And *Desert Solitaire* is autobiography, though autobiography elevated into art.

"You need the way lighted," he continued. "If you think you know all the ones who have lighted your way, you're nuts. You don't know, because you can't. But of course you can know *some* who have. Wallace Stegner and Edward Abbey are two who have lighted my way."

It pleased me to think of writers, dead and alive, as members of a community. Not as competitors or "influences," but as part of what Keats called "the immortal freemasonry." Or, put more simply, one big club.

When talk turned to the environmental state of the West, Wendell challenged me. If I really wanted to think deeply about the meaning of Wallace Stegner as I traveled, then I needed to think about how we use the land.

"Land use," he said. "I think the people who confront it are the relevant people today. And the specialists—the preservationists and the literary specialists—are becoming less relevant."

By preservationists I assumed he meant environmentalists who only fought for "wilderness" and by literary specialists I assumed he meant those writers who restricted themselves to poetically celebrating the same. My own work, and thinking, had started with a focus on the lyric celebration of nature but had grown more muddied and complex in recent years. I knew that for both Wendell Berry and Wallace Stegner, abstract notions of nature and wilderness were not enough. To think deeply also meant to think practically.

As the afternoon deepened, we began to hear a deep rumbling outside. Gray thunderheads were rolling in. After a while, Wendell said he had to head down to the barn to get the sheep in, and he invited me to join him. We climbed into his truck and drove to the barn with Maggie, his border collie, in the truck bed. When we arrived at the barn, Wendell asked me to hold open the metal gate, but then, glancing up at the lightning, said, "On second thought, you better not."

I was glad not to be electrocuted by Wendell Berry. I watched Maggie herd the sheep directly into the barn, marveling at the way she snapped to and followed Wendell's orders.

With electricity crackling in the clouds, I looked out over the fields and green woods above the Kentucky River, where Wendell Berry had tried out and lived many of the same concepts of home that Wallace Stegner advocated. After he left Stanford and returned to this place, Wendell laid out his agenda, if anything so artful can be called an agenda, in two striking and beautiful essays, "The Long-Legged House" and "A Native Hill." The "plot" of these essays is the central myth of Wendell's life, which goes this way: he was born in a rural community, where his family had lived for many generations. As he grew up in the land it grew up in him: he paddled its rivers, farmed its fields, learned its people. But with the dawning of college and career he began to enact the traditional American exodus, leaving the small town behind to become "bigger." For Wendell Berry this meant a career in literature that led him west to Stanford, overseas to Europe, and finally landed him in New York City. He was teaching there, clearly on an upward trajectory, when a radical notion occurred to him. What if he, and his young bride, were to return to Kentucky? What if he were to stake his claim not in some big city but on his native ground? His fellow writers and professors scoffed, don't be ridiculous. They quoted Thomas Wolfe, telling him he couldn't go home again.

But he did just that. And his return to Kentucky, his return to his hometown and family land, proved to be not a regression but a stroke of genius.

When I had brought this up earlier at the table, he had smiled and said: "You make us sound too foresightful and knowing. We came because we *wanted* to."

He added: "One day I realized I could be perfectly happy if I never wrote anything."

Upon his return home he became a farmer, but crops were not the only thing his fields yielded. Though he might not have *needed* to write anything to be happy, it turned out that out of his home ground, where he would settle and remains settled today almost fifty years later, grew words and sentences—a true profusion of stories, novels, essays, and poems. With his return he began to *learn his place.* And to worry and grieve over it. The land he had romped through as a child he now studied, deepening his knowledge of the birds and trees and reacquainting himself with the fields and woods and people. Wendell Berry believed that most Americans are displaced people. He defined himself, in contrast, as a "placed person."

There is little doubt that his evolving philosophy of home owed much to his old teacher, and that this was an example of Wallace Stegner lighting Wendell Berry's way. I thought of Stegner's book *Wolf Willow,* a nonfiction account of his return to his own childhood prairie home in Saskatchewan. "I was trying to be the Herodotus of Cypress Hills," Stegner would later say of the book. "Because I didn't want to be a man from nowhere."

The book wasn't strictly history; this was Herodotus joined at the hip to Montaigne, a kind of historic memoir. The knowledge of home was deep, the historic research vast, but what drove the book was the quest for personal identity, and that identity was tied directly to place. It is in the first chapter of *Wolf Willow* that Stegner wrote his famous line: "I may not know who I am, but I know where I am from."

The influence of this idea was great. Going home again, the drive to find a community and a place where he belonged, would remain a recurrent theme in Stegner's work and one he would hand down to a new generation of writers.

After reading *Wolf Willow,* Wendell Berry sent Mr. Stegner a letter in October 1963:

"I would like to do as well, sometime, with the facts of my own little neck of the woods," he wrote.

Which is exactly what Wendell proceeded to do in his own work over the next several decades. As it turned out, his neck of the woods provided a fount of stories and ideas.

In fact, you could make a fairly good argument that the next big movement in the field generally called nature writing was a return to home, to region. That in the time since, hundreds of capable writers, with Wendell Berry perhaps foremost among them, have tried to make something of the facts of their little necks of the woods. In their celebration of a particular place, in their seeing the world in their backyard, all of these writers are children of Thoreau. But they are also children of Stegner.

There was one crucial difference between the teacher and the student, however. Wendell Berry came from a tradition of rootedness, generations of people who farmed the same land. Wallace Stegner came to the idea of rootedness through its opposite.

Later, back at the table, I asked Wendell about this.

His answer surprised me. I had been focused on the negative example of Stegner's father, George, who could never settle, but Wendell mentioned the positive one of Hilda, his mother.

"In her he managed to see someone who planted perennial flowers in the yard and who tried to stick around to see them bloom. That's very tender."

It occurred to me that if you believe, as Wendell Berry does, that literature is a vast ecosystem, a tangled mass of roots where we never know exactly who is influencing whom, then more writers than know it have been influenced by the fact that George Stegner rarely let Hilda stick around to see those flowers bloom.

AFTER I SAID good-bye to Reg Saner and left Boulder behind, I headed south past Rocky Flats, the radioactive nuclear trigger plant turned park. Rocky Flats has an ugly history of plutonium leaks, and while it has been twenty years since it shut its gates, you never really close when your soil holds particles of a material with a half-life of 24,360 years. I passed the still-eerie, long-contaminated ground where Ed Abbey linked arms with a thousand other protesters, Reg Saner included, who were trying to get the leaky plant shut down before it turned Colorado a different sort of green. From there I drove down to Golden, taking the big turn up toward the divide, deeper west into the real Rockies—mountains that Abbey, always poking and teasing, called "overrated."

They did not seem overrated to me. I felt the usual, expected lift, though it was true that these days if you want to look beyond the mountains' glory you don't have to look that hard. I could see significant patches of dead trees, some from fires but more from bark beetles, which had made inroads into the health of Colorado's ponderosa and other mountain pines. Spruce beetles had also migrated down from the north, while another beetle, the Piñon Ips, was busy killing trees farther south in the Rockies and in the desert. The shorter winters gave both the beetles and fires a head start on the year. More startling, as I looked around, was the almost complete absence of snow in the high country. There had been rain in late winter, which is always appreciated in this arid place, but rain doesn't do as much good as snow out here. Rain comes and goes, charging off somewhere, sometimes barely sinking into the hard, dry soil. Rain also can become something far from nurturing, as recent floods have made clear. Snow, on the other hand, is its own storage system. Snow is time-released, becoming water in hydrating doses throughout the spring and summer. But snow is now in short supply. Worse, the remaining snow is often darkened by dust, dust from human activity ranging from road building to recreation to mining to home construction. This may not seem like much unless you think about it for a bit and understand that white snow reflects heat while the darker patches pull it in. What this all adds up to is a warmer Earth and less snow and an even shorter winter.

I turned up the radio and tried to drown out my own spoilsport brain. Ascending one side of the divide and descending the other, I didn't stop until I entered the steep canyon of Glenwood Springs, where I took a brief break, pulling off the road and dipping into the Colorado River, which was cold though not nearly as icy as the creek in Eldorado. It was then, drying off after my dip in the river, that I received an unexpected gift. I had considered driving on to Utah, or at least to Grand Junction, but there on the riverside I received a phone call from Adam Petry, a former student of mine whom I had contacted a few days before and who now called to tell me that his roommate was out of town. Which meant that he had a spare bedroom in his cabin up above the mountain town of Paonia. I had other plans but this . . . this sounded too good. *A cabin in the mountains.*

The drive to Paonia turned out to be one of the most beautiful of my life. First I headed out of the strange horizontal slots and slices of Glenwood Canyon and up Route 133 into the high country, excited by the fact that it was a road I had never traveled on before. Great gray slabs of mountains alternated with intense red rock and green forests. Mount Sopris loomed above it all while below its scree slopes enormous fields of aspen soughed in the wind, their leaves doing the usual dance, flipping from darker green to light. I passed a half dozen magpies and a single Steller's jay, birds that let me know I was back in the West. I felt preposterously happy. Forty minutes passed and I didn't see a single house. And then a joyous message appeared on my phone: CELL SERVICE NO LONGER AVAILABLE. I could no longer be tracked!

To the naked eye this looked like the same West I had left behind fifteen years before, and in some ways it was. Caught up in my surroundings, I was in no mood for talk of the region's doom. One of the reasons we can still read Abbey and Stegner, it seems to me, is that theirs was not the standard environmental theme of The End of the World. Yes, they understood just how dire the environmental picture was, just how high the stakes were, but they also never failed to take some fundamental joy in the places where they found themselves.

This may be more obviously true of Abbey, who excelled in the arts of reveling and exalting. But Stegner was no slouch when it came to celebrating his home landscape. It is why he, for all his hard-eyed realism, called the western landscape "the geography of hope."

It still is. It still pulls us in. My exhilaration over being in a beautiful place with few other people around me was not false. But at the same time it was getting harder to ignore the snakes that were squirming through Eden. For one thing, there is a fundamental irony at work. More and more of us keep pouring into the region, in no small part because it seems relatively empty compared to the rest of the country. What attracts us is what we then ruin. Meanwhile, we can't seem to get it through our heads that the land can't support human beings the way other parts of the country can. That's one of the things that Wallace Stegner spent a lifetime trying to tell us: this is *not* your green East and you can't treat it or live in it as if it were. In the introduction to *The Sound of Mountain Water,* he writes:

> The history of the West until recently has been the history of the importation of humid-land habits (and carelessness) into a dry land that will not tolerate them; and of the indulgence of an unprecedented personal liberty, an atomic individualism, in a country that experience says can only be successfully tamed and lived in by a high degree of cooperation. Inherited wet-land habits have given us a damaged domain.

In other words, we come to the West as if it were any other place. It is not. It is fragile, vulnerable, and, as Bernard DeVoto said, disaster-prone. Not just local disasters like a tornado wiping out a Midwestern town, or even a hurricane raking the East Coast. But potentially region-wide disasters. In May, I had flown out to the University of Arizona Library in Tucson to study Abbey's papers, and as we crossed New Mexico I found myself staring out the right side of the plane down at a dry, cracked moonscape that looked like it could sustain a human population of about 3. Then I saw the cloud, or what I at first thought was a cloud. What it was in fact was smoke that seemed to cover the whole state, smoke from the massive million-acre fire in the Gila National Forest. A fire of that size, which would have set records just a decade before, is now commonplace, fueled by drought and the dense fuel loads resulting from fire suppression.

Now, as I drove up into that world of thin air and aspen, I wanted to simply take in the sights. That is, I wanted to keep reveling. And the strange thing was that I could, despite my brain and its ideas. I constantly marvel at my, and most of our, ability to both delight in the world and bemoan its fate. Reg Saner has written: "Perhaps resistance to what geological time implies has been instilled by DNA to nudge us aside from that kind of reality." In other words, we might be able to intellectually understand that the West has lost 18 percent of its trees over the last twenty years, and at the same time be overcome by the quaking of a single aspen leaf. It's a strange world, and I pulled the car over to step out into it. A whole mountainside of quivering aspen greeted me, untroubled by the loss of their brethren. It was quiet except for the wind in the trees, and there was no one around, no cars coming, so I took a celebratory leak by the side of the road.

Perhaps in times ahead, reveling, or at least sustained reveling, will get harder. Perhaps it will become more difficult to ignore darker truths, to stop ourselves from seeing things, ugly things, that deflate us. Some of these are the very same ones that Wallace Stegner warned of, but some are things he never had to worry about during his lifetime. For instance, he did not have to worry about those millions—did I say millions? Sorry, billions—of pine bark beetles chewing up the innards of pines and spruce throughout the West. He did have to worry about dust—any westerner did—but he did not have to worry about winter regularly ending earlier, and massive clouds of man-created dust covering the thinning snowpack and transforming it from a reflective white shield into a darkened heat absorber, heat that, along with the beetles, abetted the massive die-off of western trees. And finally, while he might have been saddened by the loss of those trees, his sadness would not likely have focused on seeing that loss as part of the cycle of increased atmospheric CO_2,—the loss not just of beauty but of storehouses of carbon.

Of course Stegner knew the basics—more than the basics, he knew the fundamentals—and he had an uncanny knack for putting those fundamentals together to see the big picture. But he didn't have *our* fundamentals. The puzzle might be the same but some of the pieces are brand-new. And these days the few who can really put things together the way Stegner could are frankly scared stiff. The picture is as simple as it is scary. One equation goes like this: high temps + beetles + less snow + darker snow + more fires + more carbon in the air = Well, equals what? No one knows exactly.

Perhaps the scariest thing of all is that most scientists currently studying this landscape say that the recent rash of fires and floods, drought and dust bowls, are not aberrational. That they were common enough *before* climate change ratcheted things up another couple of degrees. Which means that rather than treat these events as freaks, it is better to consider them the cyclical norm. It is now foolish to regard a "normal year" as one without disaster.

It would be wrong to see a silver lining in the current cycle of drought in the West—there is none—but at least drought can sometimes force us to see things as they are. In flusher times there are parts of the West that can whistle along and ignore reality, pretending to be something they're not. But that will soon be impossible. We will be forced to strip away our illusions, to prepare ourselves, as much as possible, for what is to come.

AFTER THE MOUNTAIN pass, I followed the north branch of the Gunnison River down into the town of Paonia, then up again on a dirt road called Dry Gulch Creek to a small wooden cabin in the hills. So often on trips like this I have found that my already high expectations are exceeded. All I had wanted to do after my cross-country drive was find a place to rest, maybe a hotel in Grand Junction. Instead I was driving into a mountain-rung cabin, my fantasy of a western rest place.

I ended up staying at the cabin for two nights. That first evening Adam and I drank beer at the dining-room table. Adam was a former student of mine who moved to North Carolina to study with me and who eventually became the managing editor of *Ecotone*, the magazine that I founded. He was born in Missouri but had been living in the West after he graduated from college, working in the Wyoming oil fields as a geologist. He never quite adapted to coastal North Carolina: it was too flat, too humid, too *eastern*. I remember that he wore a cowboy hat to the final reading he gave before graduating, and if there was something a tiny bit corny about this, there was also something right. Now, in jeans and T-shirt, and having grown out his sideburns in Wolverine fashion, he looked more comfortable, like his clothes fit him better. And I swore that as we talked, I could hear a slight western twang in his voice that I'd never heard before.

Adam certainly wasn't the first person whose self changed when he changed regions.

"Our where determines our who," Reg Saner once wrote.

I mentioned this to Adam.

"I guess I just feel so much more comfortable here," he said.

I slept like a baby and early the next morning went for a lung-searing bike ride up to the base of the nearest mountain. I splashed creek water on my face and came back to find that Adam had made me a plate of eggs, peppers, sausage, and onions. Without much difficulty, he talked me into staying a second night. I spent the afternoon reading, taking a short hike, and gathering my notes together from the first part of the trip.

The next morning, after another good night's sleep, Adam shoveled some more eggs into me and handed me a book. Adam was well versed in Abbey and Stegner—their books lined the shelves of his bookcase—and for him they were essential writers. The book he handed me was his copy of Stegner's essay collection *The Sound of Mountain Water*, and he showed me a quote that he had underlined.

I read:

> These are things one might begin with, but I should rather begin with how it feels to be out on the road again, dry camping in the desert, hitting the road after five years of rationing and restrictions, doing what a good third of America is doing this summer of 1946, if the polls and the prophecies mean anything. For many people—and I sympathize with them—one of the least bearable wartime deprivations was the loss of their mobility. We are a wheeled people; it seems to me sometimes that I must have been born with a steering wheel in my hands, and I realize now that to lose the use of a car is practically equivalent to losing the use of my legs.
>
> Returning to the road after a layoff of several years is like re-establishing intimacy with a wife or a lover. There are a hundred things once known and long forgotten that crowd forward upon the senses, and there is the sharp thrill of recognition in all of them.

I thanked Adam for the benediction, and then hit the road.

As I drove, the quote proved perfect fuel for pondering. It wonderfully scuttled my easy assumptions of Stegner as the patron saint of homebodies. *Born with a steering wheel in his hands!* Stegner as Springsteen. I thought of Abbey, too, who always had a bit of George Stegner in him, constantly moving from place to place during his adulthood, looking for the Big Rock Candy Mountain not by striking it rich but by finding the perfect place to quiet his restless mind. Abbey never did, of course, unless you count his final rocky grave in the desert. He was fond of Churchill's phrase "bloody peace," which referred to the way that despite our longings for peace, our imaginations never seem capable of being content without stimulation.

Adam's quotation even relieved me of a little of the guilt I had been feeling about taking a long carbon-fueled road trip during the age of climate change. True, when Stegner was doing all that driving he didn't know that by burning fuel he just happened to be bringing about the end of the world. But the unavoidable truth is that I love driving. It has always been one of my great pleasures, particularly in the wide-open West. There is something about driving, even driving great distances, that is perfectly suited to the human mind. We can stay still and move at once, quietly thinking while taking down the miles. "We humans are an elsewhere," wrote Reg Saner. If so, then what better way to be than on the road?

Now, armed with a large cup of coffee in my right hand, steering wheel in my left, I pointed my Toyota Scion down into the red-rock landscape of Utah, and soon I was dropping off I-70 and heading south on Route 128. That last phrase may sound like a relatively simple one, but not for anyone who has actually driven that road. If you have not—or if you have (sadly) not been to Utah at all—then there is simply no way to describe it. Coffee-table books won't do. Neither will all the sci-fi movies or the SUV commercials that this landscape is often featured in. It's a world that has to be seen, a world of vivid color that for some reason can never entirely be captured on film: a world of oranges and purples and reds. And, of course, it's a world of rock: strange looming rocks that rise above you, inhuman shapes with inhuman scale.

Transcendence is a gift, not something consciously sought. But why not go to the places where the gift is most often given? For Stegner and Abbey that meant this particular state above all others. It is about Utah that Abbey wrote his greatest book; about Utah that Stegner wrote many of his.

I pulled over by the side of the muddy Colorado River, where a lone great blue heron stood guard on the opposite bank, the only other sentient being within view. Above me loomed a row of orange rocks that looked like every figure in a chess set: rooks, queens, kings, bishops—all of them. The thing was that even the pawns in this set were about five hundred feet tall. And it wasn't as if I were imagining the things I saw, like the way you imagine shapes in clouds or knots of wood; here you couldn't *help* but see the shapes. Black stains of desert varnish, the dark coating often found on rocks in this arid environment, ran in smears down the red walls. After I got back in the car and continued down the winding road above the river, that red turned to white-yellow humps and then to a great slag heap of darker red. Meanwhile, the heads of gorgons and the long legs of lounging rock warriors waited around every corner.

Across the river and about a thousand feet above me, over the ridge to my west, was Arches National Park, where Edward Abbey lived during his season, or seasons, in the wilderness. "Abbey's country," the author of *Desert Solitaire* modestly called it. Abbey's country it has become.

I continued south, along the river, and then saw something truly unexpected. Thunderclouds over Moab, and choppy ocean waves in the Colorado, and what even looked like rain falling ahead. The wind whipped through the cottonwoods and tamarisk that lined the river. I had never been there at that time of year before—"monsoon season" the locals called it, when that bone-dry place got a substantial percentage of its annual eight inches of rain.

I passed the turn-off to Castle Valley on my left. The Castle Valley community, nestled right up against the sheer walls of red rock, was the home of the writer Terry Tempest Williams. In many ways, Tempest Williams was the natural heir to Ed Abbey and Wallace Stegner, and she had spent decades both writing about and protecting the land she loved.

Using Wendell Berry's terminology, it was clear that Wallace Stegner had lighted the way for Tempest Williams. In many of the battles that she had fought, she had Stegner to look back to as both model and exemplar. For instance, in 1955 Stegner, in an effort to stop the building of a dam in Colorado's Dinosaur National Monument, edited a book that described the wonders that would be lost if the dam were built. Working with the publisher Alfred Knopf, who contributed an essay, Stegner organized and edited the contributors' work and the photographs, wrote his own essay and introduction, and pulled *This Is Dinosaur* together in two short months, pushed by the urgency of the moment. Stegner wrote in his unpublished autobiography: "That little book, distributed to every member of Congress, had a part in stopping the Upper Colorado River Storage Project in its tracks, and in uniting the previously dispersed and weak environmental organizations into a political force that by the 1970s was formidable. It also confirmed in me an environmental activism that has taken precedence over every interest except writing since that time, and has sometimes taken over the writing too."

It would not be going too far to say that that first fight, and victory, provided a template for the battles to come, and the use of *This Is Dinosaur* as a tool for lobbying was part of that template, one that would be continued and refined over the next decades. Forty years later, in 1995, Terry Tempest Williams, working with the Utah writer Stephen Trimble, put together *Testimony: Writers Speak on Behalf of Utah Wilderness*, an anthology of the work of twenty writers whose purpose was to help preserve 1.9 million acres of land in southern Utah. Just as with *This Is Dinosaur*, the book was distributed to every member of Congress. It was part of the effort that led to the creation of the Grand Staircase–Escalante National Monument. At the monument's dedication on September 18, 1996, President Bill Clinton held up the book and said, "This made a difference."

If the Grand Staircase–Escalante was Tempest Williams's most significant environmental victory, her most significant book was *Refuge*, which braided together the stories of her Mormon family's struggles with cancer, the land, the birds of Utah, and the flooding of the Great Salt Lake. Soon after I first moved west, *Refuge* joined the other books on my bedside shelf. Tempest Williams wrote not just about the land but about her own cancer, and that resonated with me. After I read her book, I wrote to her, and, she, generously, wrote back. Since then I'd had the pleasure of meeting her on several occasions, and she had always encouraged me in my work. She had, it would be fair to say, lighted my way.

Before the trip, I'd e-mailed her to see if I might stop in when I drove through, but it turned out she would be away. She did offer something though—quite a lot of something, actually. She e-mailed back a kind note with a sentence that soon began to take on, for me, the properties of a koan.

"In so many ways Ed was the conservative," she wrote, "Wally, forever the radical."

I turned this over in my mind for a while. Was she simply being playful and contradictory? Or did she mean it? Had she mistyped? I wrote her back and asked.

"I meant it," she replied.

On the ride out, I'd started thinking about this idea fairly obsessively—treating it like a riddle to ponder. After a year of reading the two men, I had begun to regard them as, in some respects, polar figures. I saw myself as flitting between the two poles. In many ways I saw all of us as flitting between the two poles. At one end is Wallace Stegner, the man of order, the man of culture, indeed The Man. At the other end is Edward Abbey, the man of wildness, the counterculturalist, the fighter of The Man. These labels are true, to some extent, but as Terry Tempest Williams was perhaps reminding me, they were too simple. If we accept them, we start to worry that the reasonable man is not passionate enough, and that the passionate man is unreasonable. I was greedy and had returned to Stegner and Abbey to see if it was possible to have the best of both.

Of course, it could have been that Terry Tempest Williams was just having some fun. After all, Abbey, the supposed conservative, was serious about his anarchism, having studied the works of Kropotkin and written a thesis called "Anarchism and the Morality of Violence." He then set about putting those principles to use by practicing, and writing about, environmental sabotage, which eventually inspired Earth First!, a truly radical organization. Paul Abbey had taught his son to not be afraid of holding unpopular political stances, and he had taught him well. Ed Abbey often stated that he had a deep belief in absolute freedom: freedom from government, rules, laws. It was a young man's belief that Abbey held on to until he was old.

Abbey was also an advocate of free love, husband of five wives and father of five children. In the 1950s, by the time Stegner briefly became his teacher, Abbey's lifestyle could perhaps be best described as "cowboy bohemian," and in the older pictures he actually looks more beatnik than cowboy. He fit the bill, right down to the jugs of wine and many women, and clung to the idea of sex, free and unrestricted, with the passion of principle. "A priapatic," he called himself. A sex addict, we would call him now (and he would snicker at us). For someone so trigger happy about marriage, it was odd that he could hardly conceive of the idea of loyalty to one woman. In fact, he couldn't suppress a laugh when he repeated the first of his five wedding vows. In his journal he wrote:

> How boring is monogamy. How can any honest man deny it? Never get enough. More than anything else, one desires variety. Variety. Novelty. Fresh young stuff everywhere and none available. Maddening, maddening.

As for Stegner the radical, after leaving Salt Lake City he married Mary Page and stayed married to her for the next sixty years, and was known to all as a model of old-fashioned propriety. It was the same with work: he got a job and kept it. True, there was some movement, mostly upward, during his early adult years, when he taught at the University of Wisconsin and Harvard, but by the age of thirty-seven he had taken the job at Stanford, and would soon after build the house in the nearby hills where he would live until the end of his life.

"Radical," in fact, was a word he came to despise. He believed, along with his fellow hard-nosed realist Samuel Johnson, that most of the cures for humanity are palliative, not radical. He had little patience for anything extreme. The poet and essayist John Daniel called him "a liberal of conservative temperament." Back in Kentucky, Wendell Berry had described Stegner's antipathetic relationship with Ken Kesey, who embodied the '60s for him. Stegner disliked writing that "throbbed rather than thought." Indeed, his lowest point at Stanford came in the mid-'60s with the rise of the hippies and campus radicals, which he saw as the downfall of a great university.

Back in Kentucky, the night after I talked to Wendell Berry, I sat down in a bar in Lexington with Ed McClanahan, who was one of the original Merry Pranksters. At about the same time that McClanahan had begun to experiment with LSD and cavort with soon-to-be Prankster leader Ken Kesey, he also became officemates with Wallace Stegner.

"Stegner was a buttoned-down fellow," McClanahan said. "A very tightly controlled person. Which is not to say he was not a kind man."

He told me about the split that occurred between Kesey the student and Stegner the teacher. According to McClanahan, Kesey gave an interview to Gordon Lish for the magazine *Genesis West*, in which he suggested that Stegner's work had suffered due to being lionized by his students—that it had all gone to the professor's head. Almost immediately Kesey understood he had screwed up. The very next day he brought a big red apple by Stegner's office. McClanahan was there but Stegner was not, so Kesey gave the apple to Dolly Kringle, the secretary. Later, when Stegner came in, Dolly handed it to him.

"I don't know what he did with the apple," Ed McClanahan said to me. "Threw it at Dolly? But he wasn't in a forgiving mood. He just looked at Dolly without smiling and said, 'Well, he said it, didn't he?'"

After that Kesey came to represent all that was wrong with the '60s: the drugs, the recklessness, the trashing of hard-won traditions.

Abbey stood on the other side of this divide. There was no one less "buttoned-down" than Abbey.

Now, as I drove south to Moab, I found myself thinking, oddly, not of the split between the men's books or careers, but of two separate parties they had thrown. Stegner, though a paragon of responsibility, was no teetotaler and would at times let his well-combed hair somewhat down; he was even known, according to his biographer, Jackson Benson, to entertain by singing and "dancing a little soft shoe." In 1937 he threw a party when he learned he had won a first-novel contest sponsored by Little, Brown and was awarded $2,500 and the publication of his first book. In Stegner's fictional version of the party that followed, re-created in his last novel, *Crossing to Safety*, the Stegnerian character, Larry Morgan, buys more bottles of booze than he ever has before in his life, and his friends pop Champagne and make toasts to his glorious future. But the party—"quite a party"—has an unexpected end when his wife goes into labor. Two days later their son is born.

Stegner's party, then, began with the start of his career and ended with the birth of his first and only child. Or, as he put it in his autobiography, "My new family responsibilities and my new literary life began together." The fledgling novelist and father was twenty-eight years old.

Abbey's party was quite different. It too is re-created in fiction, in his late autobiographical novel, *The Fool's Progress*. In the novel, Abbey describes a sacrifice made on the day of the party, and his fictional wife's reaction to it: "She stopped and stared. Her husband, with blood smeared hands, forearms, face, knelt at the side of a blazing pit. Behind him a naked child hung upside down from a dead tree."

While Abbey could be extreme, there was in fact no child sacrifice. What his wife mistook for a child was a slow-cooking goat.

Then, as the goat continued to cook over the coals, a wild celebration broke out, made up of a crowd of artists, writers, and University of New Mexico students who drank all day, burned down the outhouse, and then leapt over it like pagans. The party didn't end until the wee hours of morning, when the Abbey character kicked over some embers and burned down the house. This is fiction, of course, but it is actually a composite of two real events in Abbey's life, as his biographer Jim Cahalan has pointed out. The first was the actual party where the goat was cooked. The second occurred in 1954, when Abbey and his second wife, Rita, were serving as caretakers of an old adobe home—a task that it would be hard to argue they performed well considering that they burned the house down soon after they moved in (ignited by a fire Abbey set in the stove).

I guess the point was that I didn't quite know how to tease out an answer to my koan, at least not yet. Of course, you could cite Abbey's frequent rants against immigration and his adamant belief in the right to bear arms, but I still had a hard time calling him a conservative. Somewhat to my own surprise, I actually found it easier to imagine Wallace Stegner as a radical. I thought of Wendell Berry's decision to not make ambition his personal deity. "The life that men praise and call successful is but one kind," wrote Thoreau. Wendell Berry knew this and acted on it, and in doing so he had a model who lighted his way: his old teacher. Rather than cash or fame, what was important was knowing a place, belonging to a place, committing to a place. Even, in Wendell Berry's language, *marrying* a place.

Like his student, Wallace Stegner was a placed person, defining himself against his placeless father. "The old man could never say anything without sounding like he was daring you to contradict him," Stegner wrote of Bo Mason in *The Big Rock Candy Mountain*. In a way, Wallace Stegner's whole life was lived as a contradiction to his father. Like so many of his ideas, Stegner's ideas about home grew out of his childhood. Having witnessed the failure of a thousand rugged individualists, his father among them, as they battled the inhospitable landscape, he came to believe in community. Having grown up in movement, he came to value staying put.

Where is home? Stegner asked near the end of *The Big Rock Candy Mountain*. Is it where we were born, where we spent our childhood, where we hang our hat? For too many Americans, especially the American who fathered him, it seemed to always be around the next corner. "The whole nation had been footloose for too long," he wrote at the novel's conclusion. "Heaven had been just over the range for too many generations. Why remain in one dull plot of earth when Heaven was reachable, was touchable, was just over there?"

It is a question that remains central for many contemporary American writers, not to mention many contemporary Americans. And it is this idea of home that perhaps starts to unlock Terry Tempest Williams's riddle. Perhaps to be radical in this country is to try to be rooted. Perhaps to be radical is to not flit after the next fancy over the hill, not to give into the culture's constant come-ons of "more," but to truly commit to one's place, one's family, one's mate. Perhaps that was what Tempest Williams had suggested.

And in a fractured, rootless, overheated world, is it wrong to consider these notions radical?

PARADISE, LOST AND FOUND

I followed the river and road down into Moab and encountered a different sort of spectacle: a great cluster of strip-mall tackiness where every sign hollered "Adventure!" RVs rumbled down the streets and a hundred gaudy signs tried to draw in tourists like beckoning recreational prostitutes, selling, instead of sex, rafting and biking and jeep tours. Think Vegas for outdoorsmen. Beamed down onto Main Street, an extraterrestrial could be forgiven for concluding that the word *adventure* was the most common in our world.

Moab has always been a boomtown, starting with the discovery of uranium in the 1950s, when it briefly reached a population of 9,000, or almost twice today's numbers. When uranium prices dove with the shift away from nuclear energy and the end of the Cold War in the '80s, the town floundered: unemployment skyrocketed and the population fell. But the town reinvented itself fairly quickly as a mountain-biking mecca, hosting the first fat-tire festival in 1986, and the chamber of commerce, realizing they were on to something, began to advertise it as a recreational haven. Today Moab is a center for biking, off-road vehicles, rafting, rock-climbing, skydiving, and anything else even vaguely adventurous, while playing host to dozens of annual festivals that include the Jeep Jamboree and the Moab MUni Fest ("MUni" of course being short for mountain unicycling).

The town's other main business is Edward Abbey. Or as my friend the writer Luis Urrea once called it, "The Dead Ed Industry." The last time I was here I stayed up at the Pack Creek Ranch in the La Sal Mountains, and the caretaker there said to me: "Ed Abbey was a hypocrite. His books brought more people to Moab than all the ads by the chamber of commerce." Certainly, I admitted to the man, he had brought me.

Despite the clutter and all the beckoning signage, I was happy to be back. I'd told myself that I would camp outside of Moab, but my hands had other ideas, turning the steering wheel so that the car pulled into the parking lot of a Sleep Inn off Main Street. My hands had a point: thunderclouds still threatened and the rain would have made camping unpleasant and possibly dangerous due to flash flooding.

After I'd thrown my bags in the room and washed up, I headed up to Arches National Park. Of course it's obligatory for someone writing a book about Edward Abbey to make the pilgrimage to this particular park, the setting of his greatest book, but it's also a place that has in some ways fulfilled Abbey's worst nightmares, and now seems to celebrate not just a wild red-rock landscape but the rise of the automobile. Abbey called these incursions of cars into national parks "industrial tourism." Could he have imagined where this would lead? Arches, which saw about 25,000 people during Abbey's entire stint as a ranger from 1956–57, now has almost a million visitors each year.

For all its beauty and grandeur, it is a hard place to view without irony. You try to find a spot to create some quiet, some personal relationship with the unearthly landscape, to drink a beer and maybe smoke an honorary cigar, and revel in the desert quiet. But then another line of cars comes ripping up the paved road. Or, as happened to me, a camper full of kids and parents landed right where I'd tried to have my little ceremony. Meanwhile there were no doubt other earnest Abbeyites in other parts of the park trying to worship in their own ways, also part of the larger crowd. It was like getting into a traffic jam on the way to Walden Pond (which I've also experienced), and soon I felt a dark mood descending.

Though this place was relatively unpeopled during the two seasons he worked as a ranger here, Abbey, too, did his share of grumbling while living in the park. Grumbling about tourists, although back then they had as many in a year as they now do in a week; grumbling about cars; grumbling about familial obligations (his second wife and first son were back in Hoboken, New Jersey); grumbling about his own precarious mental state, always just a step away from the melancholia he both feared and romanticized. The journals from that time tell a story of a man fighting depression, a brave man but an inconsistent one.

"The spoiler has come." This line from Robinson Jeffers, an early twentieth-century poet whose work had a great influence on Abbey, came into my mind as I walked away from the camper. But who was I to complain about all the people? I was no less a spoiler than the family that now spilled out over the rocks. Maybe it was simply a case of too many of us in the world, of the fact that for something to feel sacred we must feel it is *ours* and only attainable to a few. Is every traveler on this overstocked planet now by definition a tourist?

Soon I was driving again, gawking up at three giant sandstone towers that someone had named, perfectly, the Three Gossips. If this stunning landscape had lost its power to stun me, it still impressed: great sand doodles of rock, huge eye sockets in rock walls, muscular bulges of stone. I hadn't shaken my bad mood when I reached Balanced Rock, but there was only one other car in the parking area, which seemed promising.

And then something strange happened. All day bulky clouds had crowded the sky. But now the sun, just about to set, dipped below the line of clouds in the west, and the whole place lit up. In particular, Balanced Rock lit up. It *glowed* orange, and I noticed my own feet now taking charge, hurrying me closer to it. The only other person at the site was a man in a muscle shirt who had ignored the warnings about not stepping on cryptobiotic soil, and who was standing right below the rock itself, snapping pictures furiously. He no doubt resented the intrusion of another human and, respecting that, I walked around the other side of the rock, giving us both a half privacy.

Ravens shot by. Bats and swallows, too, both after the same insects. The rock *was* amazing: a fifty-five-foot-high boulder of slick rock balancing atop a more quickly eroding seventy-one-foot-high mudstone base. Dark was coming in like the tide, but the rock, high enough to catch the sun, stayed light, as if it were holding the day inside it, turning that intense, almost-edible orange you only find here. It occurred to me that I had been too cynical too quickly. The sunset line blazed and turned the distant La Sal Mountains pink. Something opened up inside me.

On the walk out I almost bumped into the muscle-shirted photographer. But I now felt more benevolent toward my own species.

"You had some good luck with the light there, huh?" I asked.

"You betcha," he said. "Got some real good ones."

Soon I was grumbling again, caught in a commuter line of red-ember taillights snaking out of the park. But I left glad I had come.

Maybe *inconsistent* is the wrong word for Edward Abbey. *Imperfect* may work better. Wendell Berry defined Abbey as an autobiographer, and *Desert Solitaire* is autobiography, though of course it is what Wendell called *selective* autobiography. We are treated to the wild thoughts of a man alone in the wilderness. There is no mention of the fact that there were times when Abbey's wife and young son shared his solitary trailer with him, and not much of the fact that the other half of the year was spent trying to salvage his marriage, working as a welfare caseworker in Hoboken. No matter. Paradise is never really paradise, idylls never truly idylls. In *Desert Solitaire*, Abbey created a character, a fiction, of a man living in nature, a man passing his days watching cloud formations, a man living bravely and in solitude. But his own life was never so simple. Not only was he about to undergo his second divorce, but to tell the truth he sometimes didn't do all that well in solitude, his brain turning on itself.

Of course, Abbey wasn't trying to tell the true and full story of his life. While he wrote about the exhilaration of living far apart from others, he still had his daily battles with anxiety, still had his regular worries.

But he had his moments, too. His elevated moments, his inspired moments, his transcendent ones. That was the important thing. It was out of those moments that he would build a great book.

Perhaps you could unravel many of the differences between Wallace Stegner and Ed Abbey by considering their attitudes toward "moments." Abbey disdained soft mysticism and his one experience with LSD was flat and uninspiring, but in other ways he fell in line with the '60s, the decade that celebrated the moment in so many forms: the ecstatic, the present, the sexual. Stegner, meanwhile, believed that even in the present we should respect the past and consider the future. Not that he didn't enjoy life—it seems clear he did—just that pleasure was fairly far down on his list of priorities.

If a sort of bristling impatience enlivened Stegner's early years, there is a different feel to Abbey's beginnings as a writer. Back in May, when I traveled to Tucson to work my way through the Edward Abbey collection at the University of Arizona, I spent a week with his journals and got some sense of what it was like to occupy that wild, shaggy, slovenly but often brilliant mind. I understood how a mind like that might not do so well when left to its own devices. As a philosophy major, Abbey prided himself on doing "the work of brooding," but the brooding in his writing was leavened by descriptions of landscape, and by creativity and humor. Because while Abbey brooded plenty, he was at heart not a philosopher but a maker. And it would turn out he was better at portraying a character named Ed Abbey in the act of philosophizing than he was at philosophizing itself.

I was struck, and even caught off guard a little, by just how smart the man was, how contemplative and well read. Also striking was the constant wordplay, including the jokes and bad puns, the frequent references to women he lusted after. Spread over it all like a mist net was all that melancholia and moodiness, something dark and slothful and, for all his love of outer nature, decidedly inward-turned. It felt darkly adolescent and, to me, familiar.

There was reason for depression, other than a simple genetic predisposition for it. From the time he left the East for good in 1948 and landed in the Southwest until the publication of *Desert Solitaire* twenty years later in 1968, Ed Abbey was involved in an immense struggle. The struggle was the brute effort to become a writer. True, he was involved in other things too: halfheartedly working toward his degree, getting married and falling in love a couple of times, working at various park ranger jobs and as a welfare counselor and, briefly, as a factory worker, roaming around the desert in old cars and trucks, and making a good many lifelong friends. But underneath it all, and seeping through it all, was a driving ambition that belied his claims of sloth: *he wanted to make something great.*

It's true that this effort was sporadic, and that his habits were never consistent. "I write best under duress," he confided to his journal. Then: "I write *only* under duress." Later when he taught creative writing to graduate students at the University of Arizona, he advised them to write regularly, every day. He was an intimidating teacher, but one student got up the nerve to ask if he did this himself. "No," he answered simply.

But words were set to the page, if not consistently then persistently. The journals filled up, little schoolboy notebooks crammed from end to end with scrawling cursive sentences, and the effort put into the first novel is impressive. During a Fulbright fellowship in Scotland in 1951, the twenty-four-year-old Abbey scribbled notes

about the need to write the book, notes that swing wildly between
pep talk and parody:

> About time my friend about time to think about the book,
> the first spasmodic effort of the reluctant soul harrowing itself
> for something to say; do I have something to say? Your god-
> damned ass I have something to say!
> What?

And:

> Everything. I'll throw everything in. Whole hog. Hog wild.
> A great big fat beautiful obscene book, the most hilarious,
> tear-jerking, side-splitting, throat-choking, belly-busting, heart-
> breaking book ever written. Don't forget the book in the book.
> (The proper place for parody.)
> Throw everything in? Maybe you better throw in the towel.

The trouble is that these journal notes show more life, and more
Abbey, than *Jonathan Troy* ever did. It was a novel that would embar-
rass him for the rest of his life, and for good reason. Thomas Wolfe
threw a long shadow over youthful writers in the mid-twentieth
century, longer than Hemingway's in some ways. Abbey's first
effort swells with both earnest Wolfian romanticism and chronic
self-obsession.

The larger point, however, was not the quality of the thing but
that he managed to complete an actual book. It might, as Abbey
himself said, be "juvenile, naïve, clumsy, pretentious" with "all the
obvious faults of the beginner," but for all but a few writers there is
no other way to get beyond those faults than to travel through them.
At the very least momentum was gained, and by the time the book
was published he had already written a good part of the *next* novel,
which, in its cinematic sparseness and external, nonautobiographi-

cal plot, seems a clear reaction against what had come before. *The Brave Cowboy*, and the book that followed it two years later, *Fire on the Mountain*, pit anachronistic cowboy heroes against the banal but destructive forces of modern life. It is fitting that *Cowboy*'s hero, Jack Burns, is killed on his horse when hit by a truck carrying a load of toilet seats down the interstate. Both of these next books are taut, full of action, scene-driven. Themes that will become recognizably Abbey's, in very different forms, are here: a preference for the old ways, an anger at what progress has wrought, a willingness to fight against ridiculous odds, the need to die a good death.

There is a hint of screenplay to these books—they are *boy* books, *action* books—and it is not entirely shocking that *The Brave Cowboy* was made into a movie starring Kirk Douglas, who would later say it was the favorite of all his more than a hundred films. You can't help but think that this taste of success influenced the direction of Abbey's fiction, and he admitted that he had half an eye toward film when he wrote *Fire on the Mountain* (which was, in fact, later made into a TV movie starring Buddy Ebsen). This tendency would get its full airing in the action-packed, cartoonish *The Monkey Wrench Gang*, which while not yet made into a film seems built for it.

Abbey was learning his chops as he crafted these tight, short books. But something else was going on at the same time that would ultimately prove even more important. All that roaming through the West had brought him into contact with some of the most beautiful places on the planet. And new words and sentences were coming, words and sentences that seemed to spring directly from the land. In 1956, the same year that *The Brave Cowboy* was published, he spent his first season as a ranger at Arches. On August 26 of that summer he wrote: "This is the thing. The desert is a good place—clean, honest, dangerous, uncluttered, strong, open, big, vibrant with legend." In his journals, and in his subsequent nonfiction, he retains some of his early sensual romanticism: "The more I dim my eyes over print and frazzle my brain over abstract ideas, the more I want and appre-

ciate the delight of being basically an animal wrapped in a sensitive
skin: sex, the resistance of rock, the taste and touch of snow, the feel
of sun, good wine and rare beefsteak and the company of friends
around a fire with guitar and lousy old cowboy songs." Counter-
balancing this is something harder, something leaner. He is learning this leanness in part from the craft of fiction, but also from the
desert itself, which seems to be offering up its own aesthetic. Three
years later, on August 15, 1959, Abbey, now living in Albuquerque,
described what it would mean to "write like the desert":

> Conrad. To write of—no, to do for the desert what he did
> for—of—the sea. But I must avoid his rich flowing organ-valved
> almost lush (tropical) style. Emulate his passion for the exact.
> My style: something almost harsh, bitter, ugly. The rough com-
> pressed, asymmetrical, laconic, cryptic. Cactus. Old Juniper.
> Rock, dry, heat, the stark contour.
> *NO FOG. NO GODDAMED FOG.*
> Combine intensity (not density) with clarity. *Clear* and
> *intense.* Like the desert landscape, the desert light, the desert
> atmosphere—clear, intense and infinitely suggestive. Hard dis-
> tinctions, precise outlines—but each thing, suggesting, some-
> how, everything else. As in truth each thing does.

This was a beautiful, and incredibly self-aware, description of
one of the effects that Abbey would create in his coming work. He
would gain the clean intensity he was looking for, but would also
retain some of the remnant romanticism, including a little lushness
and even, despite his intentions, a few shreds of fog. Sparseness and
abundance would both come into play. The key would be the coun-
terpoise of these elements, the contradictory dancing back and forth
that could never be contained within third-person boy action novels.
The key in fact would be the embracing of the first-person voice, the
voice he had long been sharpening in the journals.

From a distance an artist's life can have the cleanness of pattern, and we can see how the "subject" is developing in ways that please us, in part because we know the end result. It's not so easy for the artist him- or herself, trapped as they are in their own lives. The big prize for Abbey, as it was for Stegner and Wolfe and most every writer of the twentieth century, was The Novel, and when he scrawled down his desert notes he was still almost ten years away from making his breakthrough and turning to nonfiction. The scribblings in the journal were just that: scribblings. What might seem like success to some—three published books with one made into a movie—was not success to him. Kirk Douglas might be a new fan, and might say upon meeting Abbey that he looked like Gary Cooper, but otherwise he was virtually unknown. And he was poor, struggling to pay rent and alimony. Heading into his forties, he still had the worries, and the reactions to those worries, of an adolescent. This, too, is endemic to the writer's life, where any kind of monetary success, if it comes at all, usually comes late. He knew he loved the spare, brilliant light of the desert and he dreamed of writing like the place itself. But he wasn't sure of much else.

THERE IS A different feel to Wallace Stegner's early years as an artist. One of his favorite quotations, and one that he repeats over and over in his books, is from Henry James: "Order is the dream of man, but chaos is the law of nature." While he admits to the world's chaos, order remains the dream. The quotation has more than a little biographical significance: it was out of the chaos of his own childhood that Stegner created the order of his adult life.

It is a tricky business trying to retrace how a personality develops, imagining a little nurture here, a dash of nature there. With Stegner some things were there right from the start: his love of books, his assiduousness in poisoning gophers. But it seems clear that so much of the man was forged during his difficult early years. It was against the image of himself as the family runt that he would create the respected, responsible man. And if he was fashioned by those years, then so was something else: his belief that individuals have a hand in their own fashioning. He would hold on to this conviction his entire life, frequently using what would come to seem dated words like *will* and *determination*.

A tough-minded view of life seems almost inevitable, given the circumstances. The transition from boyhood to manhood was not a gradual one for Wallace Stegner. His brother Cecil died of pneumonia soon after high school, and two years later his beloved mother died from cancer. And as his family in Salt Lake unraveled, his mother and brother dead and his father broke and increasingly desperate, he began to create his own family, marrying Mary Page, who would be his companion for the next sixty years.

The young family headed east, if not exactly fleeing the West then perhaps not minding putting some distance between themselves and their troubles. I have described Wallace Stegner as someone who charged through life, but there is one odd detail that complicates this picture. For such a willful and determined man, it was remarkable what a role that luck played in Wally Stegner's fate. He was finishing his degree at Utah in Salt Lake City, contemplating taking a full-time job selling carpets and linoleum at his friend's father's shop, when a professor at the university pulled on an old contact to get him a position as a grad student at the University of Iowa. He had not set out to be a writer, or at least had not yet fully admitted that ambition, though he'd already won a contest at a local paper that led to the publication of a short story, but he arrived in Iowa at the moment that the Iowa Writers' Workshop was born. This was the Depression, and there were no jobs to be found, so he stayed within academia after graduating.

The next stop on the family's eastern migration was Madison, Wisconsin, where Wallace took an untenured job as a teacher. In

Madison, Stegner was let go after one year, but during that year he and Mary met the couple who would become their closest friends, Peg and Phil Gray. The well-connected Grays would lead them farther east, to Vermont and then to Cambridge, and once again Stegner's luck—as if in counterbalance to the ill luck of the family he left behind—held. A former roommate from Iowa, Wilbur Schramm, managed to get him a position on the staff of the Bread Loaf Writers' Conference, and the young westerner was soon hobnobbing with Robert Frost, Archibald MacLeish, and perhaps most important of all, Bernard DeVoto. Connections made there—more luck!—led to him being one of the first group of Briggs-Copeland lecturers at Harvard.

But settled in the exotic East, Stegner's mind roamed west, and on top of his heavy teaching load he worked obsessively on *The Big Rock Candy Mountain*, the autobiographical account of his wandering childhood. He would later write that he had a "good part of it done when my father made it imperative, and gave it its fated ending" with the murder and suicide in 1940. This was the forever-imprinting event: his father, who had written his son increasingly desperate letters begging for money, shooting himself in a shabby hotel room in downtown Salt Lake City. But not before killing Dorothy LeRoy, a woman he was in a relationship with. In this way—brutally, unceremoniously—Wallace Stegner was cast out into the world.

Stegner admitted later that the novel in which he tried to capture this event was not "a literary effort but an act of exorcism." The book was published in 1943, and two years later the young Stegner family moved back west, leaving Harvard for California, where he would start the Stanford Writing Program.

If he had not burned to write at first, had almost backed into it really, once he got rolling, and especially once Page was born, he applied himself to his own pages with a startling ferocity. Work and production were the watchwords of those years. In the five years from 1937 to 1942 he published four novels and a work of nonfiction called *Mormon Country* while also teaching four classes per term. Not everything went as planned and the novels didn't sell very well, but he didn't have time for complaining. There was work to do, dammit.

AFTER A NIGHT at the Sleep Inn, I got up early and dressed in Lycra. It was hard to imagine either Abbey or Stegner approving. I looked ridiculous, I suppose, especially given my current girthy profile. A middle-aged man in black, skintight clothes.

My destination was Slickrock, the world-famous mountain-biking trail that crawls over the land above Moab. Before it was a sandstone playground, of course, it was something else. "Abbey's Country," perhaps, but Stegner's Country too, and Stegner's next book after *Big Rock* would in fact be *Mormon Country*, a historical account of Utah and the Mormon religion.

What it wasn't was Gessner Country, and I found I was gasping for air within a hundred yards of starting to pedal. I had been younger when I last rode here, and braver apparently, since the prospect of climbing up the Slickrock walls, and trusting that the tires would stick as I climbed, unnerved me now as it hadn't then.

My last visit had come four years before, during the dying days of the Bush administration. Around the time I was boarding my plane west, in November of 2008, a 1,235-page manuscript landed with a thud on the desks of environmentalists all over southeast Utah. This was an eleventh-hour surprise from Bush and company, courtesy of the Bureau of Land Management (BLM), a plan to open up millions of acres of public land, not just to the extractive industries but to off-road vehicles. As a comic capstone to this episode, Bush, calling himself "the mountain biker in chief," also proposed opening up hiking trails in national parks to mountain biking.

While the now ex-president may have pushed things to the point of the absurd, his agenda brought up some interesting questions. When we look at the present-day West it's easy to wag a finger and say, "Bad drillers," but, as a sometimes Lycra-clad mountain biker myself, I wonder: where does our recreation culture fit into the West's overall economic and environmental picture? Are we helping or hurting? Is the beauty of our public lands just another resource to exploit—like natural gas, gold, silver, oil, or uranium? In "Thoughts on a Dry Land," Wallace Stegner wrote: "We are in danger of becoming scenery sellers—and scenery is subject to as much enthusiastic overuse and overdevelopment as grass and water."

During that trip I talked with Rob Bleiberg about the boom in recreation. While Rob has loads of respect and sympathy with the ranchers and farmers he worked with, he also warned me not to be too hard on the Lycra set. He pointed to the town of Fruita, which neighbored his home in Grand Junction, and which had become a mountain-biking hot spot.

"Well, they come here to play but then maybe some of them decide to stay. And then maybe they get involved in the town. They come here because they love the land and more than a few of them end up fighting for it."

It was an interesting thought. The possibility that recreators could become citizens, that some of the Lycra-clad could be numbered among the stickers. It even made a kind of sense. Being outdoors has always defined being western, and who says that outdoorsmen can't straddle a Stumpjumper instead of a stallion? Stegner, speculating on how a western town might move from temporary to permanent— that is, how it might fight to "make itself into a place and . . . likely remain one"—suggested that it would help for the town to have, on top of the traditional enterprises, a university and a writer or two who actually comes from and writes about that place. In updating this equation, was it so crazy to suggest adding a few hikers or mountain bikers to the mix?

Thomas Michael Power, a professor and former chair of the Eco-

nomics Department at the University of Montana, doesn't think
so. One of the arguments against wilderness areas in the West is
that they take potentially lucrative lands out of the hands of those
who might use them for economic gain, thereby stymieing the local
economies. But Power's studies suggest that preserved wilderness
lands actually spur the creation of nearby businesses and services,
from bike shops to restaurants to rafting tours—what has come to be
called the "amenities economy." More recent studies suggest it goes
beyond mere amenities. People tend to move to beautiful places, and
money tends to follow people. This, of course, happens even more
in our current computer economy, where companies often consider
beauty when they decide where to locate. "Thus it cannot be said
that environmental quality is only an aesthetic concern to be pur-
sued if a community feels prosperous enough to afford it," writes
Power in *Lost Landscapes and Failed Economies.*

It is worth pausing on this point as we consider the relative "wildness" of the West. The fact that beauty can be an economic benefit, even when we are not ripping things out of the earth. That we
can make hard-nosed, practical gains by leaving something alone.
Before I left on my trip, I talked to Ben Alexander, a friend of Rob
Bleiberg's and the associate director of Headwater Economics, based
in Bozeman, Montana. He pointed me toward a fascinating study
that found that, in recent years, human service jobs had grown by
345 percent in non-metro counties that had more than 30 percent
of their nearby lands protected as federal lands. These are mainly
human-resource, not natural-resource, jobs, which provide a potentially more reliable and steady model for economic growth, less given
to the extractive industry's highs and lows. And there is also this: a
community that depends on the beauty of its environment, while in
danger of becoming scenery stealers, will also be less likely to allow
the exploiters and extractors to soil that beauty. Of course, Power
and Alexander are not advocating a complete shift from a goods to
services economy and acknowledge that the amenities economy has

"to be maintained at an appropriate scale." But perhaps a bike shop and a coffee shop, as well as jobs in education, health care, and other professions, could be added to more traditional businesses, and to that potential university, to fill out Stegner's list of what might bring long-term viability to a western town. A larger question, of course, is whether such a formula will prove durable enough, particularly during troubled times, to withstand the short-term temptations of the extractive industries.

It was time to get away from Slickrock, and also to get away from that famous and mythical creature, "It All." While Moab is a fine town, it is also an example of Dr. Power's "amenities economy" run wild, seen through a funhouse mirror, with little regard for "appropriate scale." Moab, at its best, is a jumping-off point.

Dark, ragged clouds threatened up above the La Sal range as I drove south on Route 191 and then west on 211 toward Canyonlands National Park. Not long after the turn west the bottom dropped out of the world and I headed down, down into it, into the heart of the canyons. The flash-flood signs in the wash took on more than the usual urgency given the rain of the night before, but the weather also excited me: in the American West, the sudden introduction of that missing element, water, changes everything, sometimes for good, sometimes for bad. These arroyos I crossed through might look like wide and gentle paths to most easterners, but were in fact fallow creek beds, looking docile but waiting for water. When it finally came they could show off their true nature and roar like a train.

The one ranch I passed, which Rob Bleiberg had once told me belonged to the Redd family, relied on acreage of a magnitude that would be preposterous by eastern standards. Heidi Redd had sold it to the Nature Conservancy at a large discount to preserve and protect it, and so that she could stay on (though no longer the owner).

The ranch itself held over 5,000 acres, but its cattle grazed on the 250,000 acres of grassland leased from the government. It was good luck for the Redds to have Indian Creek running through their land, though what today looked like a gentle stream could in other moods turn angry. To understand why this land is so vulnerable you have to understand the fundamental lack, a lack of water that alternates with a sudden, occasional overabundance, like a dehydrated man choking on his first gulp from a canteen.

The reason this land I was driving through was so vulnerable, to mining and driving and the tires of mountain bikes, to people in general, is that it is so dry. And like dry skin, it cracks easily and heals slowly.

Ravens hopped across the road, casually getting out of the way of the car. I passed no one, which excited me. At Arches I had grumbled about wanting to be alone, and now I had my chance. No one else, I supposed, was brave or maybe stupid enough to camp here on a stormy day in monsoon season. At the moment I wasn't worried. Great mythic slabs of rock, red monuments, lined the road to the north. Bulging ramparts, with orange and yellow-red scree sloping down at their feet. As I drove on and downward the valley opened up and I entered the land of rock needles, towers shooting up eight hundred feet into the sky, spires and pinnacles. I stopped and got out before the entrance to the park proper. The sun broke through as I took out my binoculars and stared across at the canyon walls of Chesler Park.

It was then I saw what I had hoped for: silver streaks running down the troughs of orange cliffs. Waterfalls. Not one, not two, but half a dozen. Silver water against red rock. Water in a dry land.

I turned off a mile before the park entrance and followed the dirt road onto Bureau of Land Management (BLM) land. My usual campground, the one I camped at with Nina before we got married, and with my friend Mark Honerkamp, was down by Indian Creek, but it would not be wise to descend all that way to the creek given the weather. With enough rain the creek would not be content to stay within its bed. So instead I set up my tent at Hamburger Rock, which matched its name almost exactly, an H. R. Pufnstuf village of bulbous sandstone where I could sleep under a ledge during what might be a wet night. There was still some light, so with the tent up, I decided to bike down to the creek. Muddy red water flowed over pockmarked rock before dropping over falls. I looked up to where I knew I'd see an Anasazi kiva and, sure enough, there it was. Farther up was the ledge where Honerkamp, Nina, and I once climbed to watch the lunar eclipse. ("That's the last sight we'll ever see," Hones said when the sky went dark, leaving us blind atop a rock cliff.) I rode my bike down into one of the side canyons, got lost, fretted that I had not brought along a first-aid or snake-bite kit. I was learning that as you get older there is more to be afraid of, or at least more to worry about. But I made it back to camp in time to drink a beer on top of Hamburger Rock and watch the last glimmer of sun. I sat out on a ledge roughly the shape of the head of a loggerhead turtle. Small junipers gnarled out of rock.

I realized how much I'd missed the place. If the West really "faces you like a dare" as Stegner said, then here it was. I was happy to be without phone or Internet, just scribbling down my thoughts in my journal, but then decided it was time for bed when the winds picked up and the first streaks of lightning blazed across the southern sky. Clouds came alive, illuminated from the inside by the lightning. I was a little worried about getting soaked, but between my tarp and the ledge of rock I thought I'd be okay. To my surprise I slept deeply. At least until I got up in the middle of the night to take a leak and heard the close howling of coyotes. The sand was wet, but overhead patches of stars blazed between the clouds. I suspected I would live until morning.

I woke alone in the desert. My tent was dry but evidence of rain was readily available. When I went exploring I found red froth churning down Indian Creek. This is what this red, parched land spends

most of the year waiting for. The sound of running water filled me
with a bubbly Champagne happiness that almost counteracted the
lack of coffee. I took a morning bath below the falls, though it didn't
leave me clean so much as coated. To an outsider—there were none,
fortunately—it might have looked like I was wearing a red, caked
onesie, even tighter on my skin than yesterday's Lycra.

I took a long bike ride—three hours—through the dry land. I
headed north on the dirt path toward Moab. I saw no one, just red
dirt and red rock, tower after tower after tower. My environmental outrage upon seeing the crowds the previous day was somewhat
tempered by the fact that I had now not encountered a human being
in close to twenty-four hours.

The night before I had been nervous while riding into the side
canyon, but while I was in essentially the same circumstances that
morning—all alone with no first aid—I felt nothing but exhilarated.
Maybe that was stupid. And maybe it was stupid to keep pedaling and
pedaling, farther and farther away from camp. But my "keep going
around the next corner" gene had been engaged. Pumping my legs,
sweating, I stared out at sights I felt privileged to see. All alone, I felt
immensely happy and looking back I still do. How wonderful that
once you shut down your nagging brain, moments like these are still
available. I rode over red rock, out to an overlook of the Needles, feeling like I had eaten hallucinogens, not a granola bar, for breakfast.

We pay a lot of lip service to the word *freedom*. But for me the
essence of the word comes from these moments. Just you and the
beautiful world and a long day ahead to do whatever the hell you
want. It was what pulled in Abbey, and a million others, too.

It is also the reason so many of us are resistant to restraint, to
regulating and policing our public lands. "Lawlessness, like wildness,
is attractive, and we conceive the last remaining home of both to be
in the West," wrote Stegner. Yes: we come west for that feeling of
wildness, of lawlessness, the sense that we can do what we want and
do it on our own.

The problem comes, however, when one person's freedom impedes another's. This problem is exemplified, in southeast Utah at least, by the rise of the off-road vehicles (ORVs). As alone as I felt right then, I knew there were days when this same road was a motor course, and the quiet filled with the roar of a speedway. I could see it right there in front of me in the many tire treads in the sand.

During my trip four years earlier I had spoken with Liz Thomas of the Southern Utah Wilderness Alliance. "Mining and drilling are the biggest environmental issues in northern Utah," she told me. "But off-highway vehicles are the biggest issue in southeastern Utah, hands-down. Right now there are twenty thousand miles of route in Utah. If you look at a BLM map it looks like a bloodshot eye."

The public BLM lands are the lands I had slept on the night before, the lands I was riding through, and they are the lands that for many of us—from hiker to mountain biker to rancher to ORV user—make up the real essence of what is left of wild Utah.

Bike tires can cause damage too, it's true, and mountain bikers aren't somehow morally superior to ORV users. I understand that I am rightfully open to charges of hypocrisy as I go about indicting my fellow recreators. But unlike our ex-president, I have no interest in opening up trails in national parks and other public lands to biking, and if someone told me I had to keep my bike off these trails, I'd be okay with that, too. What I want to preserve are not just beautiful places but the possibility that an individual can, in this overheated, overcrowded world, find a place to be quiet and alone. To have their own freedom. Is this really too much to ask? Shouldn't there be a few places left to get away from motors? From the incessant roar of machines?

Quiet recreation—mountain biking, hiking, river rafting, backpacking, fishing, even, relatively speaking, hunting—bring almost a billion dollars into Utah each year. We can start there if we like, though anyone who has spent time here knows that this red rock has a lot more to offer than financial gain. In his famous "Wilderness Letter," Wallace Stegner, writing to the Outdoor Recreation Resources Review Commission in 1960, extolled the spiritual resources of wilderness land beyond any obvious *uses* for recreation or extraction or development. Stegner wrote of this wilderness ideal: "Being an intangible and spiritual resource, it will seem mystical to the practical minded—but then anything that cannot be moved by a bulldozer is likely to seem mystical to them." He urged the commission to consider "some other criteria than commercial" when it came to putting aside wilderness lands, stressing open spaces not just as a counterbalance to "our insane lives," but as something integral, and vital, to our national character.

You could argue that responsible drivers of ORVs are following the better impulses that Stegner describes, and many of them are. But the problem of motorized recreation is one of sheer scope. The increased use of Bureau of Land Management land for ORVing, and the great range of the new motorized users, has led to the destruction of thousands of acres and hundreds of Native American archaeological sites. The dry land cracks under those wheels and the dry land doesn't heal.

If one person's freedom can destroy another's, consider the roaring freedom of off-road vehicles, which make up only 7 percent of the Moab area's recreators but have access to 81 percent of BLM land. Those who stay on the existing roads do minimal damage, but since freedom and exploration are central to the activity's appeal, heading off-trail and splashing down riverbeds, for instance, is common. As for sheriffing the motorists, or the bikers and hikers for that matter, the last time I had been here there had been two BLM agents in the Moab office in charge of overseeing the area's 10 million acres.

During that trip, I had a long talk with Bill Hedden, executive director of the Grand Canyon Trust.

"If you go out on just the absolutely legitimate roads, you could drive every day for the rest of your life," Hedden said. "The problem is that Moab invites everybody in the world to come here and go crazy for these festivals. Whole families in campers towing four ORVs. Then their kids ride out into the desert and create a zone of destruction. And the desert doesn't heal."

Earlier that year Hedden had accompanied Jon Huntsman, then Utah's governor, out to Canyonlands National Park. Afterward, the governor, an ORV user himself, called damage done by off-road vehicles that did not stick to set trails "an abomination."

For 93 percent of Moab's visitors, who have come to encounter not motors but nature, ORVs do not mean freedom but its opposite. Many of us can't shake the feeling that loud, motorized vehicles don't belong in the wilderness. Ranchers and other Old Westerners, and now ORV drivers, have long resented having the government tell them what they can or can't do on public land. But with greater numbers and greater use, it may just be that championing regulation and restraint, while not quite as sexy as championing freedom, is the key to preserving the smaller freedoms that are left. Conversely, allow for unregulated freedom and you end up with Moab or worse. Not the freedom of the wild but that of raw commercialism.

So what is to be done? If to think deeply is to think practically, then mere fretting or hand-wringing doesn't help. One solution that Bill Hedden has proposed is a massive zoning of BLM's millions of acres, some areas being designated for off-roading, some for biking and hiking, and others preserved as pockets of true wilderness. This might have rankled Ed Abbey's old-time sense of freedom, as it clearly rankles the drivers of ORVs, who don't like the word *no*. Working against any effort to zone is the determination to open it all up, and the local government's old-school belief that the lands are theirs to do with as they will. In other words, as Stegner well knew, the wild-man myth is working to destroy the last wild lands.

The other obstacle is getting people to really believe that this is a land in crisis. This is a hard concept to get your head around if you, like me, were at the moment alone in a spectacularly beautiful place without another human being around for miles. But this was the old beginner's problem of judging the West by eastern standards. We wonder: how can this giant really be threatened by us, the few and the puny?

It can because this giant—and the animals and plants that live on it—is already involved in a daily precarious daily fight for survival. It can because this giant is perpetually dehydrated, starved for water, and easily scarred.

LATER THAT DAY I packed up the tent and threw my bike on the rack, bidding adieu to Hamburger Rock. Soon I was driving north up 191, heading toward the La Sal Mountains in hopes of talking to a man whom I first knew as a character in a novel. I decided not to call Ken Sleight ahead of time but rather to ambush him. Sleight was the eighty-three-year-old former river rafter and horseman who was the inspiration for Seldom Seen Smith, the adventurous and laconic "Jack Mormon" who co-starred in Abbey's best-known novel, *The Monkey Wrench Gang*. Seldom Seen was one of the band of eco-saboteurs who roamed the western landscape protecting its beautiful places by whatever means necessary, none of them legal. Ever since the book had been published over thirty years before, people had sought out Ken Sleight in hopes of meeting Seldom Seen, so if anyone knew about the confusion of fiction and nonfiction, reality and myth, it was Sleight.

I had first met Ken Sleight on my trip here four years earlier, and I think it's fair to say we hit it off. That day started at around nine in the morning, when I went to interview him in the aluminum-roofed bunker above his horse pasture—he offered me a Milwaukee's Best after cracking one of his own—and ended many hours later with both of us yelling at the TV as Sarah Palin prattled on during the vice-presidential debate with Joe Biden.

I pulled into Pack Creek Ranch—fjord-green in summer—with its aspens and pines, and pastures of goats and horses, all with views of red-rock towers and arches below. Huge thunderheads collected above, up atop the majestic La Sal range. No wonder this had been one of the places Ed Abbey loved. After I parked, I talked briefly with the new caretakers, who generously showed me the cabin where Abbey wrote when he stayed there. They pointed out that Abbey, a tall man, must have bumped his head a lot on the low roof. I thanked them and wandered up past the chickens in an open field to the "shop," the Quonset hut where Ken held court. I found him in basically the same spot where I'd left him four years before, as if he hadn't moved since. He was sipping whiskey out of a coffee cup, sitting behind a desk that was cluttered with papers, old computer files, and two computers, one defunct or at least unplugged. Despite the heat, he wore a blue checkered flannel shirt with a blue dungaree shirt over it, and he smiled widely upon my arrival. True, he looked a little older, but basically none the worse for the wear: shaggy white eyebrows, hunched shoulders, ears that stuck out like jug handles, a big thatch of white hair. Best of all, he even seemed to vaguely remember who I was.

This time no beer was offered, which was fine with me with a long drive ahead. I apologized for taking him by surprise, telling him I just wanted to say hi before leaving town. He suggested I take a seat and so I did, across the desk from him in the cluttered office. And then, with just a little prompting, he was off and reminiscing about his old friend.

"I knew about Abbey for a while when he worked at Arches, but I didn't meet him there. Then he got laid off at Arches and the Park Service hired him for Lees Ferry. When I came down to put my boats in at Lees Ferry, there he was. He came over to talk to me and my girlfriend. He helped us rig out. We sat on the edge of that boat talking until two or three in the morning. Talking about how we would get rid of that damn dam. That was the beginning of *The Monkey Wrench Gang*, I think."

It was the Glen Canyon Dam that he was referring to, the dam that Abbey hated more than any other. I asked Ken about his fictional alter ego, Seldom Seen Smith.

"It's a novel. It's not all that Abbey believed just because he put it down on paper. Seldom Seen had some parts of me, but he wasn't me. It was a caricature, but I didn't mind. I knew it wasn't me.

"He liked to take a lot of notes, see. How many he threw away I don't know. But he would gather the sense of the thing.

"He had a kind manner about him. But he would turn away from people. Especially after he got sick. You can't do everything. Sometimes he wouldn't respond to people the way they wanted him to respond. He would get criticized for that.

"He did a lot of writing right here in my roadside cabin. And in the little cabin next to it. If I came up and heard him typing, I would stay the hell away. And I'd try to keep other people away. Everyone wanted to know Ed, and Ed appreciated my buffer. That I would push people off. A couple times I really did have to push. If he wanted to he could have done one interview after another. But that way he would never get any work done.

"But he was a kind man. A good friend. Of course he had his opinions. He got out in front. On the front lines. He liked antagonizing people. He criticized the environmental community. Some of them loved it. Others didn't. And of course he antagonized the ranchers. He wrote a letter to the editor here about raising cattle on the mountain, called cows 'stinking bovine.' The editor got over thirty letters back."

Ken paused, rubbed his chin, and stared back at me with an expression you could describe as a friendly glare.

"'Are they thinking?' That's what he would always say. What he wanted to know is 'Are they really thinking?' Regardless of what they think of me, I want them to *think*."

The best times with Abbey, he added, were by the campfire while on the river.

"He could speak around the campfire with no inhibition. We were close, like we were in the same family. Like brothers. Just speak what you feel. That's what he did. I would speak too, but he knew so damn much more than me. He was a mentor to me, a teacher. You don't hear that too much, but he was to a lot of people. He had a way of bringing you into these conversations, and when it was over you realized you had learned a hell of a lot. He could be serious, could be playful. He changed all the time, and quick. But I always knew which Abbey I was talking to."

To me it sounded a lot like the way he was on the page, joking one minute and serious the next, all mixed together. I mentioned something I had read recently. How some scientists speculated that gathering around fires was the original unique characteristic of human beings. Not language or metaphor or tool use but the social circle, the gathering around the flame, the place where all those other discoveries were communicated.

"Yup, that's right. Around the campfire you have a lot of spirit and it comes out in different ways. Kidding each other, serious thought. Singing. Politics, nature, jokes. Everything mixed, like you say. Campfires are a medium of expression all their own."

"Abbey had that nice resonant voice, and that turned a lot of people on," he added. "He had no use for small talk. In conversation he always wanted to dig a little deeper. To get the answer. And he'd listen when you talked. You had to watch it too. A lot of times what you said could end up in a book."

Ken spoke for a while more and then quietly stared off at the far wall. I decided I had taken up enough of his time and stood up to shake his hand. He asked me about my project, and when I gave him a brief description he surprised me.

"You know Wallace Stegner stayed here once too," he said.

"Here?"

"Yup, right here in Pack Creek. I always regret I didn't get a chance to really talk to him. Or really to just listen. I would have liked to just sit there and listen to the man."

He walked me over to my car and I thanked him and we shook hands. I drove down the mountain, out of the La Sals, and back north toward Moab. My goal was to get to the town of Vernal in northern Utah, a town that was booming on oil and gas, not recreation. On the way north I pulled off the highway and into Arches to say a last good-bye, but I didn't stay long since I wanted to reach Vernal by dark. So I bid a hasty good-bye to paradise, climbed into the car, and stepped on the gas, driving northward toward something else altogether.

WRITERS, LIKE OTHER human beings, have plans. Goals, destinations. But what happens often enough is that it is the misdirections and sidetracks on the way to those goals—the getting lost—that prove most fruitful. This is not a soft, groovy concept but one as tough and real as evolution. David Quammen, in a brilliant appreciation of Abbey in *Outside* magazine shortly after his death, retells a story that Abbey himself liked to tell about how *Desert Solitaire* came to be. After a New York editor had rejected his fiction and suggested he "write something he knew," Ed went back to his "condemned tenement in Hoboken" and "typed up, out of nostalgia, an account of a couple of summers I had frittered away, playing the flute and reading Dreiser, in the Utah desert."

Quammen writes: "Swallow that intact at your own risk. But do note Abbey's persuasive insistence on a central point: the creation of the book was somehow unpremeditated, offhanded, uncalculated. In writing it he surprised himself, I believe, with the lovely discovery that his powers of observation, his unadorned passions and convictions, most of all his singular voice, could be shaped into an act of literature just as potent—just as artful, even—as an assemblage of invented characters and plot."

David Quammen would know about the way that writers evolve in unexpected ways. In his twenties he had moved to Montana and become a fishing guide while setting out to be a novelist in the style of his hero, William Faulkner. But when two of his clients turned out to be the editors of a fledgling magazine, *Outside*, he was invited to write a column for that magazine, and in this way learned that he was actually a nonfiction writer. Abbey, too, would become something other than what he set out to be. He would later make a point of disparaging his nonfiction as "just journalism." It wasn't. It was something special, unique, and it remains so. He had unintentionally trained during all those years wandering the desert and writing in his journals, and in *Desert Solitaire* that journal voice would have a chance to get directly at the things he had until then just circled around.

Without *Desert Solitaire*, I would never have heard of Abbey, nor would millions of others. So what is this book that Wendell Berry and others claim will last?

The story is simple enough: a man living alone in the desert apart from the values, and other denizens, of the modern world, speaking about what has gone wrong in American life and how what is still right is often found in nature. "No, wilderness was not a luxury," Abbey wrote, "but a necessity of the human spirit, and as vital to our lives as water and good bread." The plot was not really a plot: in one chapter someone gets lost in the desert, in another Abbey sees some snakes, in another he has breakfast, in yet another he throws out scene and setting altogether and rants against the use of cars in national parks in the manner of a cranky letter to the editor. If a traditional plot can be at all ascribed, it might be that the protagonist has found paradise here, alone in the desert, and that the forces of progress are marching forward to make sure that paradise is lost.

Abbey rolled his eyes at the way that every writer who mentions a twig or bug is called "the next Thoreau." And yet with *Desert Solitaire* the comparison with *Walden* seems unavoidable. It starts with the similarities between the two books, both of which celebrated years in the wild. Here was Thoreau at Walden but a Thoreau for the modern world, a Thoreau with a more outrageous sense of humor and a fuck-it spirit, a Thoreau with a gun and pickup truck, a Thoreau with a beer in hand and a trailer instead of a cabin.

"I love a broad margin to my life," writes Thoreau, and what is Abbey's life at Arches—lounging with a hot cup of coffee on the trailer steps, wandering among his rocks—if not one with a broad margin? Both men suggest an alternative way of living, a less harried, fretful way, and also suggest that their contemporaries have made a seriously wrong turn in their choices of life.

What people don't remember who have not read Thoreau since high school, or who have never read him at all but just use his name as cultural shorthand, is how wild and confident his voice can be. The two men, a century apart in time and a world apart in temperament, had obviously distinct voices, but they shared this: those voices were complex, unpredictable, and confident. In his biography of Thoreau, Joseph Wood Krutch speaks of the "magisterial confidence" of the writer's voice. Krutch describes how the "sense of being right" despite the world thinking him wrong pervades Thoreau's book, and how purely joyous the book often is. "Joy is a symptom by means of which right conduct may be recognized," Krutch writes.

We feel that joy in the pages of *Desert Solitaire*, too, with Abbey's voice ringing out in all its varied tones. And what Krutch says of Thoreau is true of Abbey: he makes "no sense of distinction between the serious and the comic, the temporal and the eternal." Puns and meditations, ontology and fart jokes, it all gets thrown in. In the fiction the jokes sometimes fall flat, forced, but here they work because they are part of something larger, and that something larger is one man's complex character and complex voice. It is a voice always ready to contradict itself, like a stream rushing one way while eddying another, so much so that, even though it is definitely one man talking, the voice sometimes seems more dialogue than monologue. One line might be so Whitmanesque and sensual that it would make other modern writers, and readers, cringe. But in the next line he could be as blunt as a truck driver. And in the next he would throw in a joke, or a bit of philosophizing, or a stunning description of a juniper or flowering yucca.

There is a famous passage early on in *Desert Solitaire* in which Abbey, walking through Arches, picks up a rock, throws it at a rabbit, and, to his surprise, kills the animal. Abbey, being Abbey, does not shrink with guilt over this act. Instead he characteristically runs through a gamut of emotions and thoughts, ending with a kind of exaltation:

> For a moment I am shocked by my deed; I stare at the quiet rabbit, his glazed eyes, his blood drying in the dust. Something vital is lacking. But shock is succeeded by a mild elation. Leaving my victim to the vultures and maggots, who will appreciate him more than I could—the flesh is probably infected with tularemia—I continue my walk with a new, augmented cheerfulness which is hard to understand but unmistakable. What the rabbit has lost in energy and spirit seems added, by processes too subtle to fathom, to my own soul. I try but cannot feel any sense of guilt. I examine my soul: white as snow. Check my hands: not a trace of blood. No longer do I feel so isolated from the sparse and furtive life around me, a stranger from another world. I have entered into this one. We are kindred all of us, killer and victim, predator and prey, me and the sly coyote, the soaring buzzard, the elegant gopher snake, the trembling cottontail, the foul worms that feed on our entrails, all of them, all of us. Long live diversity, long live the earth!

Above all else this voice tells the truth. Throughout his work Abbey was honest about his own faults, admitting the way lust preyed on him, admitting his grumpiness and impatience, admitting his anger at the ways of the modern world, admitting his own intolerance. Those faults, freely admitted, gain the trust of readers, and join a concert that includes an active intellectual curiosity, a ready sense of humor, and a deep appreciation and love of the land. So while all we are really reading are just marks on the page, what we get is the illusion of a person talking to us. Abbey is more than any writer I know, this side of Montaigne, alive on the page. Cut his sentences, as Emerson said of our first essayist, and they bleed. Our modern curator of the essay, Phillip Lopate, once compared being in a Max Beerbohm essay to being in a video game of the writer's mind. Well, there's no video game quite like Abbey's. Read other essayists after him, E. B. White for instance, and they seem too tame, too civilized, too controlled. You appreciate their subtlety and craft but you get none of the raw joy, none of the silliness, none of the fun of Abbey. Next to his, theirs is prose with a pole up its ass. Abbey *let loose*, if not in person where he was known to be shy, then on the page, where it counted.

The miracle is that his work does not more often come off as mere ranting. Any fool with a pen can go on a tirade, write a let-

TWO VERSIONS OF ABBEY AT ARCHES: SOLITAIRE AND WITH FAMILY, SECOND WIFE, RITA, AND SON JOSH.

ter to the editor, and there were times that Abbey can sound like that too. But rarely. "Our moods do not believe in each other," said Emerson. All of Abbey's statements, no matter how boldly put, are open to second thoughts, or at least second jokes. Not that he changes his mind, but that he can come to the same material with a different part of his mind.

Obviously this sort of writing had been done before, in fact had been done in the sixteenth century by Montaigne himself, the first writer to let us see his mind at work. But there is an important difference. Though we saw a man behind Montaigne's thoughts, up there in his study with his Latin quotes tacked to the beams, the essays themselves proceed solely in the realm of thought—in his head. Like Montaigne, Abbey follows his own voice where it leads, twisting and turning, and not overly concerned with following where it first set out to go. Like Montaigne, we can see him thinking, and contradicting himself, and there is pleasure in that. But Abbey also *dramatizes* thought. That is, he turns thought into a kind of action. He works out his thinking on the page, but just as important is the artifice of making readers feel they too are working out those thoughts. It doesn't hurt that the narrator who is thinking these contradictory thoughts is also walking in the desert, interacting with plants, animals, and other people. In this way he becomes the show, his own main character, both watcher and watched.

In doing this, Abbey revitalized—and more than revitalized, made thrilling—a new/old type of literary nonfiction. Never one to be fenced-in by genre, he combined autobiography, the personal essay, nature observation, and a smattering of editorializing. He casually made this form his own, taking it and shaking it out, making it new. He also made it funny, and for that I at least am eternally grateful.

Abbey knew how to take a naturally funny scene and build it up through a kind of Marx Brothers piling-on. One of the best of these occurs in *Desert Solitaire* when Abbey, sitting around a juniper fire and awaiting the full moon, has his solitude broken by the whining of a jeep and the approach of a survey crew. The crew is there to map out a new road into the park, and when Abbey asks why a road is needed in a place no one comes to, they give him incredulous looks.

The head of the crew is "a pleasant-mannered, soft-spoken engineer with an unquestioning dedication to his work," and therefore "a very dangerous man." He explains patiently that if a new road is built, then many more tourists could visit the park. Then he stares at Abbey, "waiting to see what possible answer I could have to that."

Abbey concludes: "I had an answer all right but I was saving it for later. I knew I was dealing with a madman."

To some it may make a difference that Abbey's years in Arches were not exactly the nature idyll they seem in the book. After all, the modern biographical impulse is to tear down: there are those who love to mention that Thoreau brought his laundry home to his mother's house, as if this somehow undermines *Walden*, and that same type likes to point out that Abbey was a moody SOB who spent half his desert year in New Jersey, going through a divorce while paying little attention to his wife and son.

But the proof of how much more there was to the year is in the book itself. Joseph Wood Krutch says that in real life no one could be as "sustainedly incandescent" as the Thoreau portrayed at *Walden*, and of course no one was: the sentences "had been written down as fragments" and then Thoreau had done the work of "arranging brilliants that had been hoarded over the years."

Abbey, too, was hoarding brilliant fragments while at Arches, sentences that he greedily returned to when constructing *Desert Solitaire*. That there was no real sustained golden age at Arches hardly seems to matter, any more than does the fact that Thoreau did not spend all his days at Walden skipping around the pond in fits of ecstasy. What we do know is that both men had golden moments, and it was out of those moments, and more specifically out of the sentences they created from them, that their books were built.

Which leads to the most amazing thing of all, something that to me at least seems not far short of miraculous. That through the simple act of reading, those moments can be resurrected. That we can suddenly be back in the desert or at the pond. That those moments, long dead to the authors, are still fully alive and available to us.

OIL AND WATER

If you have never seen a fracking boomtown, it can be hard to picture. You drive into a town that at first seems like any town, until you slowly notice that on this particular Main Street there are far too many hotels. Then you start to see the oversized white trucks, the hundreds of Rams and Rangers and Silveradaos that prowl the crowded streets, most displaying Texas and Wyoming and Oklahoma plates (even when you are nowhere near these places). You also note that the drivers of the trucks are twentysomething men, who, like their trucks, are almost all white. When you try to get a room, you quickly learn two more facts: the prices are double those in the other rural towns you have traveled through and it is likely you may not be able to get a room at all. Once the hotels here might have been a haven for tourists, a place for families and kids to come and stay the night before a rafting trip. Now they are unofficial camps, camps filled with the men who drive the white trucks.

If you are one of the lucky few to get a nonsmoking room, do not rejoice too quickly. When you walk into that room, the smell of smoke will likely ooze from every fiber of polyester bedspread and carpet. The previous room-dweller may or may not have been fined for this infraction, but if he was it was not a great worry, not to him. Money is not a problem in these impromptu hotel camps. This is a culture unto itself, a culture that in some ways feels a whole lot like what cowboy camps must have been like a hundred and fifty years ago, only with trucks instead of horses. While you try to sleep, the men will congregate outside your door, talking loudly and smoking relentlessly and, quite frankly, scaring you a little. If you are like me, you might chain lock the door and crank up the TV.

So it was on my first night in Vernal, Utah, in July of 2012. After saying good-bye to Ken Sleight in early afternoon, I made the four-hour trip north. On the way into town, driving through the mountains and the red-rock canyons, I played a little game, tallying up two points for each tanker I saw, one for each white truck. It was close for a while, nip and tuck, but by the time I hit the neighboring town of Gusher and the landmark Chug-a-Lug Café, the white trucks had prevailed.

On the drive north I'd been listening to CDs of Stegner's *The Big Rock Candy Mountain*. I'd read the book years before, during my class with Reg Saner, and had returned to it as I wandered the West. Stegner often said that his father had a "sticky memory," and the son's was every bit as sticky. *The Big Rock Candy Mountain* was nothing less than a massive, almost encyclopedic, re-creation—and exorcism—of his early years

Back in North Carolina I'd spent a couple of months reading Stegner's earliest books, those that preceded *Big Rock*. I thought that the first prizewinning novel, *Remembering Laughter*, was a tight drum of a book, sharp but lyric. The other early novels were weaker, but I knew the novels were not the point, and that later in life Stegner thought of all that early writing as simply "blowing out my pipes." The real work consisted of the autobiographical short stories of the frontier, and the big novel they were leading up to, a novel in which he would sometimes use those stories, almost whole-cloth, as chapters. Like many writers before and since, Stegner saw the writing of a large novel as the big prize, "the heavyweight title" as Norman Mailer later called it, and though Thomas Wolfe and Wallace

Stegner are about as unlike as two human beings can be, there are Wolfian rhythms near the end of *Big Rock*, particularly in the travel scenes, as Stegner tried to invest grandeur into his bildungsroman. In the end, *The Big Rock Candy Mountain* was, quite frankly, the story of Wally Stegner and his family—so much so that later the author said he was almost "as uncertain as any outsider would be what in my story is fictional and what is historical."

The ideas embedded in the book, those same ideas that first came to the young Bruce Mason as he drove back from Iowa, are the seeds of Stegner's later thinking, notions of aridity, community, and landscape that he would continue to develop over the next fifty years. This is a novel, however, not a tract, and at the novel's heart is not an idea but characters. Those characters include young Bruce himself and his saintly mother, Elsa. But at the core of the book is the violent and mercurial Bo Mason, the fictional father, an often unpredictable and scary man who comes alive on the page, bristling with joy, wildness, and fury. His own father didn't give him much, the young Wally often griped. But he gave him the gift of hard work, and perhaps more important, he gave him his main character.

There is an appealing mountain-man rawness to Bo Mason, and when he comes onstage the blood of the book rises. Bo is hungry; he *wants* things. To Stegner, the thinker and visionary, the Bo type was the whole problem with the West—the prototypical boomer who rushes to a place, scores or tries to score, and then rushes to the next. But while the moralist in Stegner might have seen Bo's story as a cautionary tale, the novelist knew that in his father he had struck gold. And if in many ways the son was unlike the father, he was not entirely devoid of ambition himself. He, too, *wanted* things, just different things.

George Stegner, or Bo Mason, would have felt right at home in Vernal, Utah, population 9,000. As I drove into town I joined the white-truck parade that cruised down Main Street through classic strip mall shops and the overabundance of hotels, like the Holiday

Inn that local rumor had it was rented out for a year in advance by Halliburton *before* it was completed. The drivers of the trucks were here for the same reason I was: the boom in drilling for oil and natural gas. Here was a place that embodied Wallace Stegner's vision of the West as boomtown. It was a town full of Bos, a town full of hunger—that is, full of a kind of palpable urge for more. It teemed with the eagerness to extract, to strike it rich, to take.

There was plenty for the taking. The vast dry lands south of Vernal hold about half of the state's active rigs for both oil and natural gas, and present a veritable smorgasbord of energy extraction: shale aplenty, fracking—where new technology allows for a return to old fields—and even their very own poised-to-open tar sands. These tar sands, like their more famous cousin to the north, focus on the open mining for bitumen, a heavy, black, viscous oil to which the feathers of migrating birds have been known to stick.

While some of the methods might be new, Uintah County has been Utah's main oil producer for more than seventy years, and as far back as 1918 *National Geographic* extolled the area's potential for yielding fuel: "Campers and hunters in building fires against pieces of the rock had been surprised to find that it burns, and investigation showed that they contained oil." In other words, what is happening here is no nouveau drilling affair, no young Bakken sweetheart in first flush, freshly wooed, but a long on-and-off-again affair that has been going on for decades.

In Vernal there are signs everywhere of how Big Oil has wooed the town. Not long after I arrived, I drove over to Uintah Basin Technology College, a beautiful sandstone building with the streamlined look of a brand-new upscale airport. I decided to tour the hallways of the school, playing the visiting professor, and peeked in on a class called "Well Control," where a movie was being shown that, unlike the grainy safety films of my youth, had the production values of Spielberg. If all that didn't tip the place's hand, then certainly the dioramas of oil derricks and the prominent placement in the lobby of the name Anadarko, the giant Texas oil company that is the area's main employer, did. Anadarko's particular bouquet to the school and town was a $1.5 million gift for construction and faculty endowment.

"Energy is fundamental to our existence," the plaque in the foyer proclaimed. "It is as important as clean air, water and affordable food." Amen.

From the school it was a short drive over to the rec center, a looming spectacle of oaken beams and concrete and great sheets of glass that revealed within Olympic pools and running tracks and climbing walls and squash courts. It looked as if Frank Lloyd Wright and Frank Shorter had gotten together to build their dream house. Right down the street was the Western Park Convention Center, which covered thirty-two acres, one of the largest buildings of its kind in the West. On top of that, Vernal sports shiny new schools and municipal buildings and baseball parks. Anadarko alone paid $14 million in county property taxes the previous year, and raw total income for Vernal and Uintah County from oil and gas far exceeded this number, as a result of sales tax, production taxes, mining royalties, and lease payments on federal land. In other words, the rec center and other buildings are not gifts outright but the metaphoric equivalent of Big Oil saying, "Here, honey, go buy yourself something nice."

This is all without even mentioning the word that all defenders of oil and gas speak first and last: *jobs*. The word is sacredly uttered. And it's true: jobs have been gained—hundreds of them—and when I drove into town, Uintah County had the lowest unemployment rate in the state at 4.1 percent. But no one talks about what type of jobs these are, or the fact that, as the white trucks attest by way of their license plates, many of these jobs are for people coming from somewhere else. (It goes without saying that most of the profits are heading elsewhere too.)

After taking in the rec center, I paid a visit to the chamber of commerce. There, when I mentioned my concerns about the environmental consequences of the oil boom, a young woman named Misty smiled at me from behind the counter and said: "It's an oil field town and everyone makes money from the oil field. Tree huggers should go somewhere else." I climbed back in my car and was drawn like a magnet to a big sign that said: I ♥ DRILLING. The sign pointed toward a small shop called Covers & Camo that I soon learned specialized in custom truck-seat covers, its windows bedecked with stickers, shirts, and displays, all professing love for the pursuit of gas and oil. Inside, wearing a big straw hat and a T-shirt sporting the same words that adorned the sign outside, was George Burnett, the affable, slightly manic owner. I talked to George for a while and was surprised that his business really had nothing to do with drilling.

"I was working retail up in Montana in my twenties," he said, "when the Juice Guy came to town. You remember the Juice Guy? He gave these seminars and had these infomercials about the benefits of juicing. Well, I loved what he was doing and wanted to bring the same passion to my work. I worked for him for a while and then went to work for myself."

His own passion, it turned out, was to become a kind of Tony Robbins of seat covers. George had opened his first shop, called Mr. Trim Seat Covers, back in Provo, Utah, a decade ago. But then the economy started to crater and no one could afford trucks, let alone covers for the seats of trucks. A friend told him about Vernal, where economic prospects seemed to be moving in the opposite direction from the rest of the state and where the latest boom would mean not just plenty of trucks but truck owners with plenty of money to spend. Business was slow at first but then, calling upon his Juice Guy training, he found his gimmick: I ♥ Drilling! He put up his signs, made his T-shirts, and suddenly he was the talk of the town, everyone honking their horns when they drove by his shop. Only a few drivers gave him what George called "the single-finger salute."

After we finished chatting, I browsed for a while, taking in the large wall map of the United States with pushpins for every active

THE OIL PROGRESS PARADE IN VERNAL, UTAH, 1953.

rig in the country along with a state-by-state tally. Texas still led the oil league by a wide margin, with 933 rigs, but I noted that North Dakota and Pennsylvania were on the rise, with 203 and 85 respectively. Utah had only 39.

I was confused by the small number of rigs, but when I asked my host about it, he explained patiently that an active rig and a well site are quite different things: a rig drills for oil that a well site will continue to extract. In fact, though the number of rigs might seem small, just to our south there were 2,477 producing wells, with thousands more expected to open up soon.

George then turned from the map and pointed to his pride and joy, an old photo that he'd had blown up and made into a poster. The photo showed three women in hard hats and one-piece bathing suits riding on a truck bed that featured, along with the women, an undeniably phallic ten-foot-tall wooden oil derrick with black papier-mâchè oil gushing out of its top. The black-and-white photo was from 1953's Oil Progress Parade down Main Street in Vernal, an event that George, in his genius, had exactly re-created the previous summer, right down to the derrick, one-pieces, and vintage truck. Hundreds of people had come out to cheer. It had been both a display of civic pride, and, I suspected, an in-your-face challenge to those few left in town who objected to oil's dominance. At the top of the list of the event's funders was Halliburton.

For all the town's riches, there was some fear that boom was becoming bust before their very eyes, with oil prices falling and natural gas suddenly abundant. The town suffered from Dakota envy, understandable given the numbers on George's wall. If a bust was coming then it wouldn't be the first time. Since its initial boom in 1948, Vernal has been riding these waves up and down, the boom of the 1980s crashing hard and then rising to crash again in the early 2000s. During those hard times no matter how the town ♥ed oil, it hadn't ♥ed them back. There were no oil parades during that bitter span of almost two decades, when the money that the town had grown used to had flown back to Texas. If a lesson was to be learned, it was, it would seem, one of caution, but as soon as oil returned the town threw itself back into its big arms. That was the W. boom, including a last-minute gift of three thousand more leases, which then turned into the Obama boom, and continues on to this moment. It was this recent boom that they had come out to celebrate at George's parade last summer. But for all the bunting and cheers, they had learned to be wary. Did oil really ♥ them? They had been burned before.

I thanked George and walked next door. From Covers & Camo to the Dinosaur Brew Haus is less than a fifty-yard walk, and I was about to learn that not everyone in town was quite as gung-ho about oil as my new friend George. The place was bustling as I jockeyed my way through the crowd and ordered a beer called Hop Rising. My working method as a writer over the last few years has boiled down to the first line of a joke: A man walks into a bar. I'd found this a good way to take a town's temperature and, sure enough, before I'd had two sips I was listening to a tall, bearded man, an obvious energy apostle, describing the joys of fracking.

"What the eco types will tell you is that it contaminates the water," he yelled over the bar's din. "But if you know anything at all about it you know that the water's here. And the gas is here." He held one hand down low and another up higher to illustrate.

I listened to him for a while, saying little, and then he got bored with his own proselytizing and moved on. Almost immediately I found myself talking to the next guy down the bar, who turned out to be a geologist. Though he, too, worked in the oil fields, he was skeptical when I told him the theory I'd just heard about the distinct levels of gas and oil.

"That's great," he said. "But just ask that guy one question: 'What happens if there is an earthquake?'" He didn't seem to be predicting an earthquake as much as tweaking those in town who spoke with the fervor of certainty.

After a while the crowd thinned out a bit and I took a seat near the wall. It was then that I began my education in the relative diversity of Vernal's citizens. Above me was a picture of a raft in the middle of some impressive rapids and next to it another picture, this one of a rugged man, gray at the temples, obviously a river guide, in front of a scene of craggy rock and whitewater. Then, eavesdropping on the table next to me, I learned that there were still people who had been drawn to Vernal not for oil but for water.

I introduced myself to the table full of river guides, telling them I was a writer and that I was specifically interested in ways that the oil companies had curried favor with the town and its citizenry. There were hoots of laughter, and soon they were trying to outdo one another.

"Well, there's the fancy golf tournament," said one. "The Annual Petroleum Invitational!"

"And the rodeo and concerts," said another. "Oil Corp's Country Music Explosion!"

When the laughter died down one of the group pointed up to the picture on the wall of the older river guide. He explained to me that it was a photo of a legendary local riverman, Don Hatch, but that his son John, exemplifying the town's strange mix, had gone into the oil business.

Misty at the chamber of commerce had said that tree huggers should get out of town, but here was a table full of them, mixing easily with the roughnecks. The residents of the bar at least, if not the town, were a strange blend, and belied the cliché of oil not mixing with water.

"WHAT WOULD YOU do if you were a high school kid and had a chance to make a hundred grand in the oil fields?"

Rob Bleiberg had asked me that question four years earlier in Grand Junction: What would *I* do given the choices? Is it surprising that a high school kid, told he can make great money in the oil fields, drops out and takes the chance? And is it surprising that a town rushes toward the goodies that Big Oil doles out? In Pinedale, Wyoming, another boomtown, the students at the local elementary school all have new computers to go with their new school buildings. That's hard to say no to, hard to shrug off as we go on our merry environmental way.

But if we are going to celebrate the gains, then we had better look hard at what has been lost. Property taxes and crime have soared along with employment. The incidence of rape in Vernal exceeds that of the rest of Utah, which exceeds that of the United States as a whole. At the same time, air quality has dramatically worsened, and last winter's ozone levels in this rural county rivaled those of Los Angeles. These very real problems are counterbalanced for the citizens by the gifts the boom brings. But what happens when boom turns bust? When Big Oil leaves and the problems remain?

The truth is that I'm not sure I will ever really make sense of what I saw in Vernal. I originally went to the town in part to talk with Herm Hoops, a rafting guide who had lived in Vernal for more than forty years. But we got our dates mixed up, and while I was in the West he was back east. It wouldn't be until five months later that I would finally return to Vernal and get a chance to shake Herm's hand.

When I did return, right before Christmas, I would find him in the driveway of his home just outside of town. He was working on a raft and wearing shorts and a T-shirt despite the afternoon chill. Herm was a big man with a thick beard and an easy manner, and he immediately invited me into his home.

"When I take people down to raft Desolation Canyon, the single thing they talk about now is the number of oil wells they see," he told me. "That's not what they paid for. They paid to get away from it all. Not be in the thick of it. They say oil is good for business. Not for *my* business."

He added that he now preferred solo river trips to guiding groups.

"That way, I only have to deal with one asshole," he said.

We sat in his living room, a cozy place with a lit Christmas tree, a glass case featuring Civil War figurines, two kittens who crawled all over me, and a fine view of the sun's late red glow on Split Mountain in Dinosaur National Monument.

"When I first came here in the '70s it was a beautiful place. A lazy Main Street lined with cottonwoods. The old booms had faded and the two top businesses in town were agriculture and tourism. People came to see the Dinosaur quarry. People came to float on the river."

He held out his large hands, palms up.

"And what are we left with now?"

Certainly not tourism, I thought. A tourist, like me, would be hard-pressed to find a hotel room in Vernal. As it had been in July, it was in December.

And then there were the busts. Unlike some, Herm remembered what it was like after the last one. Storage lockers of people's possessions being auctioned off. Houses foreclosed on. He understood that we all needed gas and oil, he said, and he was not against drilling. But what was lacking, he told me, was perspective and long-term thinking. What about saving and investing the boom money? For him, the whole town was exemplified by the archetypical Vernal high school student, the one who drops out of school, lured by the chance to make money working out on the oil field, and who does make money—good money—and buys a house, a big truck, and some ATVs.

"And what happens if that job goes away?" Herm asked. "He is left with no education, many debts."

At the last public meeting, where Herm questioned the oil orthodoxy, a boy just like that stood up and said: "If we don't keep drilling, how will I pay for everything?"

There it was in a nutshell. Herm wasn't trying to drive oil out of town. At the same town meeting he had merely suggested that Vernal proceed with some restraint, and consider investing its money for the future. For that he was shouted down and later received death threats in the mail.

The truth was he was simply stating what he had seen over the last forty years. Big Oil brought its gifts and its gifts were shiny and, for the most part, irresistible. But it also brought crime, prostitution, spousal abuse, and a Main Street culture that embodied the minds of the twentysomething males who came to town to work the oil fields. That and the fact that Herm had been around for many spills, had seen oil and chemicals foaming and floating down the Green River. *His* river.

Somehow that made him a little less giddy than most about Vernal's prospects.

"I've been through it before. They come into your neighborhood. They change your neighborhood. Then they move away. And we're left to pick up the pieces and pay the bills."

———

WHILE IN VERNAL I toted a book along in my backpack, a book that, for a change, was not written by Abbey or Stegner. This was instead a collection of Bernard DeVoto's environmental writing called *The Western Paradox*, and its pages practically bristled with energy, insisting on being read. The sentences, written from the 1930s to 1950s, spoke directly to Vernal today. For instance: "The West does not want to be liberated from the system of exploitation it has always violently resented. It only wants to buy into it."

It occurs to me that to read Bernard DeVoto is to, perhaps, briefly think Wallace Stegner less original. Or, if you accept Stegner as the apotheosis of the western environmental prophet, as many now do, then DeVoto must be cast in the John the Baptist role. Regardless, Stegner grew out of DeVoto. Both sharp and aggressive, both fancying themselves realists (they were), wanting to strip away myths, they shared a vocabulary and to a certain extent a philosophy.

DeVoto's enemies argued that the land was vast and that taking what the vast land had to offer was a westerner's birthright. They also said that by doing so the people could strike it rich. That was, and remains, a hard argument to fight against.

DeVoto didn't care if it was hard. He had watched too many places be cored out. Too many places where the citizenry was suckered in by the dream of riches, only to be left empty in the end. Locals might convince themselves that it was a mutual commitment, a marriage of sorts. We ♥ each other. But despite the companies' promises, despite the vows they made, there was never any true commitment to the places they were emptying of fuels or minerals. Of course, it wasn't just the land that would be emptied out but the towns.

DeVoto could point to history and ask a simple question: Can you show me a single example of a time when a company *didn't* leave after taking all it wanted? A single time when a company took care of a town it had left?

Here in five words is his summary of the extractive industries: "All mining exhausts the deposit."

DeVoto shared with Stegner an ability to see the big picture. But he shared plenty with Abbey, too: a tendency toward overstatement, a willingness to bloody noses, a love of tweaking the overly proper and accepted. Stegner once called DeVoto the "Lone Ranger," and one can easily imagine DeVoto standing alone in the 1940s and '50s, keeping a mob of vigilantes (politicians, developers, ranchers, oil men) at bay as they clamored on about taking back "their" land. Stegner joined DeVoto in the fight, but it wasn't until Ed Abbey came along that anyone took to the fight with anywhere near the same cantankerous spirit.

Abbey, coming later, witnessed the plundering of the West in full force, the mines and coal-fired plants, the roads and smog, the damming of every wild river, the burgeoning population. His overall "platform" might not have been quite as thought-through as DeVoto's or Stegner's, but he had read and subsumed those who came before, and his reading mixed with his evolving anarchism. He was enraged by what others shrugged at, and saw the plunderers for what they were. And like DeVoto he wasn't about to back down from a fight.

An example is a speech that Abbey delivered at the University of Montana in Missoula on April 1, 1985. In the heart of cattle country, and to increasing boos and jeers, he told the crowd: "Western cattlemen are no more than welfare parasites." After a childhood of romanticizing cowboys, he had come to see them as what they were: a highly subsidized special-interest group—a group of about 35,000 individuals who controlled 400 million acres of *public* land, land that after it was used was left "cowburnt" and useless. The cows did "intolerable damage to our public lands" and went about their job of "transforming soil and grass into dust and weeds."

Abbey's solution to the problem was a characteristic one: we should open hunting season on all cattle on public lands. But the joke hid the real point—that instead of cows those lands could be inhabited by wild creatures, elk and wolves and bear and deer.

LARGENESS OF THOUGHT does not come naturally to most of us. It isn't easy to see the big picture. Many don't even try.

But there are times when the big picture is hard to avoid, and my second day in Vernal was one of those. On Monday, July 12, I woke early and drove over to the Vernal airport to meet Bruce Gordon of EcoFlight, a nonprofit organization that sponsors flights over the western landscape. I would now have the chance to see Vernal from above, and by that I don't mean snootily.

Soon we were up in the air in Bruce's small plane, looking down at the land laid out below us like a map. It was a startling experience: what was theoretical became actual. These were the places, the oil fields, that I had until then just been thinking about.

"For most people who are driving through this area they just see a few sites from the road and have no idea," said Bruce. "But from up here you can see the extent of it."

I thought of a friend of mine who had just moved west, a former stockbroker who knew a thing or two about booms. When I told him what I was writing about, he was mystified.

"How can you worry about the West? There is so much land. And so few people. How can they possibly hurt it?"

He was apparently as-yet unschooled in western aridity, and therefore western vulnerability. He didn't understand: scar this dry landscape and the scars remain.

We saw evidence of this not ten minutes outside of Vernal. The land quickly rose and grew wilder, the Green River twisting beautiful and snakelike through a landscape of purple and yellow. At first glance I could almost believe my friend was right. All that great empty, unpeopled space, still looking like "the geography of hope."

But on second glance you could see the rectangles, the straight, squared lines that didn't quite fit in nature, and that turned out to be the hundreds of drilling pads and evaporation ponds and holding tanks dotting the area. This was where the white trucks all went during the day before coming back to rest at night in front of the hotel rooms.

My traveling companions in the small plane, along with Bruce, were a documentary filmmaker named John McChesney and two members of the Southern Utah Wilderness Alliance, Ray Bloxham and Steve Bloch. I pointed down. The land below was scarred so badly that in places it looked as if someone had taken a knife to a beautiful woman's face.

"They used to say that the vegetation would eventually reclaim the sites," Steve said through the headset. "But scientists no longer think so. Not enough water for the vegetation to regrow."

Not enough water. Stegner's and DeVoto's refrain. There is nothing new under the sun, you could say, except of course that there is something new here: fracking. Which requires water, millions and millions of gallons of it, while also directly threatening aquifers.

"Not Enough Water" could have been the whole country's motto during that summer of brutal drought, but it had been the West's motto forever. Native people had built civilizations adapting to this fact. The conquering Europeans, for the most part, tried their best to deny it. One thing that still made this denial possible, in the several decades before the last one, was that we were, unbeknownst to us, experiencing one of the most flush periods the region has ever experienced. Not anymore. The twentieth century was one of the three wettest of the last thirteen. The twenty-first is something quite different.

The river below us, the Green, wending its way through the oil lands, would soon join with the Colorado and help water the West. Three-quarters of that water goes toward agriculture or, more accurately, agribusiness, turning previously brown lands green through irrigation. Millions of gallons from these rivers are also destined for Phoenix and L.A.

The history of the West, Stegner said, has been a history of pretending. But in a land of so little water, even less water from either the sky or melting snow tips the balance and reveals the place for the desert it is. Some argue that this year, the hottest on record so far, is a freak year. Remember, they say, that the year before gave us one of the largest snowpacks ever recorded.

But most scientists studying the western climate believe the freak will become the norm. Researchers recently concluded that the extended dry period in the West over the last ten years is the worst in eight hundred years—that is, since the years between 1146 and 1151. *Eight hundred years!* If we were just talking about another decade of this or, worse, a decade of the type of heat we were seeing in the summer of 2012, the results would be catastrophic. But climate scientists believe it will keep getting hotter. If so even drought-resistant plants will die, reservoir levels will continue to fall, crop production will drop. Worse, as vegetation withers, it will no longer be able to absorb carbon dioxide, further exacerbating climate change.

And now to this precarious and combustible mix we have decided to add fracking. We have chosen to do this not with caution but on a massive scale, and to do it right next to our precious rivers, right smack in the middle of aquifers. We go into these places and use, mixed with the millions of gallons of water, a secret recipe of chemicals, many of them poisonous to humans, which we then force into fissures of rock with high-powered blasts to flush out the fuel we are seeking. The man in the bar had warned about earthquakes, but fracking is, in essence, a small seismic event, designed to blast out minerals. We have decided to inject poisons into the ground, then shake that ground, in a region where potable water is more precious than gold. But not, we have decided, more precious than oil.

One thing is crystal clear. Though fracking is unproven technology, we are not treating it that way. Instead we are conducting a vast experiment all over the country, from the hills of Pennsylvania to the deserts of Utah. Since we are moving into unfamiliar territory you would think, if we were wise, that we would carefully monitor any and all results. We are not. When people in the fracked area complain that their water is fizzling out of their taps in a foamy mix, smelling of petroleum, the companies are quick to offer other water sources, like cisterns, but not quick, of course, to question the enterprise itself. In fact, the corporate response to the contaminated water supplies and groundwater has been consistent. They tell the landowners and anyone else who complains that *they are concerned* but that they will not slow down until there is conclusive proof that what they are doing is dangerous and poses a health risk. This is standard operating procedure in today's world, but it is also, to any-one with a dollop of common sense, an ass-backwards way of doing things. "Despite the troubles people are having, we'll keep going full-speed ahead until someone proves to us the trouble is real," they tell us. Never, "Maybe we should slow down until we learn the facts."

The plane banked south, down toward the Book Cliffs and Gob-lin Hills and Desolation Canyon, and we saw a few hundred more rectangles. Rectangles up in the high forested mountains, where the highest concentration of black bears in the state roamed. Rect-angles near the Sand Wash, where rafters who put in to retrace the journey of John Wesley Powell were now serenaded by an industrial hum. Rectangles near the unique Ute defensive armaments on rock spires near the river, cliff towers that are unique to the region, and rectangles near the largest known Ute petroglyph panel in upper Desolation Canyon.

Rectangles were not all we saw, of course. For the rectangles would have been lonely if they didn't have the big white trucks to keep them company. And to get from rectangle to rectangle the big white trucks needed roads. So what had once been roadless wilderness was now a spiderwebbed wilderness. The roads were everywhere, includ-ing one being built that would lead to the new tar sands right below the beautiful Book Cliffs. This particular road, called Seep Ridge, would be forty-nine miles long and paved, the land scraped a hundred feet wide to provide for a fifty-five-mile-an-hour freeway in the midst of this formerly raw wilderness.

The geography of hopelessness, were the words I scribbled in my journal.

And this is what I thought: We are a short-term people, hungry for now. But the West is a long-term place. A place where the stones in an Anasazi cliff dwelling sit just as they did a thousand years ago, and where nothing rots and decays. Here you can see the scars cutting across the dryness. And here you will see the same scars in a hundred, or a thousand, years.

I thought of how Stegner and DeVoto understood that water was the most precious resource of all, and how below me the Green and the White Rivers, the only major water sources for miles, ran through what was now an industrial hive.

Near the end of our flight, I asked Steve a question: who owned the land we had been looking down at? He told me that part of it was Indian Reservation land. A small part private. But most of it was public land, including Bureau of Land Management land and US Forest Service land. In other words, the short answer to my own question was: *We* do. It belongs to all of us, our American land, our heritage.

I knew it would not be wise to make that case too loudly back in the hotel lobby in Vernal. I wouldn't have wanted to walk out of my hotel room last night and announce loudly from the balcony that this land is *my* land, *our* public land, that the oil companies are coring out for profit. "*Your* land?" most of the people of Vernal would respond incredulously. "*Your* heritage? *Your* birthright?"

It is *our* land, they would counter. *Our* birthright. And, they might add, if we want to trade our birthright for a fancy rec center then we damn well will. It is an argument that is hard to counter, and I have no doubt it will ring out here forever. Or at least until the wooing is over, and Vernal, along with its deposit, lies exhausted.

———

I T WAS ON the Green River below us that Major John Wesley Powell began the epic journey that would lead him through the Grand Canyon in 1876. Powell fought heroically in the Civil War, losing his right arm, but became famous by leading the first group of Europeans, and possibly the first humans, on rafts down the Green River and then the Colorado River through the Grand Canyon.

Wallace Stegner's breakthrough book was a biography of Powell, and it was Bernard DeVoto who gave Stegner the necessary nudge to tackle it. DeVoto, who had failed at writing serious fiction but then turned the fictional techniques he'd learned to his Pulitzer and National Book Award–winning history books, provided a model, a cheerleader, a nag, a noodge. Stegner had met many challenges, personal and professional, always wading into deeper intellectual waters as he moved from Salt Lake City gradually eastward to Harvard and then back west to Stanford, and his great mental capacity, and gift, was for expansion, for growth. But it was by turning toward Major Powell as his subject that his instinctive grasp of the West turned into something much larger and more comprehensive.

Why Powell? Because he was, in a word, perfect. Perfect for Stegner as subject, man, and model. Though Powell's celebrity had faded by Stegner's day, what made him appealing as a subject went far beyond his river adventures. In fact, what drew Stegner in was what came after the trip through the Grand Canyon: Powell's work as the head of the Geological Survey of the Rocky Mountain Region and then as director of the US Geological Survey. It was in those roles that Powell articulated his ideas about the American West, ideas that were at the time radical and that now seem prophetic. They were also, for Wallace Stegner, a kind of confirmation. Here was a wide-ranging thinker who saw the West as he did: a fragile desert landscape that should be regarded and treated differently from eastern lands.

While Stegner still defined himself as a novelist, it would be by bringing novelistic tools to Powell's life that he would tell one of his most compelling stories. Like Edward Abbey, Stegner in mid-career would be surprised to find himself cast as a nonfiction writer, specifically a writer of biography, history, and memoir, and it was in this new role that Stegner would mine a deep vein of western history. Writers have plans, we have said, but sometimes the world turns us in unexpected directions and the smart writer, the alert writer, listens to where the world is telling them to go. Stegner's movement began with *One Nation*, a book about race in America that required that he drive all over the United States and report on what he saw. What he saw was injustice everywhere, and he reported this honestly. It was a serviceable book, admirable. What it led to, by turning the author toward nonfiction and research, was something greater, perhaps Stegner's greatest book, *Beyond the Hundredth Meridian*. On the surface a biography of John Wesley Powell, it is really much more. It is the first time, to my ear, that Wallace Stegner sounds fully like Wallace Stegner, a masterful storyteller and historian and biographer, effortlessly moving between these various modes of writing, ranging from a history of the western frontier to a study of water in the West with, as if Stegner were just showing off, some astute art criticism thrown in. The book is, Stegner insists from the start, a biography not of a man but of his career and, more important, "of ideas." Powell's overarching vision of the American West, filtered through Stegner, was of a place where individuals are left to fail if left to their own devices; where only an honest assessment, not a romantic dream or an overlaying of eastern notions on western land, can make the land livable.

But if Stegner's book is so idea-driven that it might be a manifesto, it begins as a boy's adventure story with Powell and his nine companions rafting down into an unknown canyon world. The adventure story is brought alive in scenes by a writer who at that point had published eight novels and who knew the waters, both figurative and literal, having taken more than a few river trips himself. This allowed Stegner to both aptly describe the one-armed Powell steering the wooden boats through deadly rapids, and to say of him: "Losing one's right arm is a misfortune; to some it might be a disaster, to others an excuse. It affected Wes Powell's life about as much as stone fallen into a swift stream affects the course of the river. With a velocity like his, he simply foamed over it."

When Powell made it back to civilization he found he was a national celebrity, but not being the type to bask, he immediately parlayed his fame into an impressive career. For others the exploration of the Colorado might have been their life's climax, but for Powell it was just the beginning—in particular, the beginning of his understanding of western lands. While he would always be best known for running a river in a wooden boat, it was what he did in the years from 1881 to 1894, in his role as director of the US Geological Survey, that would place him, in Stegner's eyes, right at the top of the pantheon of western environmental thinkers. What he did was wade into the halls of Congress and consistently, unflappably, stubbornly, but *reasonably* place scientific fact before a body of politicians who practically wallowed in irrationality, self-interest, and superstition. During that time he continued to fly the flag of reason and fact, putting the public good over private interest, despite those who tried to tear him down. And he put forth a vision of the American West as an arid to semi-arid land where humans, if they were to inhabit it at all, would need to understand certain facts, facts specific to that particular place.

The physical courage that held Powell in good stead rafting through the canyons translated into intellectual and political courage when he emerged. The late 1800s were a time of gung-ho expansion and the irrational belief of ideas like "rain follows the plow," the asinine notion put forth by boosters that annual rainfall would naturally increase once the ground was cultivated. The governor of Colorado, William Gilpin, whom Stegner skewers in *Beyond*, was a particularly passionate believer in this theory, giving speeches that painted the West as a kind of Garden of Eden, a land just waiting for anyone with an ounce of gumption to go and claim. Land speculators back east picked up on this idea of adjustable climate, which fit like a puzzle piece with the notion of manifest destiny. The railroads, too, would later use it as part of their advertising for the westward drive.

In the face of this vision, Powell put forth another. What was needed above all else, Powell believed, was to know the land, to understand the land, and to react accordingly. This had practical consequences: while a cow might properly graze on a half-acre in the lush East, it would require fifty times that amount of land in most of the West. It followed that the standard acreage of settlement should be different, and it followed that settlement should take into account sources of water. Powell's goal with his survey was to clearly map out the western lands, to determine what land could be realistically used for agriculture, which meant also determining where irrigation dams should be placed for best effect. In other words, his goal, to use Wendell Berry's phrase, was to think about "land use" and to do so on a massive scale. Specifically, Powell wanted to think out the uses of land that would be the most beneficial and fruitful for the human beings living there, and for the entire ecosystem (though that word did not yet exist). From the Mormons, Powell learned how "salutary co-operation could be as a way of life, how much less wasteful than competition." In the late 1880s, Powell wrote a General Plan for land use in the West that "reached to embrace the related problems of land, water, erosion, floods, soil conservation, even the new one of hydro-electric power" that was based on "the settled belief in the worth of the small farmer and the necessity of protecting him both from speculators and from natural conditions he did not understand and could not combat." It was a methodical, sensible, scientific approach, essentially a declaration of interdependence between the people and their land, and the miracle is that it came very close to passing into law. But of course it met with fierce opposition from those who stood to profit from exploitation, from the boosters and boomers and politicians who thought it "unpatriotic" to describe the West as dry. After all, how dare he call their garden a desert? What right did he have to come in and determine what only free individuals should? Powell was attacked in the papers, slandered in Congress. According to Stegner, Congressman Thomas M. Patterson of Colorado referred to Powell as "this revolutionist," and the overall attack on Powell "distinguished itself for bombast and ignorance and bad faith."

If the story was the perfect one for Stegner to tell, it didn't hurt that the yahoos whom Powell opposed, and who opposed him, espoused something that sounded a whole lot like the irrational strike-it-rich philosophy of George Stegner. Of course that view prevailed. Congress defunded Powell before he could achieve even his first goal of fully mapping the West. Given the legislative body's behavior in recent years, we may think that we have a monopoly on venality and corruption in Congress, but the gang Powell was fighting could teach ours a few dirty lessons. Our current climate deniers have a long, proud history. In describing that Congress of the late 1800s, Stegner quotes Mark Twain, who saw the prototypical congressman as having "the smallest mind and the selfishest soul and the cowardliest heart that God makes."

But if Powell was going down, he would go down swinging. Those on the Right love to accuse those on the Left of being soft, but Powell, who today would be called a liberal or even a radical, was as tough and as real as you can get, whether climbing up to the rim of the Grand Canyon with one arm or fighting for his annual allocation of funds. When his enemies finally ambushed him it was only after decades of forcing them to acknowledge, for the first time in American history, really, that science was a force to be reckoned with in politics. Powell stayed committed to the facts and "devoted himself to a region and attempted to bring it into focus" right up until his death in 1902. And while he ultimately failed to translate his biggest ideas into law, he provided a model of a large thinker not giving in to smaller ones, a reasonable mind fighting the superstitious.

Stegner had always been a confident writer, but there is a new sense of mastery in the pages of *Beyond the Hundredth Meridian*. The book changed its writer. It did so technically, particularly in his uses of compressed time and synecdoche, learned in part from DeVoto but also from the writing of his own earlier books, techniques that would see their full flowering in experimental nonfiction like *Wolf Willow* and in the late fiction, where time is always working on at least two levels, pulled in and out like an accordion by the author.

Just as important is what writing the book did to Stegner's thinking. *Beyond the Hundredth Meridian* is a visionary story of the West, but it is also a biography of Powell's beautiful mind. Powell was, according to Stegner, "incorrigibly sane," a man who tried to dispense with fable and "dispel the mists," a man who saw the facts and not the romance. The real enemies were not just greedy and stubborn congressmen but "credulity, superstition, habit." In many ways Stegner subsumed Powell's own thinking and brought it into a new century. Ideas that were before then half-formed for Stegner became habitual. Like Powell himself, Stegner had a "bolder, generalizing imagination" than most who struggle to think historically, and, like Powell, he liked to apply his mind to actual problems in the actual world. Both men believed that through hard thought and focused clarity we can get at certain truths. That our minds, uncultivated, go where they will, to the till or trough, but that trained and focused, they can be put to good, and even selfless, purpose. It was an old-fashioned value and one shared by both biographer and subject.

WHEN I GOT back from the plane ride there was no room at the inn. At any of the inns. I had planned on spending one more night in Vernal and then driving farther west to Salt Lake City, but the white-truck people had commandeered all of the rooms, and my search for a place to put up my tent led me east rather than west.

Soon I was driving back into Colorado and I was also driving *up*.

Ten miles over the border I turned left and north, ascending into Dinosaur National Monument, land that, not incidentally, Wallace Stegner had played a large role in saving.

I was learning that Abbey's and Stegner's footprints were everywhere in this corner of the world. Especially Stegner's. Before I'd left the little Vernal airport, I had even gotten an unexpected Stegnerian bonus. I asked John McChesney, the documentarian who had flown with us, about his next project, which turned out to be a documentary on the western fracking boom. Then he asked me about mine.

He laughed out loud when I told him.

"I lived in the cottage behind Stegner's house in the 1960s," he said.

"No fucking way," I said.

Before I left he told me a story from that time. John was a student activist at Stanford, and was part of a group that occupied University Hall. It was pretty tense for a while; the police were called in and it looked like the situation would turn violent, but the faculty senate granted the protesters amnesty and the students went home after two or three days.

"When I got home, Wally was sweeping off his patio. That was my regular job, part of my rent. He wouldn't look at me. But I did hear him mutter one phrase: 'Ruined a great university.'"

That Stegner could be stubborn, old-fashioned, even ornery was no longer much of a surprise to me. But that the same man could also be capable of generosity and passion was also obvious. After leaving Vernal and climbing upward and eastward into Colorado, I would be spending my afternoon in one of the wild places that had been saved in large part due to that buttoned-down man. I parked near Harpers Corner and hiked out to the overlook of the confluence of the Green and Yampa Rivers. For the second time that day I got to see the Green from above—not quite as high up as in the plane but plenty high—standing on top of the canyon wall, a thousand or so feet above the place where it was joined by the Yampa.

Far below a dusty wind kicked up silver waves on the water. I knew I might have been looking down at a dam had it not been for Wallace Stegner.

It was Bernard DeVoto who first dragged Wallace Stegner into the eco-wars. At the older writer's urging, Stegner began to write a series of environmental articles in the early '50s, and those articles were read by David Brower, the charismatic single-minded executive director of the Sierra Club. Brower recruited Stegner to edit a book that would describe the wonders that would be lost if a dam were built within the borders of Dinosaur. In their successful campaign to stop the dam the two men would not just help win a battle but would revolutionize the way environmental fights were waged. Until the effort to save Dinosaur there had been something upper-crust and musty about the Sierra Club and the other environmental organizations, but with Dinosaur they would go from fuddy-duddies to fighters. Over the next decade great gains would be made and a new style forged: full-page ads would be taken out in major papers comparing the damming and drowning of the Grand Canyon to the flooding of the Sistine Chapel, beautifully photographed books would help change our national consciousness, and park land would be purchased as it hadn't been since the days of Teddy Roosevelt, culminating with the Wilderness Act of 1964.

Now, fifty years later, I reaped the benefits of that fight. I edged out close to the side of the cliff, partly terrified, partly thrilled. A gray jay landed in the twisted juniper over my head, cackling hello. If I walked to one side of the cliff I could see the Yampa snaking in, looking dried-up and shriveled, and then the Green winding to meet it. The actual joining of the two rivers was hidden from my view, modestly taking place behind a boulder. But when I walked across to the other side of my cliff, I could see the revived Green, renewed by fresh waters, a transfusion of sorts, flowing on out west, down, down, down to where I would later be sleeping by its side in my tent.

This is what we're fighting for, I found myself thinking. If rec centers and golf tournaments are important, this is important too. This was why Stegner famously called our national parks "the best idea we ever had." He was right. What could be better? To do something beyond ourselves—our species, even—that just happens to provide for the highest of needs of both species and self.

The boosters and boomers have their song about the West, a song that started long ago and continues to this day. *This is a place of excess, of resources, a place to strike it rich! Come and get it!* Powell sang another song, one that DeVoto and Stegner took up and that Ed Abbey reprised in his own warbling way. Taken together theirs is a chorus that creates a counternarrative for the West.

ABBEY WITH THE TV HE SHOT.

Back in Kentucky, Wendell Berry had said that the future of environmental thinking would stress "land use" and that wilderness preservationists would not be the relevant people. This does not mean he does not believe in wilderness. On his own farm, in fact, Berry likes to let wild woods stand next to cultivated fields. Putting land aside, like this land, is one clear *use* for it, and creating wilderness remains a key part of the environmental fight in the West. When Powell made his first maps he knew that the region demanded that some of the land simply had to be left alone. If we are looking at a big picture—a puzzle, even—then we need as much land as possible that shows us what the land would do without us. It is a key to adaptation, one clear way we can ready ourselves for the vast uncertainties of a changing climate. These wild places serve as a counterbalance, a reminder, a baseline, a template for recovery.

Much of the land I stared down at from the plane that morning and that I now stared down at from the overlook was disputed land, land that had been involved in battles to save or exploit it. For those who could never see beyond the economic argument, it made no sense to just leave it alone. At a time when we are desperate for resources, why put resources out of reach?

The same battle rages on. Why should anyone actually stop coring out the last of our lands, sucking up the last of the gas, damming the rivers? It's what we've always done. We came upon this country of plenty and took everything we could get our hands on. We didn't care what got in our way: native people, geography, climate, logic, whatever. We rationalized this as a kind of brave, bold, can-do way of being, and in some cases it really was. But in many cases it was, and remains, about *greed*. In many cases we came as raiders, pure and simple, and raiders we remain.

It is hard to argue against self-interest. Against human nature. But human nature also involves training oneself to think beyond oneself. And places like this help make their own case, their own counterargument. Abbey said our highest need was for transcendence. Well, if it's transcendence you're after, this is where you'll find it. *Up* in places like this.

The overlook created something in me, some feeling or sensation, that even the experience of seeing the ocean couldn't match. It was almost chemical: I saw the landscape and then something bubbled up, rising unbidden. I stood in a place that was almost desecrated and drowned but was not. A place that was *saved*.

The religious wording is intentional. Standing there, overwhelmed by sheer space, by the fact that I was within a vast landscape that at the moment was devoid of any other human being, the word *awesome*, in its old usage, came to mind. My hyperactive brain for once stopped its querulous wishing that it were somewhere else. The place both emptied and filled me. Sunlight hit the river, which became mirrored glass, blinding.

MAKING A NAME

H ere are Wallace Stegner's words upon deciding to leave his papers at the University of Utah, rather than at Stanford: "Any scholar who has to go to Salt Lake to study Stegner will get a bonus by being lured into good country."

Mission accomplished, Wally.

I had never set foot in Salt Lake City before July 19, 2012, but within an hour of arriving in the town I was already kind of in love. The wide, clean streets; the mountain ranges above the valley; the passes you had to cross to get to the town, at least from the east, as if entering a great fortress. All that and the fact that the whole city was atilt, like one of the villain's lairs on the old TV version of *Batman*.

As I drove into town dark clouds broiled up over the Wasatch Range. I checked in at the University Guest House, but had no time to waste. The university itself sits perched above the town, and after throwing my bags in my room, I climbed onto my bike and headed downhill. The wide roads ran straight and no pedaling was required. It was like skiing, and hard not to yell, "Whee!"

I found the small café where I was to meet Stephen Trimble, a photographer, editor, writer, and environmentalist who taught at the University of Utah, and who served as the Wallace Stegner Centennial Fellow there during the 2008–9 academic year. Only minutes after I arrived so did Stephen, also by bike. He is thin, bespectacled, smart, intense, and as it turned out he was in a bit of a hurry, generously cramming in a last-minute meeting with me before a trip out of town the next day.

Readers of Edward Abbey are often converts, people from elsewhere who read his books and move to the Colorado Plateau and call it their own. But Stephen was born here, and has spent his whole life exploring the canyon country. He attended Colorado College, which operates on the block system, with three and a half weeks of studying one subject followed by four days off, and he spent almost all of his time off exploring the nooks and red-rock crannies of his expansive home turf. *Desert Solitaire* came out while he was still in college and for Stephen the life it described wasn't the exotic, wild alternative that it is for so many people but a confirmation of the life he was already living.

"The guy took what I was doing on break and made it into literature," he told me. "Until then I had never thought of using the skills I had been developing in a profession. But now I saw an opportunity. A personal opportunity but also a professional one: 'Wow, this place I've loved for so long. I could make this my job.' And I saw I had everything I needed right in my backyard."

The book was a vivid reintroduction to a place he already knew, and in the most direct and literal sense it changed his life. Right after he graduated he volunteered at Olympic National Park for the summer, and the next fall, when a position suddenly came open, he was offered a full-time job at Arches. Two years after reading *Desert Solitaire*, he found himself working at the same park that Abbey had celebrated.

"By the time I was twenty-two I had cemented my relationship with my home landscape," he said.

We finished our beers and it seemed that that would be it. But despite his rush, Stephen had something he needed to show me.

Luckily, it was on his way home, or rather a little past his home. We climbed onto our bikes and began our ascent. It was skiing no longer but slogging, the sweaty effort to get back up the hill. Breathing heavily, I, the out-of-towner, attempted to keep up.

Ten minutes later we arrived at our destination. A grassy cemetery that, like everything else on this side of town, existed on a slant.

"It's by those two spruce trees," Stephen said, and we got off of our bikes and walked them up a path between the graves.

"I have my students read Stegner's *Recapitulation* and then bring them here," he told me.

Recapitulation, a novel published in 1979, is a sequel to *The Big Rock Candy Mountain*, in which the Stegner-like protagonist, Bruce Mason, now an adult, returns to Salt Lake City to bury his aunt. He has not been back to the city in decades, and the place releases a flood of memories. Bruce is now an ambassador—an interesting choice, really—both a politician and balancer, the sort of man with the "excess of moderation" that Abbey abhorred. Competent and powerful, he returns to a place where he was once powerless and weak, and at the mercy of a volatile, angry, capricious father. The father's fictional fate was similar to that of Stegner's actual father: he had shot his mistress in a seedy downtown hotel, then turned the gun on himself and took his own life. The novel ends at this very cemetery, where, after the aunt's funeral, Bruce finally decides to buy a headstone for his father's unmarked grave. It is, the reader imagines, an act of forgiveness, catharsis, and reconciliation.

But at the actual grave site I was in for a surprise. Stephen paused in front of two stone markers embedded in the grass. The first read: *Husband. Cecil L. Stegner. 1907–1931.* The second: *Mother. Hilda E. Stegner. Aug 31, 1883–Sept. 27, 1933.* Stegner's brother and mother, respectively.

And next to them? Next to them there was no third cathartic stone to mark the life of George Stegner, father and husband. Next to them was a lumpy plot of grass, nameless and unmarked, below which Wallace Stegner's father lay.

Stephen was pleased by my reaction. He had given me a gift of sorts, and he knew it. But he needed to run, and so we shook hands by the gravesite before he climbed back onto his bike. I started to do the same, but then hesitated. The clouds had closed in, dark-blue and heavy below, lighter up above. It looked like rain, but there were still a couple of hours of light, and I remembered that I had seen a convenience store earlier. I pedaled there to buy a cigar, then back to the gravesite to smoke it. The clouds grew darker; rain spat. The town lay below me, the mountains above. I smoked the cigar down to the nub.

I studied the two graves. Cecil, Wallace's big, strong, athletic brother, the family star, died at the age of twenty-four of pneumonia. Then came his mother, a woman whom Stegner would insist to the end of his life was "saint-like." "I love my mother," he wrote later, "and that is not anything for a psychologist to grin about." Hilda was, by all accounts (mostly *his*, as the last survivor and writer), a kind, loyal, high-spirited woman who loved her sons despite a hard life of near poverty and spousal abuse. Her last words, as she died from cancer at the age of fifty, were: "You're a good boy, Wallace."

But while the two marked graves had their own stories to tell, it was the unmarked one that held my attention. Stephen's gift had been to present me with the perfect place to consider the relationship between George and Wallace Stegner, but more than that. The perfect place to think about names and the nameless, ambition and acceptance, fathers and sons.

NOT FIVE MILES from here George Stegner, in that seedy downtown hotel, killed his girlfriend and himself in what his son later called "a neat and workmanlike job of murder and suicide." It would have hardly been national news, just an event covered in the local paper, gossiped about in town for a while no doubt, but fairly quickly consigned to time's oblivion. *Except.* Except for the writer son.

"Well, at least we don't have any skeletons in our family closet," Wallace's son, Page Stegner, said to me when I visited him in Vermont.

I had laughed—rudely, I think now—assuming that Page was joking and that having a grandfather who killed himself and his girlfriend might qualify as a skeleton.

But of course Page was right. That incident had been written about so much by his father that, far from being in a closet, it has been exposed to the harshest sunlight. It might be a skeleton, but its white bones shine for all to see.

To the extent that George Stegner is known to any living person today, to the extent that he still has a name, it is through the pages of his son's books. Whether as himself in the nonfiction or as Bo Mason in the fiction, he is portrayed as a bully, a strong and often angry man. While Stegner himself later warned about taking his fiction too literally, in other moods he admitted that *The Big Rock Candy Mountain* was in many ways an autobiography. In that novel he describes an indelible moment after Bo Mason finally returns from his wanderings to discover that his family is living in a tent in the wilderness outside of Seattle. Little Bruce Mason, still not yet five, is scared of walking the path through the woods to the outhouse, and when his father forces him to do so, the boy squats along the path instead of walking deeper into the woods. When Bo finds out what his son has done, he becomes enraged, grabs the boy by the collar, and marches him down the path, rubbing his son's face in the excrement.

Wallace, as a child, was prone to illness, a self-described runt, crybaby, and mama's boy. Sick and small and at the mercy of a man whom he watched abuse, not just himself, but, worse, his mother. It is the transformation of that runt into the ambassador—the

WALLACE STEGNER IN THE BLACK ROCK DESERT.

movement from small to big—that interests me. What drives a little boy to be a big man, or, conversely, makes a big man small? How is caring about one's good name different from trying to make a name? And how does our own smallness impede our dreams of being larger?

The rain had begun to spit and it made sense to go, to begin my climb back to campus and the University Guest House. But it was hard to leave that place where George Stegner had not left his mark. I thought about how the architecture of Stegner's thinking about the West grew out of the different models provided by his mother, the nester, and father, the boomer. His use of his family's story is fairly typical of the way Stegner's mind worked: there is always a movement toward the general, an imperative to think more broadly and openly, a preference for the long view over the short, the large over the small. This was not just an intellectual commitment but a spiritual, or at least a personal, one. "Largeness is a lifelong matter," he once said. The goal was magnanimity. But if anything got in the way of that goal in his own life it was his feelings toward his father. *Hate* was the word that often came to his mind. Hate was the concept—the feeling—that he wrestled with. How to be large when a dark and bitter smallness grew inside?

Wallace Stegner strove throughout his life to make a name, not just a known name but a good name and, more important, to create a self. Half of the genetic material he made that self with came from his father, but he consciously strove to make himself *against* the image of that man. Where the father was weak, he would be strong. Where the father was inconstant, he would be steady. Where the father cheated, he would be loyal. Where the father boomed, he would stick.

That was fine, and to an admirable degree he willed himself toward this end. But he still grew out of his father, and out of the male frontier culture that his father embodied. It was a tough culture. A culture that hated "sissies." A culture where action trumped sensitivity. A culture that laughed at anything fancy or pretentious. A culture where books, art, and intellectual conversation, the very things that Stegner was coming to love and excel at, were scorned. It was also a culture he could never entirely escape. In a particularly astute piece of self-analysis, Stegner wrote in 1962's *Wolf Willow*:

> Little as I want to acknowledge them, the effects of those years remain in me like the beach terraces of a dead lake. Having been weak, and having hated my weakness, I am as impatient with the weakness of others as my father ever was . . . Incompetence exasperates me . . . affectations still inspire in me a mirth I have grown too mannerly to show. . . . I even at times find myself reacting against conversation, that highest test of civilized man, because where I come from it was unfashionable to be "mouthy."

In short, he was taught to be wary of the very qualities that are essential to being an artist. It should not be a great surprise, then, that as an artist he is tough-nosed, a realist, able to take a punch. That he disdained the overly romantic, had no use for Whitman, for instance, while admiring the way that Bernard DeVoto could toss aside those rotten oranges and get at the essence of a thing. He admired energy, smarts, and adherence to the evidence as opposed to romantic gushing. And as an adult he contained both frontier toughness and intellectual sweep, turning himself into the sort of man he had never encountered during his youth. His father had been a ne'er-do-well but he would be a success. He would make his name.

And he did: not three miles from where the father rests under a nameless grave stands a library that houses a collection honoring the son. In creating the body of work that one finds there, Stegner relied on the one positive quality he acknowledged getting from his father, and the only one he openly admitted to sharing with the old man: a relish for hard work. Both father and son strove mightily to *make it* in their lives, though their definitions of what "it" was varied. George Stegner, though deeply flawed, had a vital animal energy, worked tirelessly, and could build or fix almost anything. He was, his son believed, ideally suited for the frontier he longed for. And what George brought to clearing a field, Wallace brought to writing. He loved to roll up his sleeves, to tackle a project, to have another project waiting when the first lay fallow between drafts. In his biography of DeVoto, he wrote: "As a matter of fact, he loved work; he could not have existed without it; and though he some-times complained about it, that was standard bellyaching, part of the pleasure." As it had been for DeVoto, work for Stegner was a stay against chaos and confusion, a time to lose himself in the intense process of making.

All his life, Stegner was a volcano of productivity. In *Crossing to Safety*, which he called his most autobiographical novel, the Steg-

GEORGE STEGNER, WALLACE STEGNER, AND AN UNIDENTIFIED MAN.

nerian narrator says of his younger self: "I was your basic over-achiever, a workaholic, a pathological beaver of a boy who chewed continually because his teeth kept growing." This fictional creation, Larry Morgan, produces a massive amount of work, but in fact Stegner admitted that he actually "toned down the facts for fear readers would not believe them." In his autobiography he writes: "In two years, besides collaborating on a textbook and writing a dozen essays and book reviews, I wrote four short stories, a novelette called 'One Last Wilderness' that killed Scribner's Magazine, a novel called *On a Darkling Plain*, another novel called *Fire and Ice*, and the first few chapters of *The Big Rock Candy Mountain*. This while teaching four undergraduate classes." He wasn't complaining, mind you: "I suspect what makes hedonists so angry when they think about overachievers is that the overachievers, without drugs or orgies, have more fun."

In *Crossing to Safety*, the Stegnerian narrator writes that "when I hear the contemporary disparagement of ambition and the work ethic, I bristle." But: "Unconsidered, merely indulged, ambition becomes a vice; it can turn a man into a machine that knows nothing but how to run. Considered, it can be something else—pathway to the stars, maybe." Ambition can lead to the stars, or at least to that greater broadening, to magnanimity, to largeness. But it still has its more primitive roots in the craving to be noticed, to be known, to have one's name recognized.

FROM THE STEGNER graves it was a hard return ride up to the University Guest House. When I got back, I took a hot shower, a nap, and again headed into town, by car this time, for a visit with Ken Sanders, owner of Ken Sanders Rare Books.

The store was ramshackle, vast and high-ceilinged, with couches and stuffed chairs in the middle for those who felt like plopping down and reading. Books everywhere, of course, in an order that was discernible to anyone who tried hard enough but known best by the proprietor himself. It was one of those bookstores that barely exist anymore in our age of the antiseptic chain store, replete with the smell of the musty pages and the sense that reading itself is, at its heart, a countercultural act. At the center of it all, sprawled on the couch next to me, was Ken Sanders, whose joking manner, smile, and Santa Claus appearance only briefly disguised the fact that he was a fount of encyclopedic knowledge of western literature, and an expert on both Stegner and Abbey. As I took a seat next to him on the couch, the first thing I noticed, high above the cash registers, were the life-size cardboard cut-out caricatures of the five members of the Monkey Wrench Gang, the work obviously that of the cartoonist R. Crumb.

"I called Crumb to see about illustrating a new edition of *The Monkey Wrench Gang*," Ken told me. "He had never heard of Abbey, and he said no at first. But I sent him a copy of the book and I guess he read it. He called me back and asked, 'Do people in real life actually go out and engage in the sort of activities that Mr. Abbey described?' I said, 'Yes they do, Mr. Crumb.'"

The activities that Crumb was referring to were acts of environmental rebellion: the pouring of sugar into the gas tanks of bulldozers, the sawing down of billboards, the blowing up of bridges.

After we had chatted awhile more, I asked Ken to play a parlor game of comparing and contrasting the two men's works. What if you had to rank the top-ten books of Stegner and Abbey?

He thought about it for a while and then admitted, somewhat reluctantly, that the body of work tilted in Stegner's favor. But he couldn't quite shake *Desert Solitaire* from the top spot.

"I'm here to tell you that what they claimed Truman Capote did with *In Cold Blood*, well, that's what Ed did in *Desert Solitaire*. Because it isn't just a collection of random essays but a nonfiction novel. Most people can't write in that genre to save their lives. It's excruciating to read the drivel that comes out these days.

"But Ed could write that way somehow. And that's something Stegner never did. He is telling you something, teaching you something. With Abbey, you are experiencing being Ed Abbey."

He mentioned their attitudes toward wilderness as an example.

"With 'Wilderness Letter,' Stegner wrote one of the most important environmental statements of the twentieth century. But Wally appreciated nature from a very academic background. Abbey just celebrated wilderness for the sheer hedonistic thrill of it all. He said the only birds he could recognize were the fried chicken and the rosy-bottomed skinny dipper."

I wasn't sure I agreed with Ken's take on Stegner; I'd read some pretty visceral nonfiction of his over the last months. But it didn't seem the right moment to object. Ken was rolling now. Customers, who likely had practical questions to ask, like where the bathroom was, were smart enough to just stand back and listen.

"Ed could make a parody of himself, like in the introductions to his essays. But in real life he was a very serious man. And what he was most serious about was writing.

"Plenty of people still haven't heard of him. I remember being at the book expo right after *The Monkey Wrench Gang* came out. I walked up to the table of his publisher. Not only couldn't I find any copies of his books, but I couldn't find a single person who knew who Ed Abbey was."

If you set foot in Ken Sanders Rare Books you would know who Ed Abbey was, or at least you would before you left. Wallace Stegner was well respected here, but Abbey was loved in this, one of the central places of worship in the greater Church of Abbey. While the names Updike and Roth might be better known to the general reading public, they do not come close to matching the cultish fervor associated with the man nicknamed "Cactus Ed" Abbey. Cults, whatever their flaws, have the power to keep names alive.

"When I give talks about Ed, my goal is to bring him back to life for a new generation," Ken Sanders said. "There is a whole new generation of readers in college now who weren't alive when Ed died. I want to introduce them to this writer who can still speak to them. He said he never wanted to write a classic. Because his definition of a classic was a book that everyone has heard of but no one has read. Well, Ed's not written that kind of classic. He's still read. We sell more of his work in the store than all other authors combined. After slow starts, both *Desert Solitaire* and *Monkey Wrench Gang* have sold over a million copies."

Before I left, I asked Ken if he had ever thought of writing a book about his friendship with Ed.

"I've thought of it," he admitted. "But I don't want to do another *I Was Ed's Chum* book."

I nodded. There was a whole cottage industry of *I Was Ed's Chum* books.

It is a tricky business being an Ed Abbey fan these days. We shift toward uneasy ground. Because Abbey is no longer just a writer whose books you read; he is a literary cult figure who has *followers*. The skeptical reader recoils: "Oh, I don't want to be part of *that*." But clearly Abbey *lives*, at least in the West. Fresh off the press just that week was an article in the *Mountain Gazette*, a journal where Abbey himself often published, in which M. John Fayhee, the editor, took no small delight in mocking the Abbey fandom: "They wore clothing that looked like what Abbey wore. They drove vehicles that would meet with Abbey's approval. They tossed beer cans out of truck windows because Abbey did." This hit a little close to home. I thought back to my days in Eldorado Springs and remembered the cans of refried beans I ate, part of the official Ed Abbey diet. I fear I was, unbeknownst to myself, a sort of groupie.

It is easy to mock the more rampant Abbeyites. But the tendency to attach ourselves to writers is a not entirely unhealthy thing. Fandom may be laughable, but it has its purposes. Stegner wrote of Bernard DeVoto that "father hunting had almost been a career for him." He meant that DeVoto sought out older writers, and was eager to sit at their knees. He did this with Robert Frost, whom he first believed was "living proof that genius could be sane" but whom he eventually broke from with the words: "You're a good poet, Robert. But you're a bad man." Stegner, in turn, would look to DeVoto as a model, a father of sorts, though a father with the wild streak of an adolescent son. It is easy to dismiss these relationships as mere hero worship, as Oedipal. But what underlies them is something better, I think. A hunger for models. For possibilities. For how to be in the world.

As we shook hands good-bye, Ken and I talked about how the Abbey legend had grown.

"He was almost as famous for his death as his life," Ken said.

I knew that after Abbey died, his friends, per his instructions, placed his body in the back of a pickup, packed it in dry ice, forged a death certificate, and took him out on one final camping trip. They drove him deep into the Cabeza Prieta wilderness and spent the night there, with Ed in the truck. The next morning they dug the grave, which two of them climbed down into to test for "fit and comfort." When they deemed it acceptable they buried their friend and poured beer on the grave as a final toast. His burial was, of course, completely illegal.

The burial, and the wakes that followed, were well orchestrated, and added greatly to his legend. The wakes, one in the Saguaro National Monument near Tucson and one in Arches National Park, were wild celebratory affairs. At the raucous public wake in Arches, for which Abbey himself had once again left instructions, Wendell Berry read aloud the letter from their former teacher celebrating Abbey. "His books were burrs under the saddle blankets of complacency," Stegner's letter said. "His urgency was a lever against inertia. He had the zeal of a true believer and the sting of a scorpion. He was a red hot moment in the life of the country, and I suspect that the half-life of his intransigence will be like that of uranium." Berry later reported back to Mr. Stegner in a letter that described how the event had been "held on a big slab of white rock slanting out toward a whole world of mountains and desert." There was much drinking and singing among the red rocks, and not too much reading of words, just as Abbey wanted it.

Writing in his journal in October of 1981, Abbey had left elaborate instructions, not just for how he should be buried, but for what music should be played, and what books read, at his funeral. He wrote: *I want dancing! And a flood of beer and booze! A bonfire! And lots of food—meat!*

Not every man leaves stage directions for his final show.

Before I left, I told Ken that when I was first planning out my trip I was pretty sure I was going to go in search of Abbey's grave. It was part of the Abbey legend, after all—that grave out there somewhere in the unknown wilderness. I knew I would likely be able to find the spot: I had good contacts, old friends of Ed's, and thought it wouldn't be too hard to figure out the location. But when I got to the Abbey library in Tucson I changed my mind. The plan had the whiff of grave-robbing to it, and, worse, of a stunt, and I decided, finally, that I would let the poor man rest in peace.

I had seen pictures, however, and knew that Abbey's grave, unlike George Stegner's, was marked. In a manner, at least. Abbey had chosen the epitaph himself.

NO COMMENT, it said.

"ANOTHER DROP DOWN the well of oblivion," was what Ed Abbey wrote in his journal when *The Monkey Wrench Gang* came out.

Neither Stegner nor Abbey were immune from the hunger for renown. Both wanted their work to be remembered. They would not, it seems to me, have frowned at the notion of my writing this book so many years after their deaths.

It is oblivion, of course, that we make our names against. Nothingness that spurs us to be something. And what is worse than being ignored? To a proud person, it is as if our existence is not acknowledged. We are *nobody*.

"I am tired of obscurity!" Abbey wrote in his journal on November 30, 1974. "I want to be famous."

Stegner, for all his striving toward largeness, shared some of Abbey's bitterness. Of course he, characteristically, framed it in a larger way. He believed that western writing as a whole was ignored, and as he became known throughout his home region he chafed against being considered regional—when considered at all—by the East.

I remembered watching a television interview with Stegner where he mentioned that something he had written had not been reviewed or recognized properly.

"Because it's provincial?" the interviewer asked.

Stegner just stared at the poor man, who shrunk as the silence swallowed him.

"No," Stegner finally replied, "because the *critics* are provincial."

Of course. It was the New York critics who were the regionalists and their region was a tiny, crowded island.

Did he have a case? Well, it should be noted that while the *New York Times Book Review* chose not to review *Angle of Repose*, they did manage to print an essay objecting when the book won the Pulitzer.

And there was one final indignity. In 1981, the *New York Times Magazine* published an article called "Writers of the Purple Sage." The idea was to finally acknowledge and celebrate the boom in western writing, to give credit where it was due, and it included mention of a young wild man named Edward Abbey.

Stegner was featured in the article too.

A caption below a photograph identified him as "The Dean of Western writers, *William* Stegner."

I HAD A BEAUTIFUL little schedule over my three days in Salt Lake. I got up, did a little writing, ate breakfast, and biked down to the library for six hours of study. I spent the day immersed in Stegner's notes, letters, correspondence, and the drafts of his novels. Then back up the hill, a nap, more reading, sleep.

One of the finds on my second day was the letters that George Stegner wrote to his son during the year before he died. Here, for instance, is one that George sent from the New Grand Hotel on March 29, 1939:

> *Wallace do your damndest to raise hook or crook $200 or more*
> *to get in on this [illegible] you can write your own ticket. I have*
> *sweat blood getting it all in shape.*
> *This is the last chance for me and if I fail in this I will end it all.*
> *Regards to family.*
>
> > *Write me at once.*
> > *I must know what to expect,*
> > *Your Dad*

Another letter contains this whopper of a line: "Will appreciate more than you know the occasional check you mentioned sending me so don't let me down I'll doubly repay you for it later enabling you to get your family well again." And: "I'm still trying hard for it's my last chance."

When I'd first read the fictional versions of these letters, in *The Big Rock Candy Mountain*, they seemed almost too much, close to overkill. Little did I know that they were nearly verbatim reproductions of the actual letters, letters that told a little of the day's news and asked routinely about how "the baby is" (one gets the sense he didn't know his grandson Page's name) but whose real purpose was to beg for money for a stake in a new mine.

Wallace was giving a speech in Iowa, the same place he'd been when he heard his brother had died, when he got the news about his father's death.

It may be too simplistic to see the son's moral code developing purely in reaction to the father. But whatever the reason, the code did develop. Stegner would never buy into the fashionable belief, exemplified in everyone from Hemingway to Wolfe, that great art and bad behavior went together. After all, "largeness of mind" was the ideal. The notion that "it is a good thing to be large and magnanimous and wise, that it is a better aim in life than pleasure or money or fame. By comparison, it seems to me, pleasure and money, and probably fame as well, are contemptible goals."

These were ideals, of course, and Stegner, a realist, knew how difficult they were to achieve. He would always be a grudge holder, for instance. It wasn't just Ken Kesey who felt his sting. The reason I was in Salt Lake, and not in Palo Alto, was that he had grown bitter toward Stanford, where everyone assumed his papers would be deposited. The reason he could never bring himself to buy a marker for his father's grave sprung from the same root.

I thought of the walk I had taken in Vermont with Page Stegner and his wife, Lynn, and daughter, Allison. As we climbed the hill from their house to Wallace and Mary's old house, Allison pointed out the ferns, the names of which she had learned many years before from Mary. The landscape was right out of *Crossing to Safety*, the last novel Stegner wrote.

When we stopped at the Stegners' old house, I asked his son if Wallace could be intimidating. Page Stegner clearly loved and respected his father, and characterized their relationship as a good one, but he admitted it could sometimes be challenging having a monument for a dad.

"It wasn't always easy growing up with a father who spoke the King's English," he said.

I remembered a letter that Wallace Stegner had written to Page in 1979. Wallace had just read the first three chapters of Page's contribution to the book they wrote together, *American Places*, and after complimenting much of the work as "first rate," went on to criticize some of the writing as too personal, with too much of a "yum-yum tone about bourbon and porkchops." The father essentially complains that the son parties too much on his pages, about "the tendency to uglify your own authorial image," and suggests something "more judicious, with less mugging and hoofing."

And then, as if anticipating Page's defensive response, brings up a writer known for his mugging and hoofing, a writer always ready to uglify his own image and to embrace the yum-yum tone.

"Of course there is always Abbey," the father writes the son. "But

Abbey is outrageous, deliberately, and even when he's throwing beer cans out into the Montana landscape he is making a point about the landscape, not about himself."

Fascinating to listen to the writer-father chastise the writer-son for talking too much about himself. Fascinating that Abbey is cited for his largeness. And fascinating too that it was the father's later work, when he got most personal through his fictional narrators, that has continued to have the greatest appeal.

But while Wallace could be intimidating and critical, my sense was that, for Page and the rest of the immediate family, Wallace Stegner was, in their eyes, everything he was in the world's: kind, steady, brilliant, loyal, hardworking, and if a tiny bit stiff then certainly caring. That picture was tempered and complicated by a familial proximity and a reality that those who know Wallace Stegner only through books could never see. When we passed a neighbor's house, for instance, Lynn Stegner, Page's wife, told me that the man who lived there had been Wally's closest friend. Wally was friends with his wife, too, and Lynn said that after the man's divorce Wally refused to talk to the man for a long time, a period of years. He didn't believe in divorce, or at least not in this divorce. I guess this is not shocking. Simple enough, really: Stegner had a clear moral code and the man had violated it.

In Vermont, Allison Stegner told me about a fifth-grade report she had written about her famous grandfather, and I went to look up the report in the library files. It was Allison's "autobiography" of her famous grandfather, written in his voice, and it featured this whopper of a line: "I try not to hate my father."

Both the trying not to and the hating formed the man. Did Wallace Stegner ever get beyond hating George? In moments, I'm sure he did. On an intellectual level he knew that his father had grown up in a violent family, received only a ninth-grade education, and was fending for himself by the time he was fourteen. And he knew that his father did his best to overcome his own flaws, that he made vows to reform after his bouts of bad behavior. In his better moods, George Stegner could be rambunctious, rowdy, joyful, fun. But there was always regression. The temper and bullying would always recur. On some deep level, striking it rich, making it big, trumped the concerns of his family. Or so the son believed.

That son could be tough on people, could hold grudges, could be inflexible. But magnanimity manifests itself in the act of forgiving, and I like to think that Wallace Stegner achieved some measure of forgiveness. Perhaps I am wrong. Perhaps, in the end, the son could not forgive the father his sin of smallness.

Do any of us ever get beyond the boundaries of the selves we start with? Can we really make ourselves into more than we are? Or do we always bump against the borders of self and snap back to the default settings that we were programmed for in the first place?

I know what Wallace Stegner believed. I would like to believe it with him.

SALT LAKE CITY no doubt has its share of problems, but over my three-day stay my crush didn't slacken. I could easily imagine living in that sloping town rung by mountains.

For Wallace Stegner, Salt Lake provided a kind of salvation. The story line of his development, the way I've told it so far, has a bit of Dickens to it: the poor frontier boy making himself into the large man. It would be easy to imagine that, with that chip on his shoulder, the young Wally vowed, "I will be great, I will surpass them all," like the biblical Joseph ready to avenge himself on his brothers. But it didn't work exactly that way. In Salt Lake City it was *belonging*, not greatness, that first served as a balm for his childhood. We imagine the truly ambitious person as having a hole that must be filled, but Salt Lake, until his family dwindled, seemed to fill Stegner up just fine. He might have had occasional daydreams about being a great writer, a big man, but mostly he envisioned marrying his local girlfriend, getting a decent job, being part of the place. "One day I realized I could be perfectly happy if I never wrote anything," Wendell Berry had said to me back in Kentucky. It was a delightful sentence, and I have the sense that the young Stegner could have said the same.

Though never a Mormon himself, Stegner was attracted to certain aspects of the religion. Criticizing Mormonism has become a popular sport, and plenty of that criticism is well deserved, but Stegner would always have a soft spot for the city and the people who took him in. Though his family would move from house to house over two dozen times in Salt Lake, mostly to escape suspicion about his father's illegal trade, the boys fit in fairly quickly. Through Mormon-sponsored programs they played basketball, attended dances, and joined the Boy Scouts, with Wally, still a runt at less than a hundred pounds, quickly winning his Eagle Scout badge. The downtown Carnegie Library was also a revelation, and Stegner, starved for culture, gobbled down books, later claiming he read a book a day. At the same time he discovered tennis, at which he excelled, and finally, at long last, grew, going in a flash from the shortest in his crowd to one of the tallest. His new tennis partner and close friend Jack Irvine got him a job at his father's floor-covering and linoleum store, and soon he had a circle of friends and money in his pocket.

As was his way, Stegner later thought long and hard about what his adopted hometown represented, taking his own experience and extrapolating. In books like *Mormon Country* and *The Gathering of Zion*, he would explore Mormonism, often with a critical eye. But he was also fascinated by the fact that Mormons had created a viable society in the desert. He took the sense of camaraderie and belonging that he experienced in youth basketball and at Mormon dances and imagined how it applied to the ways Mormons settled the land and irrigated their crops. If one of his life's central questions was how humans should live in the West, then he was pretty sure that community and sharing were a large part of the answer. To anyone who thought this answer "soft," he could point to the hard fact that the Mormons and Native American tribes both understood that it made sense to share in a land of sparseness, and that they, not coincidentally, flourished in a place where others floundered. The beehive, that symbol of Mormonism, might have repeled an individualist like Ed Abbey. But to Stegner it provided a sensible model of many working toward one goal. If Stegner was radical, as Terry Tempest Williams suggested, perhaps it was in part because he deeply believed in *sharing*. Against the false image of the rugged individualist, he held up the early Mormon cooperatives. Could it be that—blasphemy of blasphemies—something close to socialism was the best system for living in the desert? If he didn't say it directly, he certainly implied it.

I don't want to paint an overly rosy picture of Mormonism, since we can't ignore its proud history of intolerance, central and patriarchal control, and insular morality. But Stegner believed that are were lessons in the Mormon way of living if we want to listen, lessons that still might have relevance as we look toward drier, hotter times.

On my own last morning in the library in Salt Lake, I came across an exciting find, a little orange theme book that seemed a kind of road map for my attempts to understand the lives of both Stegner and Abbey. The book's cover was illustrated with pictures of boats and planes over a background like a topographic map. While Abbey was a great journal keeper, Stegner seemed to have had little time for them, and so far this had been the only one I'd come across. He kept this notebook in the mid-'70s, and in its pages he worked through many of his ideas about biography. In red ink—scrawled but legible—Stegner wrote:

Biography is the form for heroes; also for representative men. It is not the form for denials of humanity, or for cynical games. It really goes after a human life, and in something like its full scope. It cannot be unrepresentational; a black comedy biography is hardly conceivable. Farce does not match with reality and full representation; it writes only with exaggeration, distortion, etc. . . . In other words, it works with a certain type of novel, hardly at all with biography. History puts iron in biography.

The little journal contained injunctions, rules of sorts, for would-be biographers. "We look *through* the works back at the man, in order to come back to the [illegible] in something like the spirit the writer wrote them in." "The imagination of the biographer is ultimately like the imagination of any creator, but it walks along apparently prosy paths, and with materials large parts of which are themselves prosy." Stegner believed that there is no reason "biography can't utilize the techniques—and pursue the intentions—of fiction." That said, the form requires a writer "significantly addicted to the real" and: "biography, like nature photography, is an art of *found* objects." He warns against "temptations," including the tendency to "debunk a large figure" or "settling grudges" or "tell all." "If one has known his biographee personally, he is lucky. If he has to get him from reading, he has an act of imagination to perform—he has to bring paper to life." Either way, biography involves "transformation of fact by the imagination," though "imagination must work with the real."

Finally Stegner includes a list:

1. No reason for chronology.
2. None for birth-to-death coverage.
3. None for the historian's omniscient point of view.
4. As for invention—use the subjunctive.

It is worth pausing here to consider that at the time he wrote these words Stegner had just completed his own biography of Bernard DeVoto, who was, by all accounts, an immensely flawed human being. Combative, defensive, always ready to pick a fight. A man who felt bullied and so bullied others back. The perfect subject for a "tell-all," in a way. For a tearing-down sort of bio. But that was not what Stegner was after, and not just because DeVoto was a friend. His notes continued: "Malcolm (Cowley) says I made DeVoto the hero of a novel. That's not far from truth. The subject of a biography should be the hero of a sort of novel, the best sort."

And: "Heroism—if not heroes, at least representative men (yes, this is what most biogs miss), models of a sort, rarely warnings. The natural tendency of biography is positive, not negative, and it appeals to me. It is otherwise with contemporary fiction."

"What I suppose I mean to say is that I wish biographies were more like the sort of novels I like, and novels were more like the sort of biographies I like."

A little farther down the page, he wrote: "Biography must not reform truth—that much it owes to its ancestry as history—but there is more than one kind of truth, and that [illegible] it owes to its other parent, story-telling."

According to Stegner, then, the subject must be representative to be worth writing about. And what did DeVoto represent? A difficult, ornery, troubled, anxious man, who, though often afraid of the world, struggles through work and a great effort of mind to become more than his limited self. Who fights, in Freud's words, "to discipline a primitive inheritance." A small man who willfully strives toward largeness.

It doesn't take a particularly astute reader to see that there is a whole lot of autobiography in the DeVoto biography. That what this particular biographer valued, and found in his subject, was the constant, daily effort to expand, and to keep the demons of smallness at bay. To take that raw material and will it in a direction, a "positive

BERNARD DeVOTO.

direction." Largeness may be a lifelong matter, but it is also a daily grind. It requires *effort* above all, that unfashionable virtue.

The flaws of character are not and cannot be ignored. The flaws were real. Of course they were.

But so was the lifelong effort to overcome them.

ON THE WAY out of Salt Lake I made one last stop. I pulled up at the address where the seedy hotel had once stood. The hotel itself was gone and I couldn't be sure which of the two buildings stood in its place, the shiny bank or the one with the brick front and the old-time advertisement for bikes. Maybe neither. But for ambience I walked up to the brick building, a preferable object for the requisite imagining.

If you know of George Stegner at all—and if you do it is likely as the fictional Bo Mason—you know he was resilient. A kind of Jean de Florette of the American West. The failed wheat crop in 1920 was a disaster, no doubt, but soon hope was bubbling up for the next adventure, the move to Great Falls, the man newly excited about all the money that could be made from bootlegging. In his books the son made much of the fool's gold that was his father's false hope, but there was always real hope and resilience too. Until this place. This is the place where the hope and resilience ended.

I tried to picture the final scene. The lobby, the shouting. The gunshot through the pane of glass, the blood on the poor woman's coat. George Stegner, the winner of sharpshooting contests—one of his few worldly successes, the state champ—shooting two bullets, one breaking through the plate-glass door before piercing Dorothy LeRoy's heart. Then turning the gun on himself. The man, once a dynamo of energy and ambition and ideas, deciding that it was time to put an end to all that. No more imagining, no more last chances, no more big rock.

It is all over for him, though it will be a beginning of sorts for his son, who will later report his first thoughts upon hearing the news: "So now I know how that damn book ends."

HOW TO FIGHT

DO YOU HAVE DEFENSIBLE SPACE?

The looming billboard posed this enigmatic question after I'd sped through the glories of Zion National Park, having paused only once to watch an old bighorn sheep pick his way along the road.

It is a question Ed Abbey would have liked. His was a wilderness made not just for sniffing flowers but for a last refuge and hideout from the government. It was all in all a messier wilderness, a more complicated and resilient one. As a young man, Abbey rolled a car tire down into the Grand Canyon, just to see what would happen. Modern environmentalists gasp at the desecration, and perhaps they should. But I understand it. We used to think the world was so big. So indestructible. So *fun*. We still can't completely believe that it is as small and serious, as threatened and vulnerable, as we have made it.

As for me, I had been doing an awful lot of driving.

Wendell Berry had defined himself as a placed person.

I, for the summer at least, was that other thing, a wheeled person.

This was undeniable. My odometer indicted me, told me I was bad. Reminded me that gasoline, especially the burning of it, is what is destroying our world.

One of the reasons people steer clear of environmentalism is all the guilt associated with it. The creepy feeling that by doing what everyone else in one's society is doing—driving, washing the dishes, catching a flight—we are bringing about the end of the world. Part of Abbey's appeal is that, even as he lectures us about our failings, he simultaneously washes away some of the guilt. He is a big fat hypocrite and he admits it, and there is something cleansing about this.

Here is man who bought a red Eldorado Cadillac convertible in his later years and happily drove it down the streets of Moab smoking a cigar. A man who famously tossed his beer cans out the window of his truck and said that it was the highway, not the cans, that were ugly. A man who bombed over the desert in his truck like some pioneer ORVer, and who, as much as he claimed to hate the automobile, celebrated it in his books.

But here also is a man who, for all his failings, *fought.*

"We are all hypocrites," my environmentalist friend from Boston, Dan Driscoll, said. "But we need more hypocrites who fight."

What Dan meant, I think, is that too many of us, noting our own eco-flaws, throw up our hands and say, "What's the point?" But if only those with a spotless environmental record fight for change, then we will have very few fighters.

Abbey's behavior does not get me, or anyone else, off the hook. On the hook we belong and on the hook we will stay. But it does offer the hope that one does not have to be *pure* to fight. He does not absolve us of our eco wrongdoings, but we can take some small comfort in his imperfections. Somehow, despite the excoriating rants, the frontal assaults, the tireless moralizing, Abbey seems the least pious of environmentalists.

AFTER ANOTHER DAY'S drive, I arrived at the dam.

This was the place where so many of the stories I had been reading converged, a confluence of Ed Abbey and Wallace Stegner and Major John Wesley Powell, and of the current dried-out, water-starved state of the West.

The damnation of a canyon.

That's what Abbey called it. The damming of Lake Powell and the flooding of the beautiful Glen Canyon below.

As I drove, my first indication that the Glen Canyon Dam was near came in the form of three huge smokestacks jutting up into the sky, my first sight of Lake Powell a low, glassy haze of blue, wildly out of place in the desert and yet undeniably beautiful. Tropical blue against orange rock.

Just short of the dam, I stopped at Lone Rock and got to witness firsthand the sort of recreation that Abbey so often grumbled about. A line of forty campers, trailers, and trucks were parked on the edge of the water. Jet Skis patrolled the lake, shooting up their rooster tails of spray while their land-bound twins, the ATVs, whined and snarled up in the dunes. The machines seemed to be competing to see who was louder, and you got the feeling the owners liked it that way. A hundred feet out in the water stood the great, once-proud monolithic rock that gave the area its name.

The water-skiers circled the rock, and about halfway up the rock's side you could see the famous bathtub ring. The water level had dropped over the last decade but left behind evidence of its high-water mark from earlier wet years in the form of a stain created by the minerals deposited on the rock and on the rock walls all around Lake Powell. On other parts of the lake there were boat ramps that no longer reached the water. Evaporation is a huge problem here, with millions of gallons going not down the river or into the hydro-electric pumps but up into the air. Silt is an even bigger problem. Fill a tub with dirt in the bottom and soon the mud will rise, or appear to as the water sinks into it. For decades silt has filled the reservoir from below, and it is in the process of gradually changing this into a lake of mud and muck.

I could feel my own outrage building, as if by reflex. Say the words "the Glen Canyon Dam" and the environmental team all nod their heads and shake their fists. They have been properly schooled

THE GLEN CANYON DAM.

and know that it's evil, a great canyon-killing villain. I have been schooled too.

But when I arrived at the dam my first thoughts weren't environmental ones. I wondered: what if you didn't know you were supposed to hate this place? What if you hadn't read the right books? Imagine a squeaky-clean American family on a squeaky-clean American road trip, or a fresh-faced college kid driving west for the first time, getting his first look at a big western dam. Imagine they haven't been environmentally indoctrinated yet, haven't yet been taught to hate what they see. Assume, too, that they are seeing through eyes uncolored by what the dam is or does, or by what once was and now isn't below its waters. In other words, they are just taking in the Glen Canyon Dam as a physical thing. A sight to be seen.

To say that they will be impressed is not enough. *Blown away* works better. First there is the sheer massiveness. The great hulking size combined with a kind of smoothness, an otherworldly elegance. Did graceful aliens make this thing? And then there's the unreal, mind-spinning height from the top of the dam to the bottom. If they are like me—that is, not of a practical bent, unable to imagine inventing even, say, the can opener—they will also immediately wonder how the hell the thing was built. Perhaps a skyscraper is equally impressive. Perhaps, but we are used to skyscrapers. This, however . . . this is something else.

My first dam was Hoover, back on my original road trip west after college, very much that fresh-faced kid and very much without environmental knowledge, particularly of the West, and the sight of that dam is perhaps the most vivid memory I can conjure up from a trip full of vivid memories. But this dam, Glen Canyon, works fine too. If not quite as big as Hoover—a few feet shorter—it is big enough, and the tonnage of turquoise-blue water it holds back on one side—encircled by bright-orange red rock—and the 710-foot drop-off on the other dazzles anyone who looks at it with unclouded eyes. As I mentioned, I come from a tribe of nonengineers, who, if left to our own devices, would still live in mud huts, and as I walked out on the bridge that crossed the dam I found it hard to believe that members of my own species had actually built this structure. I knew I was supposed to be wagging my fist and cursing along with the rest of my squad, and I would get to that. But first I allowed myself a short moment of wonder.

I stared down at the Colorado, the same river that Major John Wesley Powell first ran. Its flow was now released periodically from the bottom of the dam, but in Powell's day it had been regulated not by engineers but by weather's whims. In 1869, the major plunged through these canyons into the unknown in wooden boats with nine other men. He had heard rumors that he might encounter falls the size of Niagara, meaning that every time he heard a rumble around the corner he knew it might be sounding his crew's doom. Powell was that oxymoronic thing, a cautious adventurer, and for most of the trip he forced his crew to portage the rapids. But near the end, as food and other supplies grew short, and after three of the men had abandoned the mission and hiked up to the canyon floor, he became, of necessity, less cautious. The plunges through the Grand Canyon rapids were no fun ride, but even the stolid Powell could occasionally find them exhilarating, especially when they all survived with minimal damage to the boats.

Edward Abbey claimed that his favorite western book was Major Powell's account of that river trip, *The Exploration of the Colorado River and Its Canyons*. In the spirit of his hero, Abbey paddled through Glen Canyon in 1959, when construction had already begun but the dam had not yet been erected. He and his friend Ralph Newcomb spent ten days and traveled 150 miles on the river. At the end of that trip they came upon a sign that announced YOU ARE APPROACHING GLEN CANYON DAM SITE. ALL BOATS MUST LEAVE RIVER . . .

Four years after Abbey's trip, in 1964, Glen Canyon was drowned with the completion of the dam and the creation of the Lake Powell reservoir, which backed up behind the dam for 190 miles, the water submerging hundreds of stunning side canyons and arches and ecosystems unknown now except, as Abbey wrote, to scuba divers. From that day on, Abbey's love for Glen Canyon and his rage against the dam radiated outward through almost all of his work. He wrote:

> There was a time when, in my search for essences, I concluded that the canyonland country has no heart. I was wrong. The canyonlands did have a heart, a living heart, and that heart was Glen Canyon and the golden, flowing Colorado River.

He had known this place and loved it, and after its drowning he would write about it in fiction and nonfiction, both mourning the canyon in elegiac prose and ranting against the dam in full tirade. Lake Powell, he contended, was not a lake at all but a fetid bathtub constructed, not for the irrigation of nearby towns but for the money procured from the electricity it produced when the water ran through its turbines. Recreation, the great gift that the reservoir supposedly gave the area, consisted of Jet Skiing and powerboating around a tub of water where biodiversity was all but nonexistent, nothing growing on the "near-perpendicular sandstone bluffs" and no plants able to adapt to the constantly shifting water line. Water level was adjusted for the purposes of electricity, so that plant life alternately starved or drowned.

Meanwhile, what was once below the dam's impounded waters haunted Abbey. A flowing river, a shoreline teeming with birds—"Living in grottoes in the canyon walls were swallows, swifts, hawks, wrens and owls"—and foxes, coyotes, bobcats, deer, ring-tailed cats. Not to mention the fern-bedecked waterfalls and hidden alcoves and Indian ruins. All drowned.

Abbey especially hated the argument that the new lake was more accessible to everyone—that, for instance, you could now putter your motorboat right up to the famous Rainbow Bridge.

"This argument appeals to the wheelchair ethos of the wealthy, upper-middle-class American slob," he wrote, believing that if the rock bridge was worth seeing, you could easily earn the view with what had been just a six-mile walk. In fact, the older forms of recreation, walking or paddling down the river for free and eating what you brought, were significantly cheaper and more democratic than the renting of motor boats and hotel rooms.

He often dreamed of a time when the river would run free again, when the lake had finally filled completely with silt and mud, and the dam would become a waterfall. This would briefly "expose a drear and hideous scene: immense mud flats and whole plateaus of sodden garbage strewn with dead trees, sunken boats, the skeletons of long-forgotten, decomposing water-skiers." But nature would take care of the mess soon enough: the winds and rains would scour the canyon clean and return it to something close to what it had been.

In his assault on dams, Abbey was to some degree working within a tradition. As far back as 1912, John Muir had protested against the building of the Hetch Hetchy Dam with these words: "These temple destroyers, devotees of raging commercialism, seem to have a perfect contempt for Nature, and, instead of lifting their eyes to the God of the mountains, lift them to the Almighty Dollar." Fifty years later, Robinson Jeffers, whom Abbey read avidly, said he would rather "kill a man than a hawk," and laid down a misanthropic baseline off which Abbey would riff. But there was something that felt new and direct, almost primal, about the way Abbey wrote about nature. It was simple, really. He wrote from two sources: love and hate. He said as much, claiming that a writer should be "fueled in equal parts by anger and love." He had fallen in love with a place and he wrote

ABBEY IN A CHARACTERISTIC POSE.

paeans to that place while cursing those who were trying to despoil what he loved.

He wouldn't have used the word *despoil*, of course. He would have chosen, as he often did, the more direct and blunt *rape*. And why not? The enemy was aggressive, rapacious, never resting. In response he had to be the same. Words were his first line of defense, maybe his last, and he piled them up like a barricade of rubble. Though he could be brutally concise, he was also a hyperbolist, and like Thoreau, varied between these two extremes: both an embracer of excess and a blunt blurter. Either way, the words seem to have been summoned directly from and in defense of the land. He is no stylist.

If Abbey didn't despise with such passion his would be just run-of-the-mill curmudgeonly grumbling. In Abbey's world Lake Mead, Lake Powell's downstream cousin that was created by the Hoover Dam, is "a stagnant cesspool" and "a placid evaporation tank," while the cars that tourists drive are "upholstered mechanized wheelchairs." He wrote: "With bulldozer, earth mover, chainsaw and dynamite the international timber, mining, and beef industries are invading our public lands—bashing their way into our forests, mountains and rangelands and looting them for everything they can get away with."

"Mr. Abbey writes as a man who has taken a stand," was how Wendell Berry once put it.

This is both instinctive and the result of a thought-out philosophy. "It is my belief that the writer, the free-lance author, should be and must be a critic of the society in which he lives," is how Abbey begins "A Writer's Credo."

He continues:

> Am I saying that the writer should be—I hesitate before the horror of it—*political*? Yes sir, I am. . . . By "political" I mean involvement, responsibility, commitment: the writer's duty to speak the truth—especially unpopular truth. Especially truth

that offends the powerful, the rich, the well-established, the traditional, the mythic, the sentimental.

IN THE 1950S, Bernard DeVoto insisted that it was Wallace Stegner's *responsibility* to fight off the plunderers, and in saying this DeVoto knew his man: that was just the right word to do the trick. Stegner responded by writing a series of articles about the way that the Eisenhower administration was violating the sanctity of the national parks, with plans to build dams within their boundaries. These culminated with the publication of "We Are Destroying Our National Parks" in *Sports Illustrated* in 1955, the same year DeVoto died.

These articles would be the ones noticed by David Brower and would lead to Stegner and Brower's historic fight to save Dinosaur. Of course, Dinosaur would be followed by that worst of defeats: the drowning of Glen Canyon. Many people blame Brower, and by implication Stegner, for selling out Glen Canyon. The most common telling of the story is that Brower, who had never seen Glen Canyon, made a deal with the Eisenhower administration. If they agreed not to put the dam in Dinosaur, the Sierra Club and the other environmental groups would not oppose a dam in Glen Canyon. Others say that the story was simpler and less sinister: Brower, exhausted and overextended from the first fight for Dinosaur, failed to adequately respond to the second. One problem was that Brower had never been to Glen Canyon, though Stegner had described it for him, extolling its beauty. It wasn't until later, when Brower rafted down the canyon with Stegner right before it was flooded by the dam, that he realized what a great mistake he'd made. Stegner's biographer Jackson Benson is rarely critical of his subject, but at this point in the story he writes: "In hindsight, it would seem that Stegner should have in this instance shaken off his moderation and more vociferously acted as advocate for Glen Canyon. If he had, Brower would not have failed to act in the clutch." In recent years, this story has been revised, with Bureau of Reclamation officials, including former bureau chief Floyd Dominy, saying that there never was a deal, that in fact the Glen Canyon Dam had long been planned and would have proceeded no matter what happened in Dinosaur. But if this made Stegner less culpable, it did nothing to stop the pain of the loss. He would return to Glen Canyon after construction of the dam had begun, and so had a front-row seat at the damnation that haunted both him and Ed Abbey, bearing witness as the great bathtub of Lake Powell filled up and Glen Canyon was flooded. With that, John Wesley Powell's journey could never be repeated.

Perhaps Stegner's biographer was right; perhaps Stegner's "excess of moderation" doomed him when it came to saving Glen Canyon. Perhaps, but of all the individuals who fought to preserve land during those years, few fought as hard or as well as Stegner. If he had his lapses, so did everyone else, most obviously the Archdruid himself, David Brower. Looked at from our distance, it is hard for anyone to throw stones at Stegner for his environmental record. Even Ed Abbey, who may not have even *liked* Stegner that much, said of him: "Wallace Stegner is the only American writer who deserves the Nobel Prize."

That these words did not come from a student trying to butter up a teacher—who could be more antithetical to wild Ed than the older, buttoned-down, conservative, hippie hater?—make them carry even more weight. Abbey admired Stegner's work and his commitment to making art, but perhaps admired more his teacher's commitment to fighting for the land.

There would be other losses, painful losses, but also more victories. In 1960, Stegner published his soon-to-be-famous "Wilderness Letter," which argued that wilderness was vital to the American soul, and that undeveloped land was deeply valuable, even when that value was not obvious and monetary. One influential reader of the letter was the new secretary of the interior, Stewart Udall, who thought so highly of it that he read it out loud at a Sierra Club gathering in April of 1961. By then he had also read *Beyond the Hundredth Meridian*, and he was determined to get Stegner to come to Washington with him. Stegner was reluctant; he was a writer with work to do, not a politician, but eventually he gave in. In DC, he worked on the beginnings of legislation that would become 1964's groundbreaking Wilderness Bill and attended meetings with Udall, during which, according to the secretary, Stegner was "never bashful." The eventual bill was in fact an almost perfect practical embodiment of the "Wilderness Letter"—a massive setting aside of lands never to be developed. For Stegner it was a heady experience, and he got "an inside look at parts of the Kennedy administration during its first energetic year" as well as "a good lesson in how long ideas that on their face seemed to me self-evident and self-justifying could take to be translated into law." He also went on a vital reconnaissance mission to Utah for Udall, scouting the land that the secretary would eventually save as Canyonlands National Park.

But the truth is Stegner lasted only four months in Washington. He might play at being Major Powell for a while, but he wasn't Powell. He was a writer and teacher, not a politician. Mary Stegner found DC cold and lonely, and by the beginning of the spring term they were back at Stanford. His relationship with Udall would continue, however, and he would help the politician write the early drafts of what was to become Udall's bestselling conservation manifesto, *The Quiet Crisis*. And for the rest of his life Stegner would keep fighting in the environmental wars despite the fact that these obligations "constantly prevented the kind of extended concentration a novel demands." It would have been nice to have turned his back on these extra obligations, but of course, being who he was, he couldn't.

For Stegner, who always valued results above mere theory, efficacy was a great virtue. Or maybe it is best to say that he valued real-world effectiveness along with theory, broad ideas applied to the practical Earth.

Stegner's could sometimes be a grumpy goodness. In a fascinating exchange of letters with the beat poet and environmental guru Gary Snyder, Stegner argues for the less exotic virtues of the cultivated western mind versus the enlightened eastern one. This included the importance of doing what one *should* and not what one *felt like.* In a letter dated January 27, 1968, he wrote: "I have spent a lot of days and weeks at the desks and in the meetings that ultimately save redwoods, and I have to say that I never saw on the firing line any of the mystical drop-outs or meditators."

He went to those meetings because it was the right thing to do. An obligation, yes, but one he valued.

"The highest thing I can think of doing is literary," he wrote a friend. "But literature does not exist in a vacuum, or even in a partial vacuum. We are neither detached nor semi-detached, but linked to the world by a million interdependencies. To deny the interdependencies, while living on the comforts and services they make possible, is adolescent when it isn't downright dishonest."

Which meant sitting in at those boring meetings where he saw no mystical dropouts or meditators. And giving talks, writing articles, and even creating propaganda when he would have rather been immersing himself deeply in a novel. He sometimes grumbled about this, of course he did. It was extra work, yet another thing to do in a life full of responsibilities. But he had signed on and he wouldn't ever really sign off. Like Major Powell, he knew the despoilers, the extractors, would never rest. You never really "won" an environmental battle, after all, just saved places that would be fought over again in the future. Since the boomers never rested he knew that meant he could do very little resting himself. Unlike many of us today, he did not take environmentalism for granted, since when he had begun to fight it barely existed. Stegner concludes his "A Capsule History of Conservation" this way: "Environmentalism or conservation or preservation, or whatever it should be called, is not a fact, and never has been. It is a job."

So he did his job.

————

During my may trip to study the Abbey papers at the library in Tucson, I'd driven up to the Glen Canyon Dam and taken a raft trip that started at the base of the dam seven hundred feet below where I now stood. The Colorado River, while overregulated and over-dammed and definitely overstressed, had still looked beautiful that day. A peregrine falcon swooped into its nest five hundred feet up the canyon wall. When I looked back at the dam that loomed behind and above us, it seemed to grow out of the roseate canyon, which of course it had in a manner. The section we were paddling was a remnant of Glen Canyon, the section that Powell, not to mention Abbey and Stegner, considered the most beautiful of all the canyons. What was left was this, "a small and imperfect sampling" according to Abbey, of the great wild that was gone.

Above us, as we paddled, loomed reddish walls splashed with hundred-foot black stains of desert varnish, a dark patina created by water seepage from great cracks. The white lines of ancient lakebeds sliced through panels of orange and pink. Bighorns grazed and great blue herons roosted; a lone tree grew out of the side of a cliff a thousand or so feet up. Green tamarisk—which most people think of as native but is an invasive species that took over the Colorado system in the 1880s—covered the banks, or those parts of the banks that were not sheer cliff. The walls of Navajo sandstone climbed claus-trophobically, seven hundred feet high at the dam but rising to two thousand by our trip's end at Lees Ferry. The river cleaved through the walls, and we—tiny we—followed the river.

To call the Colorado River the lifeblood of the West is no exag-geration: it is the only truly major river in the mountain West and seven western states could not exist in their present fashion with-out it. What will be interesting, or more likely tragic, in the coming years will be to see if they can exist with a whole lot less of it. When the river was divvied up between the states in 1922 it was based on the optimistic number of 20 million acre-feet (an acre-foot is the amount of water made up by an acre of surface volume at the depth of one foot). What those who did the divvying didn't know then was that the West was in the midst of one of the wettest centuries in the last thousand years. The estimate of total flow that they came up with has not been approached in recent years, and in fact the water supply continues to dwindle. This dwindling is the result of a drought over a decade long, but climate-change experts warn that we should not ever expect the water to return to old levels; in fact, they have predicted that the flow will be reduced dramatically, by as much as 35 percent, in years to come. Meanwhile whole cities and mini societies have grown up around their negotiated share of this particular river, including the 3 million–plus citizens of Phoenix, who, with their watered lawns and golf courses, like to pretend they do not live in the desert. A full fifth of the river's water is delivered to that city via a three-hundred-mile canal. Then there is the electric hive of Vegas, and the greatest water slurpers of them all, the residents of California. For almost a century now they have been living the illusion of plenty, but as Stegner liked to point out, in this land "aridity still calls the tune."

My raft trip that day was a planned, well-practiced affair, hardly wild, and other than getting splashed in the rapids and running into a headwind that briefly made progress close to impossible, there was nothing to it. We would sometimes hear the rumble of rapids as we rounded the canyon corners, which might have sent a tingle of excitement down the spines of some in the boat. Of course, to Powell that same noise meant something entirely different, something terrifying. Our own guide, gray-bearded, jovial Paul, was born in 1956, the same year construction began on the dam, and so never knew this as a wild river. Few people have these days. He seemed like a good man, happy enough with his job, and he spouted facts about dam and river, toeing the company line. Lake Powell may have drowned some beautiful places, he told us, but it was now a playland for

3 million people, and provided water resources for 31 million people. (Three-quarters of the water would end up in California's Imperial Valley for agribusiness, but I didn't bring this up.) We passed the Mile Four Dam site, where the walls rise 1,800 feet high and where a dam was almost built that would have dwarfed the one in Glen Canyon. (It was this potential dam site that inspired the Sierra Club to take out a full-page ad in the *New York Times* showing a drowned Sistine Chapel.)

When we pulled over at the Ferry Swale campground to look at petroglyphs, Paul and I talked Abbey for a while. Both Paul's shaggy hairstyle and his profession suggested he would be well versed. Sure enough, he was familiar with the Abbey scriptures and became slightly apologetic about his complicit role in showcasing the new, improved, regulated river. As well as the more pleasant facts he had been spouting, he knew that the ecosystems we had been traveling through had been vastly altered by the dam, and that the ecosystems upstream had all been ruined. He knew too that Lake Powell was gradually silting and drying up, its bathtub ring left by its high point now fifty feet up on the canyon walls. And certainly as a Grand Canyon river rafter Paul knew that the Glen Canyon Dam and Lake Powell symbolized everything that Ed Abbey most despised about the modern American West.

"He sure hated that dam," Paul admitted.

He sure did, I agreed. But I loved the way he had turned that hate into a kind of artistic fuel.

If *Desert Solitaire* was Abbey's best book, then *The Monkey Wrench Gang* was his most popular, and at the heart of the novel is a plan to blow up the Glen Canyon Dam and send the Colorado flowing back into the Grand Canyon. At the heart of that heart is a caricature of a man, George Washington Hayduke—a wild, hairy, passionate, deranged primitive who spoke in caveman phrases and said the word *fuck* a lot. Based on Abbey's friend, Doug Peacock, Hayduke was a Vietnam vet with a background in field medicine and explosives, a force of nature who would do whatever it took to try to restore the West to the way it was. As Hayduke himself put it: "My job is to save the fucking wilderness. That's simple, right?"

Hayduke did not work alone, of course, but was just one, as the title implies, of a gang, a gang that included Seldom Seen Smith (the Ken Sleight character), Doc Sarvis (the closest thing to a stand-in for Abbey), and Bonnie Abzug (a kind of sexpot caricature of a woman who was based loosely on Abbey's friend Ingrid Eisenstadter). Together they fought the powers that be, the forces of progress, the forces of pillage. Together they lived out an Abbey fantasy of taking on the modern industrial state by dismantling and disabling construction equipment, running tractors over canyon walls, blowing up bridges, and doing whatever else it took to slow down the demon progress.

"One brave act is worth a thousand books," Abbey wrote.

This might seem like an odd sentiment for a writer, especially for a writer whose words led to so much action. But throughout his life, Abbey chastised himself for not doing more. Not just more on the page, not mere *words*.

No doubt he underestimated how much of a difference his words actually made. True, sane writers should be skeptical about believing their words make a great difference in the world. But to a surprising degree, Abbey's words *did*. For all his own forays into monkeywrenching and protest, the most important environmental work he did was in the seeds he planted on the page.

The remarkable thing is that his fantasy of a gang of eco-fighters would be translated into reality by some of the book's readers. Even more remarkable is how many people not only took the book seriously but began to see it as a kind of training manual or how-to guide for eco-sabotage. The book, which sold more than a million copies, was read by every western environmentalist with even the vaguest of literary inclinations. As late as 1991, when I arrived in Colorado, sixteen years after the book was published, I had among my own small circle of friends a man who made it his business to smash the lightbulbs that were annually set up for Christmas display on Flag-staff Mountain (how environmental this protest was is another question); another who'd had the course of his life determined by Abbey's books and would soon begin a career as the director of a land trust; and more mysteriously another who kept the book *Eco Defense* on his bedside shelf and received the *Earth First!* newsletter but refused to talk at all about monkeywrenching, no doubt, we assumed, for fear of implicating himself or his fellow saboteurs.

Then there's Dave Foreman, who was still in the midst of eight years working as the Southwest representative for the Wilderness Society and as a Washington lobbyist when he first read the book. During those years, he had become frustrated with the traditional ways that environmental groups tried to create change. He felt that there was far too much compromise, and began to wonder if there were more creative, personal, and radical ways he could fight for the land. Soon after reading Abbey he found himself getting together with some like-minded young environmentalists who worked for both the Wilderness Society and the Friends of the Earth. The group retreated to the desert to talk about what was to be done and how to do it. When they emerged, they were committed to creating an uncompromising unit that would put the defense of the Earth above all else.

They called themselves Earth First!, a nontraditional non-organization that would use weapons similar to Abbey's gang in defense of Mother Earth. *The Monkey Wrench Gang* was their central text. The group began by fighting logging in the Oregon National Forest, where they took nonviolent action, in the spirit of Gandhi and Martin Luther King, standing in front of bulldozers and literally hugging trees. Foreman always stressed the nonviolent aspect of the protests, and he continued to do so in his book, *Eco Defense: A Field Guide to Monkey Wrenchers*, for which Abbey wrote the introduction. The book detailed the basics of how to take environmental protest into your own hands, describing techniques for pulling up surveyors' stakes and disabling machines.

Earth First! learned from Abbey the importance of symbol, and one of the group's high points was the unfurling of a great black sheet down the front of the Glen Canyon Dam that made it appear the dam was cracked, an event which Abbey gleefully attended. But a group that had romantic beginnings had paranoid endings (think *Goodfellas*), with the FBI infiltrating the organization and bursting into Foreman's home to arrest him. The FBI did a good job of painting the activists as terrorists, an accusation that became all that much more common against environmental groups in the climate after 9/11.

IF ABBEY WAS Mr. Outside, Stegner was Mr. Inside, fighting within the proper channels. The objectives of the two men often overlapped, but their *tones* couldn't have been more different. For instance, during the writing and editing of *This Is Dinosaur*, both David Brower and the book's publisher, Alfred Knopf, pushed for a more combative style, but Stegner insisted that a more moderate and temperate book, with the focus on what would be lost rather than on who the villains were, would be more effective. Abbey would have scoffed.

Wallace Stegner was impatient with the remnants of romanticism in the West, particularly with those who wrapped themselves in the cloak of the western myth so they could continue their agenda of destroying western land. He wrote: "I grew up in a cowboy culture, and have been trying to get it out of my thinking and feeling ever since." Against the myths of rugged individualism, he put forth community. Against irrationality, he put forth reason. Meanwhile, though Abbey might like to mock both cow and cowboy, that didn't stop him from occasionally putting on the romantic spurs and chaps of a western hero. Abbey, and to some extent the group that grew out of his ideas, Earth First!, used the cowboy image to battle the cowboy myth, and one of the reasons Abbey is still relevant today was that he took this do-gooding, dorky thing called environmentalism—he hated the passionless, scientific sound of the word—and made it exciting, the province of the outlaw. He also made it fun. In today's political climate, it is almost impossible to imagine the Robin Hood feel of Abbey's day. Abbey relished the fight and, reading him, others started relishing it too.

In my own life, for instance, one of Abbey's roles was that he was a gateway drug to Stegner, and perhaps this is true for many others, too. Like Stegner, Abbey thought about the West as a whole and connected many a dot, but he was never quite the global thinker his old teacher was. At first glance he might seem to have less to offer us in these more circumscribed times. Yet the funny thing is that some of his more extreme ideas have come to seem less radical. As the years have gone by Lake Powell has continued to silt up, losing more than 100,000 acre-feet per year at last count, and hydrologists believe—as Abbey did—that silting will eventually lead to a pool of mud, not water. Michael Kellett is the program director of the Glen Canyon Institute, which was founded in 1996 with the help of David Brower with the goal of one day witnessing the Colorado flowing freely through the old Glen Canyon. At a time when western dams are actually being decommissioned so that rivers can flow, experts are wondering whether it is really viable to have two enormous evaporative and silting reservoirs, Powell and Mead.

Kellett wrote in the summer of 2012:

> The trends of the last decade have dramatically changed the situation. Rising public water demand, relentless drought, and climate change have significantly reduced the flow of the Colorado River from that of the past century. Scientific studies have predicted that this situation will continue. Lake Powell reservoir, and Lake Mead reservoir downstream, are half empty. Most scientists believe that there will never again be enough water to fill both reservoirs.

Which had led to proposals like the Fill Lake Mead First project, the idea being to keep the downstream reservoir, Mead, full while releasing the upstream Glen Canyon. In other words, for the first time Abbey's wild fantasies are being considered as serious policy.

And for the first time the dream of what would occur when the dam was removed might come true. Abbey writes of that fantasy at the end of his essay "The Damnation of a Canyon":

> The inevitable floods will soon remove all that does not belong within the canyons. Fresh green willow, box elder and redbud will appear; and the ancient drowned cottonwoods (noble monuments to themselves) will be replaced by young of their own kind. With the renewal of plant life will come the insects, the birds, the lizards and snakes, the mammals. Within a generation—thirty years—I predict the river and canyons will bear a decent resemblance to their former selves. Within the lifetime of our children Glen Canyon and the living river, heart of the canyonlands, will be restored to us. The wilderness will again belong to God, the people and the wild things that call it home.

FROM THE DAM I pushed it all the way to Albuquerque and spent the night in a dive hotel. The next morning I was up early, heading up to the Santa Fe airport to pick up my friend Mark Honerkamp, or Hones as I've always call him. One thing I haven't mentioned yet is the role that male bonding played in the lives of Stegner and, especially, Abbey. As it turns out, it played a role in my life too, and as much as I'd enjoyed my solo trip so far, I was ready for company. Hones and I had been friends since 1983, when we played together on an Ultimate Frisbee team called the Hostages. Not only had he been part of my life since then, he had also gone on almost every adventure (and appeared in almost every book). By the summer of 2012, Hones had been out of work for a while, focusing most of his energies on fishing and living cheaply so that he could keep on fishing. When Kristen McKinnon of Wild Rivers Expeditions offered to comp me for an eight-day river trip on the San Juan River in exchange for writing about my experience, I asked her if she could comp *two* paddlers. Kristen, always generous, said sure.

I was late to pick him up due to a chemical spill on the highway— the whole road closed off by yellow police tape—that forced me to detour up through the mountains before cutting back to the tiny Santa Fe airport. Hones didn't seem to mind. He was armed, for the first time in his life, with a cell phone, the temporary grocery-store kind, which allowed me to call him when I made my detour. When I finally greeted him at the airport he could turn off the phone for the rest of the trip, it having served its one purpose.

Hones is a big man, 6'4", and he folded himself into my small car, squeezing in among all my belongings. In daily life, Hones can be moody, but he loves vacations, trips especially, and has traveled with me to Venezuela, Hawk Mountain (PA), New Orleans, Cape Cod, Colorado, Utah, and Belize.

We had to make a stop before we headed to the river. Jack Loeffler, one of Edward Abbey's closest friends, lived in the hills outside of Santa Fe. We dropped by and spoke with Loeffler in the open, book-filled study of his single-story adobe home.

"What Ed and I knew, on some fundamental level, is that once you've been out in it long enough, it becomes the top priority," he told us as we settled into the study. "When you're out in it fully, you recognize it's where you belong. We concluded that it took a good ten days in the wilderness until you began to change. You need to live in the spirit of nature, so that it's totally and intuitively in your system. Then you don't have any choice but to defend it."

If the words verged on the New Age, the delivery was pure Broadway. A handsome, fit, seventy-four-year-old man with a big smile and white beard, Loeffler was innately theatrical. He wore an open western shirt, kerchief, and khaki shorts. His whole demeanor was what I can only describe as oddly joyful.

"Ed was a tortured man," he told us at one point. "He was no stranger to despair."

That jibed with what I had read and thought. Though Loeffler spoke those melancholic words with a beaming smile.

"I think that is one of the reasons we got along so well," he continued. "I *am* a stranger to despair."

He exploded in a wild burst of a laugh after he said this, a noise we would grow used to by the end of the interview. His laugh sounded like the upward yodeling of a pileated woodpecker.

I agreed that he seemed to be a sunnier spirit than his friend.

"I'm a happy dude, man," he said.

I confessed to him that I was feeling guilty about all the driving I had been doing.

"Ed and I drove all over the Southwest," he said. "And worse, we took both of our trucks. I don't think we had a single trip when we didn't get stuck. As a matter of fact, we even got stuck when he was dead. We had made a vow to each other that whoever went first, the other wouldn't let them die in a hospital bed. Ed died well but when I went to bury him in the desert, with his body in the back of the truck, we got stuck in the sand. It was inevitable, I guess."

Dead bodies in the back of the truck were just one way that their camping trips were not like yours or mine. I mentioned this.

"Not only did we take two vehicles much of the time we camped, but we always brought matching .357 Magnums. So we were ready."

"For what?" I asked.

"Well, I have to be careful here. For Ed the statute of limitations has run out. Not necessarily for me. Let's just say that one of the reasons we had them—not that I would really use it for this—is that ostensibly a .357 can crack an engine block in a big piece of machinery."

This was what I wanted to know. How much of Abbey's monkeywrenching was real, how much legend or fiction? Was he just good with words or did he get his hands dirty?

"Ed did his *nachtwerke*," Loeffler told me. "That's what he called it: night work. It started with cutting down billboards in college. What you've got to understand is that rebellion was part of him, in his blood. Look, his father, Paul Revere Abbey, named one of Ed's brothers William Tell Abbey. Paul had met Eugene Debbs, who was a huge influence on him. From his father's side Ed got that strong, individualistic point of view."

What became clear to me, as Loeffler kept talking, was that Ed Abbey did a lot more than pay lip service to monkeywrenching. Loeffler described the early fights of the Black Mesa Defense Fund and the battles against the Peabody Coal Company.

"We had a rule of three," he said. They did their work in small groups, preferably two but three at most, and never confided in anyone else about what they'd done.

Both men had come to believe that American culture was "lodged completely in an economically dominated paradigm" and that those who opposed it would be punished.

"Law is created to define and defend the economic system," Loeffler said. But fighting was a moral imperative, the two friends came to agree: as obvious a case of self-defense as repelling someone who has broken into your home. That said, they would only push it so far. Abbey and Loeffler made vows of nonviolence. Doing harm to machines was one thing, human beings another.

Loeffler believed that too many people underplayed his friend's belief in anarchy, which Abbey called "democracy taken seriously." Government, any government, should be rightly feared: "Like a bulldozer, government serves the caprice of any man or group who succeeds in seizing the controls." For this reason Abbey was adamantly opposed to any control of guns. (One wonders if recent events might have led to a softening of this position, though softening, as a rule, was not in Abbey's nature.)

And there is something else in Abbey that Jack Loeffler was suggesting we not take lightly. Abbey fought the prevailing power, but he also knew why most people didn't fight the prevailing power. Comfort was a large part of it. For most of us there is a lot to lose. It was, and is, Abbey's job to make us feel uncomfortable in our comfort. He wrote: "Never before in history have slaves been so well fed, thoroughly medicated, lavishly entertained—but we are slaves nonetheless." And this was even before we slaves were given our cell phones and computers.

Right before Hones and I were ready to say good-bye, a huge crack of thunder got us jumping out of our seats. The rain pounded on the roof, a significant percentage of the rain that Santa Fe would see that year. When it stopped, Jack walked us out to the car. We hugged good-bye, which seemed in no way unnatural. I had read Jack's book, the king of all of the "I Was Ed's Chum" genre, and to be honest it had made me a little uneasy. The language was stilted in places, the dialogue between the two buddies almost Shakespearian, the portrayal of chumminess over the top. That said, no other book I'd read had brought Abbey alive to the degree it did, which was Jack's stated goal. And its description of Abbey's "good death" hit like a punch in the gut.

There was something a little groovy about Jack Loeffler, the kind of grooviness that usually sets off my bullshit detector. But the detector stayed quiet during our visit. If his book had been slightly tone deaf, Jack Loeffler in person was anything but. I was both charmed and impressed by the man. He was a force: voluble, smart, dynamic.

We left reluctantly and when we finally did, after knowing him for three hours, we felt we were leaving a friend.

The last thing he said to me was a directive regarding Abbey.

"Bring him alive," he said as we climbed in the car. "Farewell!"

DOWN THE RIVER WITH ED AND WALLY

On November 4, 1980, Edward Abbey began a ten-day rafting trip on the Green River in Utah. With him he carried "a worn and greasy paperback copy of a book called *Walden*" by Henry David Thoreau. Out of that trip came one of his very best essays, "Down the River with Henry Thoreau," the piece patched together out of journal entries of river observations and a running conversation, which sometimes grows heated enough to call an argument, with Henry David Thoreau. All his life Abbey had wrestled with Thoreau's ghost, but in this essay he did so most directly, admiring Henry as a great resister of conformity while teasing him about his sexless, preacherly persona, laughing at the man who said "all nature is my bride."

On July 24, 2012, Hones and I began our own river trip, paddling down the San Juan River, whose waters would eventually mix with the Colorado's, which in turn had already mixed with the Green's. Like Abbey, I was not traveling alone. In my dry bag, along with my field guide to western birds, were Abbey's *Down the River*, which contained the Thoreau essay, and *Desert Solitaire*, as well as an essay collection of Wallace Stegner's, *The Sound of Mountain Water*.

I spent my first afternoon on the river lying back in my inflatable kayak doing nothing. I was feeling joyous, though that is not the word exactly. Not joyous, but supremely relaxed, something that most adults, or at least the adult I am, rarely get to feel. The current was pulling me and I was staring up at eight-hundred-foot-high walls that were a similar red to that I saw on the screen of my inner eyelids when I closed my eyes, which I was also doing quite a lot of. We had been told the first rapids were a ways off, and at that moment the strong current was handling most of the work, though I dipped in a paddle occasionally to help. The river wasn't red really, but more like chocolate pudding with a shot or two of henna. A raven croaked, echoing in the canyon, and I saw signs of beaver in a side channel, and then, happily, the beaver itself. My peace was interrupted only by Hones, who was paddling along the opposite bank and who had begun to gesture wildly as if trying to bring in a wayward airplane. I finally managed to see what all the fuss was about, and noticed the half dozen bighorn sheep picking their way along the steep riverbank. I gave Hones a thumbs-up.

Part of the appeal of Ed Abbey, I've come to believe, is that he understood the lost art of lounging. Here he is in *Desert Solitaire*: "I was sitting out back on my 33,000 acre terrace, shoeless and shirtless, scratching my toes in the sand and sipping on a tall iced drink, watching the flow of the evening over the desert."

Stegner liked to suggest that the rest of us are jealous of workaholics, but certainly the opposite is true. We envy the true blow-off artists. We all like to think we could kick back in a hammock and whittle away the afternoon, but it is in fact a rare gift. And when we see someone doing nothing, even if it is doing nothing on the page, we dream that that could be us. The dream is not just that we have the time and the space, but the mind for it.

Virtue, outside of the virtue of saving wild places, doesn't have much of a role in Ed Abbey's work, and do-gooders are frowned upon. Meanwhile, sensual pleasure, which plays such a large role in Abbey's life and writing, goes virtually unmentioned in Stegner's.

It may be overstatement, but let's try this one on: We read Wallace Stegner for his virtues, but we read Edward Abbey for his flaws. Stegner the sheriff, Abbey the outlaw.

I remember an essay written by the editor and essayist Rust Hills about Michel de Montaigne and Henry David Thoreau. "Montaigne is somehow marvelously humanly indolent; Thoreau had an exceptional, almost inhuman, vitality," he wrote. "Thoreau kept in shape . . ." What does he mean by this? He means that Thoreau, though famous as someone who retired from the active world, worked vigorously on himself and his art, walked hard (four hours) each day, and wrote in his journal, striving for a higher, better life. Montaigne, by contrast, accepted his sloppy self. The song he sang was: "This is me. Take me as I am. *I* do."

Abbey, of course, plays the Montaigne role here, and while Stegner may at first seem miscast in the Thoreau role, this particular aspect of Thoreau fits well. With Stegner, there is always a sense of vigor, fitness, striving to be more.

One way to illustrate the difference between the two men is to compare their different reactions on separate river trips like this one. Abbey, near the end of a ten-day paddling trip on the Colorado, wondered if he could just stop and live there forever, roaming the side canyons, wandering naked, shooting deer and drinking river water, seeing no one. Stegner, on a similar trip, also fantasized about an extended stay in the canyon, but with one telling addition: he thought it would be a great place to roll up his sleeves and write a book.

With Stegner there is no talk of ecstasy, euphoria, bliss. Maybe that is because there is no such thing as a *steady* blissful state. These states come in moments and the moments can't be pre-planned. If consistency is Stegner's realm, then Abbey's way offers an openness to and a chronicling of moods and contradictions, of the ebb and flow of mind and self, of the dangers and difficulties of existing inside our human skin. Abbey has been accused of being adolescent, but there is a joy to this kind of honesty. A joy that might not be attained without an openness to all moods.

———

THOUGH WE HAD signed on to spend the next eight days happily floating down the muddy San Juan, ours was also a business trip of sorts. We had come to eradicate foreigners. Our purpose was to try to fight back—through poison, it needs to be added—the proliferation of non-native species, like Russian olive, that grow along the sandy banks of the San Juan River. Russian olive, a native of western and central Asia, is particularly adept at colonizing the poor rocky soil along rivers in the American West, muscling out native plants. Helping us in this noble task of repelling invaders were five Navajos between the ages of eighteen and twenty-five, three rangers, and four river guides. It went without saying that it was poetically apt that native people were doing most of this eradicating and repelling of the non-native.

Thanks to the generosity of my old friend Kristen, the owner of Wild Rivers Expeditions, we were allowed to partake of the food, equipment, and expertise of the guides while also hewing to our own less-than-rigorous agenda. We would mostly paddle the little one-man inflatable kayaks, though we were welcome to hitch rides on the big blue rafts when we liked.

About an hour downstream on our second morning we came upon a particularly verdant (or, take your pick, virulent) patch of Russian olive, green and tall as trees and seemingly growing straight out of the combination of sand and rock that made up the shoreline. The rest of the crew pulled over to do their work of poisoning, while we were given permission to paddle ahead by Ralph, the young man who was serving as the lead guide.

So we did, paddling alone, or alone together, through the afternoon.

"Do you think they'll start to resent us?" Hones asked after a while.

"They might," I said, though at the moment I was too happy to care.

We pulled over at what we decided must be the designated campground that Ralph had described to us, and I grabbed two beers out of my dry bag. It was technically a dry trip, which meant that Hones and I had to smuggle in our alcohol. This, too, was part of our agreement with Kristen, and on the first morning the guides had helped us quietly distribute about a case's worth of beer deep in the ice chests on the big rafts.

We decided to hike up one of the side canyons. The river was beautiful, the main canyon walls impressive, but we would soon discover that it was the side canyons that were the true stars of the trip. We walked into a great ascending chamber of varying stone, climbing up the pockmarked terraces of limestone, shale, and sandstone that the water ran down during storms. Which meant what we were really walking up was a dry, gradual waterfall that had been carved into the stone by rushing water over the eons. Not entirely dry though. A series of small pools, each about the size of a plastic kiddie pool, appeared in the indented rock and within those pools, miraculously, tiny tadpoles squiggled. Talk about life filling every niche. Every puddle.

We entered the final great chamber. It was like a church, a cathedral, but that didn't do it justice. We stared up at a huge limestone chute, fifty feet above us, which, during the rains, served as a water slide. At the foot of the chute was a slimy pool from remnant rains. Ferns bearded the edge of the chute, hanging down, green against red. The acoustics in the place were perfect and I stood below the falls and recited the beginning of the Gettysburg Address.

If this were a church, it was missing its central sacrament, and I found myself wishing for rain. Water was the absent ingredient, the thing that would bring this, and all the rest of the side canyons, alive. Then the church would really be in session, the place would be "activated." In minutes there would be a hundred spontaneous waterfalls up and down the river, and those falls would form temporary streams, tributaries to feed the mother San Juan. *That* would be something to see.

Water, precious water. In the West it is always the missing ingredient. Wallace Stegner wrote that "the primary unity of the West is the shortage of water."

We drank our beers, Santa Fe IPAs, by the pool, and after a while we heard the others start showing up and made our way back down to the canyon. By the time we got out of the canyon's mouth, everyone else had arrived and were spreading out over the sand, in search of their night's real estate. While this was a relaxing trip for us, our relaxation hinged on the guides' preparedness and effort, and they were already unpacking the rafts and setting up the dinner area. When we found out that we were having steaks, Hones and I offered to cook, seeing as we had been the only ones lazing about all day.

We cooked the steaks to specifications—from rare to well-done—and received many compliments to the chefs. Then, after cleaning our plates, we wandered off to our campsite, high up on the hill. The bats came out and so did a half dozen quail-like birds, called chukars, that made a gurgly racket on the opposite bank. The slice of sky above the canyon walls gradually filled with stars.

After Hones wandered off to his tent, I stayed up for a while. I rolled out my Paco, a white pad that served both as a comfortable seat on the rafts and a fantastic mattress at night, and lay back on it, staring up at the stars.

"STAND NAKED BEFORE them," Michel de Montaigne wrote in his note to the reader that preceded his famous essays. But for our first essayist this was just a metaphor. Not for Ed Abbey. Camping with Loeffler, Abbey sometimes took Montaigne one step further, never putting his clothes on. "It's such a nice day I think I'll leave it out," he said.

Elsewhere he confirms his preference for wandering around naked, for jerking off up in his solitary fire station, for throwing beer cans out of his truck, for smoking cigars, for toting guns. He drinks too much. He tends to be lazy, likes to blow things off. He argues strongly for the right to bear arms, believes in decentralized government, is against illegal immigration. He is openly lustful and sometimes writes of his desire to copulate with every woman he sees. In other words, if you are going to accept him warts and all, then you have to accept a whole lot of warts.

One appeal of tackling Abbey and Stegner together is that they tug me in opposite directions. I love the *idea* of Abbey, his wildness, but in my own life I have been saved—no other word will do, religious connotations be damned—by the way of Stegner. The way of the tough-minded, the workaholic. In fact, I wonder how much Abbey's life can offer me, a man of fifty. The standard trope would be that you're Abbey when you're young, and Stegner when you're old. But I'm not sure I buy it, at least not entirely.

If you read Ed Abbey long enough his temperament edges into your mind like weather. You sense a chronic melancholy, but also sparks of joy. Slouchy sensuality, and bursts of courage. His is a restless mind, always jumping to the next thought, the next idea, the next dream. Stegner's mind is restless too, energetic, moving briskly, fighting off a hundred mind weeds and temptations. There is a hard-nosed notion of the world as strife, a toughness, and a bristling energy. And also something Abbey lacked: a fondness for and a reliance on routine. For checking things off his daily list.

Work is always a touchstone for Stegner. Work as pleasure and work as salvation. Work fills the mind, makes chaos orderly. Work controls the uncontrollable. This is admirable but there are problems with turning to workaholism as your default setting. There can be a sense of avoidance, of running from the world. It is here, perhaps, that Abbey offers a kind of counterweight, an alternative.

Because there's bravery in Abbey's apparent slothfulness. A willingness to accept the cycles of depression and pleasure, up and down, without racing toward a solution or an ism. It is not always a happy acceptance but it is an acceptance, and that, too, is one of the pleasures of reading Abbey. A workaholic might find this quality adolescent. But there is something freeing about reading a writer who offers us something beyond the bounds and bonds of our normal lives.

In elevating Abbey I don't want to bury Stegner. Wallace Stegner knew depression and real loss, and was far too psychologically astute to hide life's messiness under a monolith called work. While he loved to quote Henry James that "order is the dream of man," he never did so without the second thought that "chaos is the law of nature." Furthermore, he was a kind and generous man, and teacher, so the portrait of the artist as an old drudge does not quite work.

At first the river seemed more of an Abbey place than a Stegner place, but then I reminded myself that Stegner was no stranger to western rivers, that in fact he paddled down this one with the legendary river guide Norman Nevills. Stegner might have had a buttoned-up side, but he also got to experience many nights looking up at the stars through the canyons, sleeping to the sound of rushing water, exhausted after a day in the southwestern sun. While these two men are different, that doesn't mean I should oversimplify, turning them into caricatures of themselves. They are complicated—and if they weren't we would no longer be interested in them. They contain parts of each other.

THE THIRD MORNING we woke to watch the sun rise, or at least show itself on the western rock wall of the canyon. The top of the wall caught fire first, turning the Navajo sandstone a bright orange. Light spread on the western rim like an incoming tide.

A quarter mile up, two bighorns made their own trails as they gamboled down the impossibly steep terrain. The sheep startled when Ralph banged a metal spoon on a pot to signal that coffee was on. I kept writing but after a while Hones appeared with two cups. I joked that he was my manservant and as it turned out we were on the same comic page. He told me what he'd said when one of the guides asked who he was bringing the second cup for: "Lord Dave."

We pushed onward. Abbey wrote about "a hard day of watching cloud formations." Our days were more strenuous than that—we paddled and cleaned and helped the rangers unpack their poisons—but there was plenty of ease, too. The little kayaks, duckies they were called, were built for napping, or at least for reclining and staring up at the red walls that loomed above us. We prayed for rain, just to see the side-canyon spectacle, and saw signs of it upstream when the color red flowed in from side canyons joining our chocolate river. Over the next couple of days Hones and I also saw plenty more bighorn and watched birds through our binoculars: hawks, turkey vultures, chukars, swallows, and a little blue bird called a Brewer's wren. Each afternoon we pulled over at some equally beautiful campground and everyone sought out the best spots for the tents in the thorny dunelike sandbars. "It's like buying a new house every day," Hones said. We looked for spots on the edge of town, when possible, and celebrated cocktail hour, though our supply kept dwindling. We also hiked up every side canyon we could find, and each night Hones slept out under the stars on his Paco Pad, though I mostly opted for my tent. Each morning he brought Lord Dave his coffee while I scribbled down my notes from the day before.

We fought for our freedom, since it seemed that too often our day's schedule was determined not just by the need to poison Russian olive but by the apparent whims of our tour leader. Ralph clearly hadn't gotten the memo that we were to be granted plenty of slack, and I, steeped in Abbey, began to bristle under his rule, wondering if we'd made a mistake signing on with a tour instead of just pushing off on our own. But the food was fantastic and we were learning a lot about the canyon. And the truth was that Ralph was a perfectly competent young man, all of twenty-three, who had the unfortunate responsibility of bossing around men many years his senior.

On the third day I lent Ralph a copy of Wallace Stegner's essays and he mistakenly dropped it over the side of the boat. He handed it back to me, waterlogged but still readable. I didn't really mind that much, it was just an accident, and I also understood that ordering us around was simply part of his job. What I minded was the *way* he ordered us around. He yelled, he pushed, he grated. On a modern river trip, safety and organization are paramount, but a good leader can take care of these things while still maintaining the illusion of freedom. Of course, if I had really wanted to be free, Hones and I would have paddled off on our own and taken our chances.

Gradually we got to know the rest of the group. There was Sierra, she of the beautiful smile and earnest sunny manner, who borrowed my inflatable mattress each night (I used my Paco Pad). She was one of the leaders of the Navajo group Rethink Diné Power, (Diné means "The People" in Navajo) that sought to combat the poverty, depression, and alcoholism so prominent on the reservations by relearning the old Navajo traditions and, most important, the language. Another of that group's leaders was Michael, a slight young man who fancied himself a shaman and who did actually seem to know the names of things and had a knack for finding arrowheads.

"The prophets came through these waters," he told me one evening. "They came through these waters and got their stories. How can we learn the traditions without knowing the place? All the ceremonies are directly connected to the landscape. Without the landscape you can't have the ceremonies."

Michael spoke only Navajo when talking with the others. He felt he had perspective on the importance of our trip, in part because of the two years he'd spent in San Diego "getting to know American culture" before returning to the reservation with a mission.

He told me the name of the San Juan River goddess was Toasdza.

He was a confident kid, though quiet.

Jordan was another kind of quiet, a proud quiet. He was Navajo too, though he was not part of the Diné group but a ranger who worked for the National Park Service in Flagstaff. Each morning he took great care washing his long black hair in the river, then flipping it in front of his head and back over his shoulders like he was in a shampoo commercial. Each night he went exploring barefoot up the side canyons in the dark and then let out war whoops, hoots and coyote howls that echoed back down to us through the chambers of the stone cathedrals.

At first he had been the hardest of the group for me to get to know, but we eventually formed a bond, thanks to our similar reactions to the tour leader.

If I was annoyed by being bossed around, Jordan was enraged.

He didn't say anything, but you could see his eyes smolder with fury every time Ralph told him not to pick up the bacon with his fingers or where to tie his kayak.

Things were brought to a head one night over dinner at a campsite called False John's. Greg, a guide who was also Navajo, joined Hones and me for cocktail hour and everyone seemed in good spirits. We had become a real group and we were sitting in one big circle. Hones broke out his Serrano peppers and put them out on the camp table for all. When people asked about them, he explained that he grew hundreds of pepper plants at his apartment in Boston, starting them under artificial light and getting them strong before replanting them outside in summer.

We had barely seen any other rafters on the trip, but while we were eating, another boat landed a quarter mile upstream and a man came walking toward us. He seemed irritated that we were there, taking the main campsite. It was the usual thing, something the Navajos had all heard before: the man wanted our land. He explained that they had been *planning* on staying at the camp where we were, that it was "a tradition" with their group. But we insisted they stay upstream. After all, it was a time-honored law: we got there first. The man walked off grumbling.

"Let them try and fight us for it," someone said.

I liked that idea. I suggested that we should walk down to their campsite in waves to intimidate them. First Hones and I would head down, the two big middle-aged white guys. Then the three rangers wearing their uniforms, representatives of the Park Service, would stroll down and have a little talk with them. And if that didn't do it, we would send a war party of a half dozen Navajos.

We were all laughing, in good spirits. But then it happened. Jordan was walking down to the boat while Ralph was sitting with a small group of us up on the beach.

"Jordan!" he yelled.

I understood that Ralph, like the rest of us, was feeling good. His yell was an attempt at jocularity, and all he really wanted to do, it would turn out, was ask Jordan to guide us on the next day's hike. But the way he yelled didn't sound like that. It sounded instead like an order. A sharp command.

Jordan glared at Ralph and said nothing.

It would have been best to let it lie, but Ralph yelled again: "Come over here!"

Jordan looked at Ralph as if he were a bug he wanted to step on.

"No," he said quietly.

A while later I sought out Jordan at his tent. I told him that Ralph and the other guides just wanted to have him lead the hike, but also confided that all the scolding and controlling was getting to me, too.

"Fuck them," he said before heading off on one of his barefoot nighttime hikes.

EVEN WALLACE STEGNER'S and Ed Abbey's utopias were different.

Stegner's dream was of a western community where good people worked together toward a common good. Abbey's dream was a solitary one, a dream of retreat. In *Crossing to Safety*, the Stegner character dismisses his best friend's vision of pastoral retreat, and offers in its stead a vision of a jail cell, an orderly day with no visitors and with time allotted for work, exercise, sleep. We romanticize nature, the realist says, because we don't have to live in it.

For most people the pastoral *is* fantasy, but Abbey made the fantasy real on many occasions. The most famous example is his sojourn into Havasu Canyon in 1949, which he then wrote up as a chapter of *Desert Solitaire*. The chapter begins with Abbey's story of a drive to Los Angeles with friends, during which they stopped at the Grand Canyon and overheard a park ranger talking about a placed called Havasu or Havasupai, a canyon with waterfalls down below. "My friends said they would wait," Abbey writes. "So I went down to Havasu—fourteen miles by trail—and looked things over. When I returned five weeks later I discovered that the others had gone on to Los Angeles without me."

I can testify that those fourteen miles are not easy ones, since I had descended them from the rim of the Grand Canyon on a hot day in May, two months before my summer trip, wearing an ill-fitting backpack bought the day before at Play It Again Sports in Tucson. I remember a lot of misery and two great joys. One joy was finally taking the pack off my shoulders, and the other was, after hours trudging through the orange, dusty, dry land, coming upon a stream of blue-green water surging through the desert dryness. It was that water, Havasu Creek, that Abbey had followed into the tiny Indian village of Havasupai, or Supai, "where unshod ponies ambled down the street and the children laughed not maliciously at the sight of the wet white man." The village is still there, still small, looking like the oasis it is—green fields and ramshackle buildings appearing suddenly, like the river, out of the desert. Abbey relates with pleasure the fact that when he arrived the Indians had just voted down the paved road that the government had proposed. There was still no road when I got there, but there had been other changes. For one, my hike down was marred by the constant metallic whirring of blades, helicopters that seemingly made the trip from the canyon rim to the little town every twenty minutes, delivering mail, goods, and tourists. The other change since 1949 had to do with the religion of the couple hundred native people who still lived in Supai. Most of them had converted since Abbey's day. They were now almost all committed Rastafarians.

Abbey had pushed right through the village to make his camp

near one of the canyon's three spectacular waterfalls. For thirty-five days he lived there alone. "The first thing I did was take off my pants," he writes. Of course. And next? "I did nothing. Or nearly nothing. I caught a few rainbow trout, which grew big if not numerous in Havasu Creek. About once a week I put on my pants and walked up to the Indian village to buy bacon, canned beans and Argentine beef in the little store." Other than that his days were filled with long walks and plenty of lazing about, maybe some note-taking in his journal. He originally had thought to sleep in one of the old, deserted mining cabins, but the mosquitoes attacked, so he dragged the cabin's old cot to within about five feet of where the creek tumbled over the edge and became a waterfall, and there he slept for the next month or so, the "continuous turbulence of the air" keeping the bugs away.

Part of Abbey's appeal to readers has always been the temptation of ease, real ease. Whether it is fantasy or not, we are attracted to the idea of Eden, a place where humans don't want to be elsewhere but wander naked and sleep next to waterfalls. Where people are happy with things just as they are. This has always been the lure of the pastoral, going back to the shepherds, or at least to the poets who wrote about the shepherds. Here is a way of life, an unambitious, unconventional, and uncelebrated way of life, that provides unexpected rewards. Here is another possible way of being, and it is hard to read about this other way without thinking, Hey, shit, maybe I could live that way too. Joseph Wood Krutch wrote of Thoreau that one of the reasons his book was so joyous was that at Walden Pond Henry was a finder, not a seeker. We imagine that Thoreau, and Abbey, have stumbled upon something that we ourselves, mired in our complicated grown-up lives, will never find.

It is a fantasy about the shedding of responsibilities and reverting to a kind of romantic savage state, and so we must imagine Mr. Stegner scoffing. But the beauty of Abbey is that he scoffed a little too. Abbey, like Stegner, had a wide realist streak, and in fact it is the dialogue of his inner realist and inner romantic that helps make reading him so enlivening. He might have extolled the delights of solitude, but he also knew the dangers. As time went by in Havasu Canyon, he noticed that his mind started turning on itself: "The days became wild, strange, ambiguous—a sinister element pervaded the flow of time. . . . I slipped by degrees into lunacy, me and the moon, and lost to a certain extent the power to distinguish between what was and was not myself . . ."

Abbey combatted his demons in Havasu in a realist's fashion: by walking and jostling his agitated brain. Part of him knew that it isn't through the mind that we solve the mind's riddles. Abbey's final walk in the canyon makes up the inspired ending of the Havasu chapter, and brought him a kind of salvation, not through idleness but through action. It is perhaps the most dramatic moment in all of *Desert Solitaire*. Not a car chase, perhaps (that would have to wait for *The Monkey Wrench Gang*), but a real life-and-death drama, a literal cliffhanger. It starts when Abbey takes a long hike into an unfamiliar side canyon and drops down over the edge of a rock slide like the one Hones and I saw. He sees no way back up so he drops down again, a longer drop this time. His hope is that he can work his way downward to the canyon floor, but when he looks over the next ledge he sees "an overhanging cliff to a rubble pile of broken rocks eighty feet below." There is no way down or, seemingly, back up. So what does our bold explorer do? "I began to cry. It was easy. All alone, I didn't have to be brave." After many failures, Abbey manages to escape the first little canyon by balancing atop his walking stick and getting his fingers over the edge, and then climbs the next by shimmying up a rock chute. He cries again at this point, "the hot delicious tears of victory," knowing he might just get out of the canyon alive. Still, there are many miles to go to return to his cot by the waterfall and he is overtaken by darkness and soaked by rains. He seeks refuge in a shallow cave, three feet high, a "little hole littered with the droppings of birds, rats, jack-rabbits and coyotes."

He builds a small fire but runs out of fuel and when the rain doesn't let up decides to sleep there.

The chapter ends:

> I stretched out in the coyote den, pillowed my head on my arm and suffered through the long night, wet, cold, aching, hungry, wretched, dreaming claustrophobic nightmares. It was one of the happiest nights of my life.

Hones slept like a baby each night on his Paco Pad out under the stars, and you got the sense he could do the same for months. Not me. I slept poorly and lived encased in a film of red-brown dirt. I also grew tired of the Groover, the metal box toilet that was the first thing to be set up when we made camp, and that had been given its name years before because of the indentations it had once left in butts (before the innovation of adding a seat).

Each day the group tended to our central task of trying to eradicate the "invaders," but the whole native-species debate made me uneasy. We had a friend back home who liked to go on about how the swans that nested behind our house, animals that we had grown to love, were "not native." It got to the point where I wanted to ask him exactly where his own family came from.

There is always the whiff of eugenics to all this talk of the native purity, or foreignness, of plants and animals, and the funny part is that it often comes from liberals who would rather choke to death than talk the same way about humans. The history of this country, from at least 1492 on, has been the history of invasives, and that goes for plants, too. It may be a fine thing to eradicate Russian olive—it's *Russian*, after all—but I noticed that we were leaving the tamarisk alone, left perhaps for the next poisoning mission. For many people, tamarisk is the virtual symbol of these banks—at least for those who don't know that it, too, is an invasive and that it replaced the native cottonwoods after scientists who thought they knew what they were doing introduced it to battle erosion. The fact is that both tamarisk and Russian olive look quite beautiful when shaken by the river winds, though for those of us who know too much it's hard to think fondly of these plants. We see them through prejudiced eyes. And to be fair: we see them that way because we know the damage they do to ecosystems.

It isn't much of a leap from botanical purity to some of Edward Abbey's less appealing ideas. Abbey, too, was dead set against foreign invasives, though the kind he was worried about were usually illegal immigrants from Mexico.

Here is the thing: if you are a fan of Abbey's work, you often find yourself apologizing for him. It's an interesting difference: people approach Stegner with an assumption of virtue, but those who love Abbey are always saying, "I'm sorry he said that." Wallace might have been a good boy, but there was something essentially disobedient about Ed. He had consistently bad manners, at least on the page. And he liked to tweak liberals every bit as much as conservatives, which is what he did famously in his essay "Immigration and Liberal Taboos." In it he describes a litany of our country's problems, including overpopulation, poverty, and the destruction of our wild places and then argues for "calling a halt to the mass influx of even more millions of hungry, ignorant, unskilled, and culturally-morally-genetically impoverished people. At least until we have brought our own affairs in order."

He continues:

> How many of us, truthfully, would prefer to be submerged in the Caribbean-Latin version of civilization? (Howls of "Racism! Elitism! Xenophobia!" from the Marx brothers and documented liberals.) Harsh words: but somebody has to say them. We cannot play "let's pretend" much longer, not in the present world.

His solution? Close the border. Or "if we must meddle," as he says in his final paragraph, let's give "every campesino" a gun and point them back homewards: "He will know what to do with our gifts and good wishes. The people know who their enemies are."

What to make of this? Should we react as Abbey predicted and call him a racist? We could, certainly. Or we could try to justify his behavior, though Abbey does not seem to want to be justified. He lets it lie there, as it is.

As I chewed over these things, I thought of an old friend of mine, the writer Luis Alberto Urrea. Luis and I went to school together in Colorado and got the Abbey bug at about the same time. But Luis would carry it a step further: an acquaintance of his would purchase Ed Abbey's '75 Eldorado Cadillac convertible from a man in Tucson, and Luis himself would drive and deliver the car to his friend back in Denver. First reading Abbey, Luis once wrote, had a "massive, perhaps catastrophic effect on me." He continued: "I went mad for Ed, but more important, and a major reasons others fell in love with him too, was the aching love he ignited in me for the land. The world. The *tierra*."

Which was why reading Abbey's essay on immigration was so brutal for him. "Ed Abbey once stuck a knife in my heart," he wrote. What was Luis, whose mother was born in Mexico, to make of sentences that attacked the culture, the morals, even the *genes* of his people?

What he made of it, eventually, was an essay called "Down the Highway with Edward Abbey," in which he vents his rage. "Ed Abbey—Aryan," he writes at one point in that essay, and then wrestles with the fact that so many who love Abbey because he is a gadfly also feel the gadfly's sting. Luis continues: "I'm trying hard not to do backflips here just to defend my favorite writer. Consider: where many writers have a pitiable need to be loved, Ed seemed to have a puzzling need to be reviled."

In the essay Luis carefully makes his way through the Abbey minefield, admitting that "writers carry the baggage of their times, their origins, and their own spiritual and intellectual laziness."

He concludes:

I admire Ed Abbey. I enjoy his books . . .
I also decry his ignorance and duplicity.
Guess what: Ed Abbey had feet of clay.
Just like me.

Not a backflip exactly. But a lot of work to circle back to the original love. It is a common enough pattern with Abbey fans of all stripes. Native American readers have to do it. Women readers have to do it. Almost everyone has to find a way to work through what they don't like to get back to what they do.

Many of us make allowances and forgive him. The funny thing is that, as Luis says, Abbey does not ask to be forgiven.

On the last evening we camped on a spot with a broad, sloping beach, a dry creek on one side and the river on the other. Our moods stayed high even after the usual conflict with the boss, who told us we couldn't sleep on the beach after we had all rolled out our pads. We didn't let him get us down. We all waded into the water and started throwing a Frisbee around, ignoring the vague rumbling in the sky and occasional spitting of rain. Pretty soon I started jonesing for a cocktail, and Hones and I climbed up on a sand bank, where we drank ginger ale and whiskey. We listened as a canyon wren went through its notes, up and down the glissading scale. Sam, the oldest of the Navajos, and his friend whom we had taken to calling "the other Michael" (as opposed to Shaman Michael) joined us. Earlier, during lunch at the Grand Gulch pull-off, I kept feeling a little bug on the back of my neck and kept swatting it. I hit it and scratched at it and scratched at it again. But it kept coming back. I might have gone on like that forever if Sam and the other Navajos had been able to refrain from laughing. But they couldn't stop cracking up. Sam had been using a long stalk of Russian olive to tickle my neck.

"My stomach hurts from holding it in," he said.

Now he told me that, even though he lived nearby in Shiprock, he had never set foot in Utah before.

"If you live in the Four Corners you are supposed to know the Four Corners," he said. "But this is a new world for me. I had no idea this was here."

Michael told us that the name of the canyon we were in was Moon Water and said that the San Juan was known as the Old Age River.

I thought of Ed Abbey and his relationship with the Navajo. Capable of spasms of bigotry, he wasn't above a few lazy drunk-Indian jokes. On the other hand, *Desert Solitaire* contains one of the best concise summaries of the brutal challenges of reservation life for the modern Navajo.

We were all having a nice time until I managed to slide off the bank, soak my last dry clothes, and impale my thigh on a beaver-chewed stick. By the time I was bandaged and back, the wind had picked up substantially, and we thought it a good idea to head back to our tents and secure the stakes.

We heard the cry of "dinner" from the crew about a second before the sky exploded. Greg and another guide fought to hold umbrellas over the food, which was delicious if soggy: refried beans, chicken, rice, the last of Hones's peppers. Thunder boomed and the sky fulgurated: one bolt of lightning appeared to split the camp in half. Almost everyone fled back to the tent but I ate my wet meal under the umbrella with Greg. I wondered where Hones was and looked back up the canyon, upstream. And then I saw it.

A waterfall. A beautiful silver-white strand, or strands, gushing down the red rock. This was what I'd been waiting for and with my plate still in hand I ran toward it. I yelled for Hones, who turned out to be eating under a cliff and had already seen the fall. Then, like an excited kid, I ran back toward camp, where other falls could be seen. One, across the river from us, started at about eight hundred feet but then turned to mist halfway down.

The rain passed through, heading downstream, but left behind the waterfalls and a strange slanting light. I grabbed my journal from the tent and made my way back to the first waterfall. Water landed on rock with a ferocious splatter, shaking the maidenhair ferns and hackberry and buffalo-berry plants, and splashing between a white oak and gambol oak, a whole tiny oasis that had grown up here just for, and from, occasions like this. I ducked my head under the water and soaked myself.

A little farther up-canyon I stood below another falls and watched it die out. The drops came from four hundred feet up, falling toward me in slow motion, and I could count individual drops like snowflakes. I stood below it as the slow, fat drops exploded on my face.

Darkness descended and with it came another miracle. The datura, the flowering night plants, began to open, their petals white and radiant.

Back at the first waterfall I ran into Shaman Michael, Jordan, and Sierra, who had decided to camp on the beach by the creek despite the law laid down by Ralph. Michael invited me to smoke some rolled mountain tobacco and I did, sitting on a rock not fifteen feet from the still-splattering falls. He told me to blow the smoke east, west, north, south, and then in front of me. I followed orders. Why not? After a while we said good night and walked out of the canyon in the pitch-dark. It wasn't until I was a hundred yards away that I realized I'd left my journal on the waterfall rock. *My words!* I stumbled back in the darkness to find them.

When I returned to camp, Hones and Greg were sitting on Paco Pads by the river. Greg told us that he had seen two sure signs of rain earlier. The first was a fat toad where he hadn't expected it (it knew rain was near) and the other was the tilted, straight-up moon, like a ladle, which Navajos say means rain is coming. We nodded. These were not signs to be taken lightly in a land where each rainfall is a sort of miracle.

Finally, Hones and Greg headed back to the tents, while I unrolled

my bag right on the beach, a final minor rebellion in the spirit of Jordan. I fell asleep to the song of cicadas and woke the next morning to
the call of the canyon wren, again working its scales. The plan was to
get going fairly early, but the creek was running now, its red flowing
into the San Juan's chocolate in a sort of minor confluence. Without
telling anyone, I decided a hike up the canyon was necessary.

I hadn't gone two hundred yards when I saw that Shaman Michael
had had the same idea. He was wearing a bandana over his mouth
and nose but invited me over to watch as he cut into the poisonous
roots of a datura, the same plant I'd watched bloom the night before.
He called it a *chohajilla*, or sacred datura, "the moon-flowering plant."
He incanted in Navajo and when I asked what he was saying he told
me he was assuring the plant that he was using it for medicine.

"It was a poison plant used by the people before the people. The
moth people or butterfly people."

The moth people apparently liked to party, favoring the datura

THE DATURA CEREMONY.

for its hallucinogenic characteristics. But according to Michael they also, counterintuitively, used it to treat mental illness. Mention of the old people, the Anasazi, reminded me that even my new Navajo friends weren't immune to the games of "who belongs here" and "who was here first." They might have been seeking their old traditions here, and I was glad for it, since this is where many of their myths came from. But the Navajos had been considered intruders in this land by the earlier peoples, the very same old ones who liked the taste of datura.

Michael invited me to stay longer, and I thanked him but told him I needed to hike on. The stream was running after all, and I had my own ceremonies to attend to.

So much of the week had been spent speculating, "What would these canyons be like with water?" Now I knew. The tadpoles, previously trapped in their puddles, were liberated. The ever-thirsty trees and ferns and flowers all drank deeply. As beautiful as the canyons had been—and they had been the highlight of the trip—it had been a little like seeing a body with the blood missing. Now I got to see the canyons *in use*. Serving their purpose. A deep orange-red like Tabasco sauce flowed down the stairways and terraces of rock.

To live in this particular landscape is to be, whether you like it or not, a water worshipper. One can imagine that this worshipping will become more fervent in the dry years ahead.

I studied the water's temple. The stairs that the stream flowed down looked made for it, and of course they were, but also made *by* it (or its watery predecessors). "I look for the forms things want to come as," wrote the poet A. R. Ammons.

I briefly worried about what was going on back at camp, but the canyon wren was up ahead, beckoning, and I decided to turn just one more corner, then another, hoping to get to the deep pool and waterfall that had to be at canyon's end. A cool wind blew downcanyon as I walked through new mud, red and wet but flaky on top, with the look of peeling skin.

I entered into one of the amphitheaters, a great carved cathedral that, after long standing empty, could finally serve its purpose. These rock caverns had been the vessels, empty and useless until now.

The canyon wren was still up ahead, trying to pull me in deeper, but I knew I had to get back to camp and not keep everyone else waiting. The previous night's baptism under the waterfall would have to do. Independence and freedom were one thing. Being a prima donna another.

Reluctantly, pulled by the world, or at least by Ralph, I turned back. I walked quickly, afraid that I was holding up the others. But about halfway down I saw Jordan, washing his hair in the red water. It seemed as surely a ritual as Michael cutting out the roots of a plant.

I asked him how he was doing. He smiled at me and said:

"I'm psyched to be done with that asshole. But I'm sad to leave this place."

I left Jordan in peace. My feelings were similar, though perhaps I would not have put them as bluntly. The truth is I no longer felt irritated or constrained. Ralph was simply doing his job, and it just so happened that his job conflicted with Jordan's and my ideas of freedom.

But I knew how memory worked. Knew how it would edit out all the dross from the trip and leave the essence, the thing itself. Later that day we would emerge from the river at the Clay Hills take-out spot and the vans would drive us back to the rafting shop, where we would linger and drink beers with the guides, basking in that feeling of having been on a great adventure together.

What I would take away from the trip were not the petty squabbles. I would take away instead the vision of the miraculous side canyons, the form they gave to red water. I would take away finding the function that fit the form, seeing the red blood flow back through the rock veins. Seeing the whole place come to life thanks to the sacred and precious fact of water.

THE DEATH AND LIFE OF MONKEYWRENCHING

During Stegner's and Abbey's heydays as environmental activists many of their battles crystalized in their fight against dams—concrete walls that blocked flow, those perfect symbols of human hubris and the destruction of the natural world. It's enough to make today's environmentalists nostalgic. These days it is not evil dams we are most often doing battle with but our own natures. This is particularly true when the "enemy" is that vague thing known as climate change. William deBuys, one of the best big-picture thinkers in the modern West, puts it well in his book *A Great Aridness*:

> Whether you are breaking prairie sod in the nineteenth century or raising a family and scrambling to make ends meet in the twenty-first, it is hard to get worked up over abstract possibilities. There is too much that needs doing, right here, right now. Even knowing the odds, people still live in earthquake zones, hurricane alleys, and the unprotected floodplains of mighty rivers. . . . Generally speaking, it is hard for any of us to get seriously concerned about what *might* happen until it *does* happen. That's why the politics of climate change are so difficult. The measurements and observation that convince scientists about the warming of the Earth are invisible to the rest of us.

If we continue down this logical road it is hard not to reach a doubly pessimistic conclusion: not only is the world warming, but there is little we can do about it, since human nature is not built for the fight. In fact, many of us respond by shrugging and returning to our sod-busting.

There is also another way that the environmental times have changed. Back in Abbey's day, the idea of blowing up dams might have sounded romantic, but in our post-9/11 world that sort of talk sounds like the fast track to jail.

Earlier in the trip I had been wondering aloud about these issues during a phone call with Rob Bleiberg when he suggested I speak to a friend of his, Jane Quimby, who'd been an FBI agent in the Grand Junction office for twenty-five years.

Jane agreed to meet me in a bagel shop in downtown Grand Junction, where Hones and I drove the day after our river trip. We arrived a little late, so Hones dropped me at the corner and headed off to park. He would occupy himself for an hour or so while I interviewed Jane.

Jane and I hit it off right away, aided by Rob, who had already drawn a caricatured portrait of me for Jane, a portrait taken more from the old days involving much beer drunk and silly things said. As for caricaturing, Jane didn't exactly fit mine of an FBI agent. She was a vibrant woman not much older than me with a shock of white hair and a great laugh. There was no creepy cop vibe. When I asked her if I could turn on the tape recorder, she said sure.

"I'm retired," she told me. I took this to mean that, within reason, she could say whatever she wanted.

After we ordered coffee, I asked her about the state of monkey-wrenching. She shook her head.

"I think there is still monkeywrenching out there, but it's mostly local now," she said. "People love their own little neck of the woods and then some oil company moves in and they say, 'This can't happen here.' So they make some sort of protest. But it is more individualized."

"'Not in my backyard,'" I said.

"Exactly. But a chill has fallen over the larger radical movements."

By this I knew she meant organizations like Earth First! and the Earth Liberation Front, ELF, a kind of natural descendant of Earth First! that had been founded in the United Kingdom in 1994.

"People joining these groups would once think, 'Hey, this is good for Mother Earth. It's going to protect the environment. And the means are justified by the greater purpose.'

"Which is all well and good until someone gets arrested. And not only gets arrested but goes to prison for a long time. Then all of a sudden it's like, Whoa, this isn't so fun after all. Maybe we've got to really think about what we're doing here or be prepared to suffer the consequences."

Jane had been the primary investigator in the famous Vail fire case, the case that would end up sending the biggest chill of all through the environmental movement. The fire was set by ELF members in October of 1998, as a protest against Vail Mountain Ski Resort's expansion into neighboring wilderness, wilderness that also happened to be habitat for the Canadian lynx. The fire destroyed a lodge and a restaurant, damaged four ski lifts, and caused $12 million in damage, though no people were hurt. The activists behind the fire were committed environmental warriors who had done their share of sitting in trees and chaining themselves to tractors. It was a point of honor within the group that, if caught, no one would snitch, and for a long time no one did; in fact, there were almost no leads at all. By the time the FBI held a coordinated meeting of agents from California, Colorado, Oregon, and Washington in 2004, the fire was almost a cold case. But it was at that meeting that the FBI committed to an aggressive policy of "shaking the trees," of knocking on doors and questioning people even when they had nothing definite.

"What came out of the meeting was this: don't underestimate the power you have when you go knock on doors."

"The power to freak people out," I said.

"Exactly," Jane said. "Let's all start knocking on doors and see what falls out. We were kind of bluffing. We'd say we need to talk to you because we have some information. And some people would say, 'Screw you.' And others would say, 'Talk to my lawyer.'"

"But not everyone?"

"Not everyone. Someone came forward and flipped. It was partly a timing thing because he had a kid. His kid was growing up and he's looking at his kid and thinking, What the hell am I doing here? This is not the kind of life I should be leading. I could lose my kid."

There were other factors involved as well. ELF members had just torched an SUV dealership in the Northwest. They had meant to burn a couple of vehicles, a symbolic gesture against gas guzzlers, but it turned into a huge conflagration, leading to more arson charges. People who usually would have been sympathetic turned against the group.

"And the suspect realized, 'We're not playing around here anymore.'"

"And by then 9/11 had happened."

"Right," Jane said. "It was huge. Nobody wanted to be called a terrorist. And now they were all domestic terrorists."

I asked her about this wide definition of terrorism and terrorists.

"Personally, I don't know that it is a fair comparison. I don't think it's apples to apples. That was a big philosophical consideration when we were going to trial with the Vail case. We were deciding whether we would label them with a terrorism tag. And this was a calculated legal strategy because if you labeled them that way it of course leads to higher penalties.

"But it was also a feather in our cap: 'Hey, look at us, we're stopping terrorism.' Whether or not you really think letting a bunch of horses out of a horse pasture and lighting a barn on fire is terrorism in the same sense of the word. That's up to people's individual interpretations. But there is political pressure within the FBI to label it terrorism.

"We decided to apply 'terrorism enhancement' to the two leaders in the case and to one other suspect. We could use it as a chip in plea bargaining."

It had been gospel that no one in the movement would rat out any other member. But once the first one turned the rest went down like dominoes.

"They had always said nobody would snitch, but they hadn't been tested since no one was caught. When push came to shove, and some got caught, they rolled on each other. Not all of them but enough.

"It was a real awakening for the movement. There was a lot of backlash. They said, 'Hey, when you're caught you're supposed to shut up and go to prison and not turn in your buddies.' But those who got caught argued, 'We've always said that, but now I'm going to prison for ten years and I have a three-year-old, and I'm not going to see her grow up because of the foolish decisions I made.'"

These were, of course, the more hard-core people, but Jane believed that this had also had an effect on those on the edge of the movement—that is, on the casual monkeywrencher.

"That kind of environmental protest has always been very generational-driven. Typically your profile would be your twenty-something kid at a sort of offbeat college like Evergreen or Naropa, where they're being exposed to a lot of offbeat things. Not to discredit those things, but they're in an academic, educational, and social environment where people are thinking outside of the box. And people are young."

Remembering my own days in that sort of school environment, I added, "There's also the sense that you can't *really* get in trouble if you are doing a good, moral thing."

"Exactly. But all of a sudden those same kids grow up and get married and have a kid and need a job. It's not to say people really lose their environmental conscience, but they do lose the desire to do something that is not only not mainstream but potentially criminal."

Further undermining old-school monkeywrenching was the fact that counterterrorism of almost any stripe had become the top priority within the FBI. Which meant that the allocation of resources, manpower, budget, and space depended on nailing terrorists.

"Someone would fly out from Washington to the Grand Junction office and ask, 'What are you guys doing about the Middle Eastern terrorism problem?' The local agent would just stare back, and finally say, 'We don't have that here.' And the Washington guy would say, 'Well, how many international terrorists do you have?' And the local guy would say, 'None.' So the Washington guy would say, 'How many domestic terrorists do you have?' and again the local would answer, 'None.'"

That wouldn't do.

"The logical response to this would be that maybe we should reassess and reallocate our resources," Jane continued. "Instead it was: 'Gee, you guys must not be able to articulate your crime problem.'"

Of course, the local agents could articulate the actual problems—they knew they had a meth problem and plenty of burglaries and some domestic violence—but what they did not have was a population that would typically produce the kind of criminal activity the Bureau was looking for. And not just the Bureau, of course, but Congress, where the Bureau had to go to justify their funding.

"We had to be able to say, 'Hey, we initiated x number of terrorism investigations.' And it became mind-boggling in terms of separating the legitimate cases from the not-so-legitimate cases. You could take something that was not a big deal and make it a big deal. Since the number-one priority is counterterrorism, everyone needs to be in the game. You could have this simple little stuff that is really nothing and suddenly you are generating interest from headquarters because they have to justify themselves. So anytime there is something that might rise to the level of worth-a-shit, they jump on it. And once the wagon starts rolling you can't stop it. You're given directives and you kind of shake your head. The tail is wagging the dog."

And so environmentalists become branded as terrorists.

"By the time we were arresting people in the 2000s it was like, 'Those people are terrorists.' Call them terrorists and pretty soon they are terrorists. And their refrain was, 'We didn't hurt anybody, we didn't kill anyone.' And that was true.

"But by then the Bureau had come out with a definition of terrorism so wide it probably fits what Rob is doing over at the Land Trust."

ED ABBEY'S FBI file was a thick one, and makes for engrossing reading.

The file begins in 1947, when Abbey, just twenty and freshly back from serving in the Army in Europe, posts a typewritten notice on the bulletin board at the State Teachers College in Pennsylvania. The note urges young men to send their draft cards to the president in protest of peacetime conscription, exhorting them to "emancipate themselves." It is at that point that Abbey becomes "the subject of a Communist index card" at the FBI, and from then until the end of his life the Bureau will keep track of where Abbey is residing, following his many moves. They will note when he heads west and, as acting editor of the University of New Mexico's literary magazine, *The Thunderbird*, decides to print an issue with a cover emblazoned with the words: "Man will never be free until the last king is strangled with the entrails of the last priest!" The quote is from Diderot, but Abbey thinks it funnier to attribute the words to Louisa May Alcott. And so he quickly loses his editorship while the FBI adds a few more pages to his file. The Bureau will become particularly intrigued when Mr. Abbey attends an international conference in defense of children in Vienna, Austria, since the conference, according to the FBI, was "initiated by Communists in 1952." Also quoted in full in his files is a letter to the editor that he sends to the *New Mexico Daily Lobo*, in which he writes: "In this day of the cold war, which everyday [sic] shows signs of becoming warmer, the individual who finds himself opposed to war is apt to feel very much out of step with his fellow citizens" and then announces the need to form a group to "discuss implications and possibilities of resistance to war."

The files contain interviews with fellow students and teachers at the University of New Mexico, who talk of Abbey's "instability and poor judgment," with one interviewee saying that as an editor he showed "a stubborn ego, a taste for shocking the reader, a lack of maturity." Abbey, according to another colleague, was "indiscreet in his individualism " and was a poor risk "from the point of view of maturity and stability." He "demonstrated a somewhat radical rebellious quality, indulging in literary immaturities." Though the interviews are mildly damning, no one questioned the subject's loyalty to his country.

One wonders how Abbey would have fared these days. Would the FBI, or the NSA, have simply kept tabs on him or actually called him in for questioning? So many of his views, and so much of his personality, match just the sort of profile we have come to associate with domestic terrorism, particularly with our new, broader definition of who a terrorist might be. It isn't just his gun advocacy, or his monkeywrenching. It's his belief that wilderness is a place where free men can retreat when the tyrants take over. Wilderness as the home of the last free people. He wrote:

> Democracy has always been a rare and fragile institution in human history. . . . As social conflict tends to become more severe in this country . . . there will inevitably be a tendency on the part of the authoritarian element—always present in our history—to suppress individual freedoms, to utilize the refined techniques of police surveillance (not excluding torture of course) in order to preserve—not wilderness!—but the status quo, the privileged positions of those who so largely control the economic and governmental institutions of the United States.

It's a type of language, and sentiment, that anticipates our government's reaction to 9/11, and that also could have, along with his other hobbies, landed Abbey in a world of trouble in our post-9/11 world. Thoreau said that under a government that unjustly imprisons its own, "the true place for the just man is also a prison." Prison is exactly where Abbey's monkeywrenching and FBI record might have landed him today.

The more you read Ed Abbey, the more you start to see him as a creature of his particular time, a time as distant from ours as Daniel Boone's from his. He came on the literary stage at just the right moment: his personal beliefs in freedom and resistance were perfect for the '60s and that remnant '60s known as the '70s. His message of aggressive nonconformity, of screw-you freedom, fit the times. It's hard to imagine that the same message would get a similar reaction today.

So is Abbey passé, as dated as bad '70s hair? Obviously I wouldn't be out here tracking his spoor if I thought so. But it is difficult, at least at first, to see how his spirit might be adapted to fit our times. For instance, isn't monkeywrenching dead, not just in an FBI agent's eyes, but as a legitimate possibility for the environmental movement? I must admit that in my own grown-up life as a professor and father I don't blow a lot of things up. For most of us who care about the environment, Stegner provides a much more sensible model.

But I don't want to be so quick to toss Abbey on the scrap heap. Looked at in a different way, Abbey's ideas about freedom are exactly what is needed today. If the times have changed, the essence of what he offered has in some ways never been more relevant. Many of the things that he foresaw have come to pass: we currently live in an age of unprecedented surveillance, where the government regularly reads our letters (now called e-mails) and monitors our movements. Abbey offers resistance to this. Resistance to the worst of our times, the constant encroaching on freedom and wildness. He says to us: Question them, question their authority. Don't be so quick to give up the things you know are vital, no matter what others say.

Before we left Grand Junction, I asked Jane one last question.

"So, let's say you were on the other team. Say you were a creative young environmentalist—a monkeywrencher, even. How would you go about fighting in the present atmosphere? How would you start a movement?"

She laughed long and loud.

"No comment," she said finally. "I refuse to answer that on the advice of my attorney."

"That seems reasonable," I said.

But as we talked for a while more about ways that monkeywrenching has persisted in different forms, we gradually circled around to a couple of possible answers to my question.

We both laughed when she brought up the reality show *Whale Wars*, but if the times demand new forms, here was one: monkeywrenching reborn as reality TV. In fact, the show's star, Paul Watson, broke from Greenpeace in 1977 to form a more radical organization called Earth Force and then the Sea Shepherd Conservation Society, in part because he favored direct-action environmentalism. Direct action means confronting the party involved in environmental wrongdoing—in the case of the show this means Japanese whalers who claim to be using whales for research—for the purpose of both blocking the activity and highlighting the activity's moral wrongness or illegality.

Imagine Ed Abbey with a camera on him as he tries to stop the destruction of wilderness. It is not so farfetched. Why not take direct action with the cameras on? The essence of the old monkeywrenching was secrecy, but now it could become openness.

The story of Tim DeChristopher highlights the new possibilities of environmental protest as public spectacle. "What DeChristopher has done is the epitome of modern monkeywrenching," Jack Loeffler said to me back in Santa Fe. "Because he fooled them at their own game."

What DeChristopher had done was walk into an auction where public land was being leased to oil companies and, posing as bidder number 70, held up his paddle and bid on 116 parcels of public land.

DeChristopher's protest had been a brilliant combination of the symbolic and the actual. It was entirely nonviolent and he didn't hurt anyone, except the oil companies' feelings, and though he had no way of paying for what he bid on, it effectively took the land off the books for a while, long enough in fact for the new administration to declare the leases illegal. But while it might seem like it would have been hard to paint DeChristopher with the terrorism brush, he still ended up in a prison in Littleton, Colorado, for two years.

In contrast to the secrecy of old-time monkeywrenchers, DeChristopher has called for a more public form of environmental protest, getting people out into the streets, with public displays of civil disobedience.

"I wouldn't say that environmental protest has died out," he told me during an interview. "There are still certain direct-action type of events where people are locking down equipment. But now it's done in a lot more public way than the monkeywrenching of old. One of the things we have learned from the last generation of activists is the importance of telling our own story and owning that story. I think especially activists now can look back on the days of Earth First! and ELF and see how much their opponents ended up telling their story and defining who they were. So a lot of the actions now are done more publicly."

This type of public activism makes perfect sense in our age of hypermedia. And I think a reimagining of Abbey's blunter, earlier environmentalism holds promise. Imagine a kind of environmental *Hunger Games*.

I mentioned to Jane that one of the reasons so many environmentalists have gone gaga over what DeChristopher did was that it suggested new possibilities—a new legend, even.

"I agree," she said. "What he did is more of a symbolic thing. Of course, it didn't really work out for him as far as the jail sentence. But he didn't know that going in. I'm not sure he appreciated the potential criminality. I don't know him, but it seems it was a fairly spontaneous decision: 'Hey, here's a paddle' and then he realizes he can really pull it off. And then the hammer comes down."

Everything Jane was saying made sense to me, but the fact that DeChristopher stumbled onto his act didn't make it all that different from other historic acts of rebellion. And within the environmental community it *was* a historic act. Like many good discoveries it was accidental, but what was discovered was nothing less than a new way of monkeywrenching. He was on to something. A way of fighting without blowing things up.

After all, blowing things up, or putting sugar in tanks or monkey-wrenching in general, never got anyone all that far anyway. True, it slowed down developers momentarily but then when the resistance dried up or the resisters got bored or went on to other things, the developers went right back to their developing. At its best it held off the enemies while public opinion formed against them. The monkey wrench itself was a symbol, and monkeywrenching has always been a game of symbols, starting with the famous Earth First! unfurling of the illustration of the crack in the Glen Canyon Dam. The goal is to stir people, rally them, and turn the symbolism in your direction. To take the phrase they love to batter you with—"environmental extremist"—and judo flip it into "environmental avenger." Or better yet, "environmental hero."

Edward Abbey may be in some ways dated, but certainly not in his use of the power of symbol.

FROM GRAND JUNCTION, Hones and I drove up the continental divide to Vail Pass, and pulled over at a rest area at the top of the world. It was there that, more than twenty years before, I once started a cross-country ski trip, a delightful all-day sojourn that ended with margaritas and burritos at a Mexican restaurant in a tiny downslope town whose name I can't recall.

Today I wouldn't be skiing, but pretty close. The plan was for Hones to keep driving to the town of Eagle while I hopped on my bike and glided down. I took my bike off the rack and was soon flying downhill on the bike path that ran parallel to the highway. When I lived in Colorado I reveled in the twin pleasures of *ascent* and *descent*, but today there would be no ascending. I dropped a couple thousand feet in a few minutes, taking a downhill skier's pleasure in flying down the mountain at thirty to forty miles per hour.

After we met in Eagle, we drove through the rest of the mountains and then down into what Stegner called the "ringworm suburbs of Denver." There we spent a late night of drinking and eating with my friend Randy, a fine host. The next morning, Hones's last in the West, we packed up early and headed to the Denver airport, where I would trade in my old friend for my wife and my daughter.

We snuck up behind Hadley at the baggage-claim carousel. She had recently turned nine and had known the man she called Mr. Hones her whole life. I surprised her, and she laughed and threw herself into my arms. Then the second surprise stepped out from behind me and Hadley hurled herself at Mr. Hones. Meanwhile I got to hug my wife for the first time in three weeks.

It was a glorious reunion.

PROPERLY WILD

Until she landed in Denver that day, Hadley had never set foot west of the Mississippi. Fifteen years before, Nina and I had gotten married in Boulder and eloped to Taos. We always imagined we would make our home, and raise our children, in the West.

We were wrong, of course. But over the next week we made up for lost time, showing Hadley our old haunts in Boulder, taking her up to the Continental Divide, and bringing her on a shorter version of my river trip on the San Juan in Utah.

"I never imagined the mountains would be like this," she said when she first saw the Rockies.

It wasn't until we were off the river—"back in captivity," as Hadley put it—that I remembered that Ed Abbey had gone down the same river with his own daughter. The essay chronicling that trip, "Running the San Juan," is an exercise in parental pride, as his daughter Susie, then eleven, paddles down the river captaining an inflatable kayak, her very own duckie.

Abbey might be a fine role model as a defender of wildness and an embodiment of resistance. Not so much as a father. There is the famous story that Abbey told and that all his biographers retell of the time he went camping in the Owens Valley with Susie a year before the river trip, when she was ten. Without saying a word to her, Ed headed out on one of his long morning hikes. Susie, thinking herself abandoned in the wilderness, grabbed her father's briefcase (that held his writing) and tried to walk to the highway. Ed, finally hearing his daughter's cries of despair, turned back from his hike and searched for her. He found her in the desert alone, wailing in terror. The stuff of parental nightmares.

"Ed was a good man," Ken Sanders had told me back in Salt Lake City. "He was extremely loyal. He was generous to his friends, to causes. He gave away about ten percent of his income and he never made that much."

But then Ken shrugged.

"Of course, he was a pretty lousy husband. And until he married Clarke, and had Becky and Ben, he was a really shitty dad. His boys grew up without a dad at all."

The letters from Abbey's grown sons, Josh and Aaron, to their father are almost too excruciating to read. The boys barely knew their father, whom they always address simply as Ed, and their attempts to impress him or appeal for some scrap of attention are heart-wrenching. At the same time, the journals reveal the deep remorse that Abbey felt at having been such a bad parent. True, it was not enough remorse to make him change his behavior, but it was genuine.

If Abbey wasn't the world's greatest dad, he was a worse husband, at least in his early attempts.

At various times he wrote:

Don't really want to be a father again—but do like going through the motions.

I believe in marriage. I love my wife. And yet I can't bear monogamy. That's the rub—for me it's unnatural. Cruel. Painful. Unbearable. I like girls; can't seem to get over it, or outgrow it, or sublimate it—in fact the more active and creative I am, the happier I am, the more I crave sexual excitement. Which means for me a new girl now and then, in bed.

And in his novel *The Fool's Progress*:

> If I were forced to choose right now, at this very instant, between a platter of hot-buttered sorority girls and/or saving the entire Northern Hemisphere, including a billion or so innocent Chinamen, which would I choose? It's a tough question.

Part of the Abbey legend is that he finally mellowed. He married Clarke Cartwright, his fifth and final wife, in 1978 at the age of fifty-two. Clarke wouldn't put up with Ed's nonsense. Together they had two children, Rebecca and Ben, and Abbey was by all accounts a doting father. I imagine that marriage benefited greatly from Abbey mellowing with age, or, more technically, the tailing off of testosterone.

In contrast to Abbey and his five wives, Wallace Stegner stayed married to Mary Page for his whole life. In fact, no one can seem to mention Stegner without extolling his marriage, and it certainly deserves extolling. Having spent his childhood watching a bad man abuse his spouse, he vowed to be a good man to his own wife. Where Abbey at times seemed to have no conscience, Stegner's was overdeveloped.

But when I met Page Stegner and his family in Vermont, I learned that his parents' marriage was more complicated than the myth. Page told me that his mother had been distant, almost resentful, of the intrusion the young Page had made into the society of two she'd formed with Wally. Sometimes she treated him less like a son than like a rival for Wally's attention. Page described Mary Stegner as something of a "professional invalid."

"She perceived early on that a way to capture and enslave my father and keep his attentions from wandering in any direction—not that he would have anyway—was to be sick."

I thought of how Sally Morgan, the fictional wife in Stegner's *Crossing to Safety*, had polio and was cared for by her husband.

"It was tangled up in his own mother's sickness and his father's response to that sickness, not being there for her," Page continued. "In some ways my mother had figured it out. So all her life she was sick. With one thing or another thing or another thing. And sometimes I have to say I don't believe she was. I mean, how do you have emphysema and get over it? I don't think you do."

It made perfect sense. What better way to assure the loyalty of someone with an overdeveloped sense of obligation and responsibility?

This was a muddying of the picture of the perfect lifelong marriage.

But Page wanted to make one thing clear. He loved and respected his father. He hadn't liked the Oedipal treatment he had been dealt in a recent biography. The biographer's inclination was natural enough: here was the only son of a famous writer and professor who was also a writer and professor himself. The imagination runs right toward anger and strife, dark Springsteen songs, the clash of fathers and sons. But that's not how it was, Page insisted.

"Well, it wasn't perfect," he said. "But he was a good dad. And he, not my mother, was the real nurturer in the family."

Loyalty and commitment were primary values not just in Wallace Stegner's life but in his fiction. Even the affairs he portrayed in his

WALLACE AND MARY STEGNER.

novels were relatively chaste. A perfect example is the kind of faux infidelity that lies at the heart of *The Spectator Bird*, which won the National Book Award in 1977. In the novel, the main character, Joe Allston, who shares some of the grumbling prejudices of his creator, reads a journal to his wife, Ruth, recounting their trip, twenty years before, to Denmark. That trip occurred just after the death of their only child, Curtis, and led to a friendship with a dishonored Danish countess named Astrid. Astrid, beautiful and enigmatic, serves as a tour guide for the Allstons, and Joe, despite himself, ends up falling in love with her.

Their affair climaxes on Midsummer Night in the Danish country-side when Joe Allston rows Astrid out to a small island. The two hold hands and kiss—just once—before realizing that there is no way they can betray Ruth. "You are not the kind who shirks things," Astrid says. The book's real climax, however, is not the moment of infidelity but when Joe reveals the infidelity to his wife all those years later. After he does, he "falls all to pieces." He claws for his coat and pushes out into the night, crying while walking up and down the couple's long driveway, which sits above the California hills like the deck of a ship. He realizes the absurdity of a nearly seventy-year-old man falling apart over what must seem like nothing in "the age of infidel-ity, when casual coupling and wife-swapping" are all the rage. He walks back and forth beneath the live oaks that arc over the drive-way, staring down at the pale heads of a field of daffodils gleaming in the moonlight. Ruth joins him and urges him to come back into the house due to the cold. "It seemed a good idea to kiss her, there in the open moonlight between the oaks, in sight of the ghostly daffodils." He does and then they walk back to the house together.

Not the stuff of racy fiction, but powerful in a way that my sum-mary perhaps does not convey. "I'd rather be your obligation than your ex-wife," Ruth says at one point, but Joe insists she is neither. While he now goes years without thinking of Astrid, Ruth is always a part of him. She is not an obligation: "I simply made a choice and it wasn't that hard a choice either." And: "It seems to me that my commitments are more important than my impulses or my pleasures." They walk back to the house, "two young people with quite a lot the matter with us." Earlier in the book, Joe Allston has defined himself as a "spectator bird," always on the sidelines and never involved, but now he sees his truer identity: a bird with a mate. A mate you can hunt up "bugs and seeds for" and "mourn over your hurts when you accidentally fly into something you can't handle."

What Stegner has done here, in a way that was obviously not lost on a certain student of his from Kentucky, was give us a literature of fidelity. Of marriage.

Edward Abbey took a different approach. He saw sex as the last frontier. He liked to point out that animals in cages procreate more often than those in the wild, and believed that modern humans, living their limited, constrained lives, are the same way. With the frontier closed, our wild lands disappearing, our lives tame and devoid of adventure, we turn to the only wild thing left.

All his life Abbey made the domestic and the wild into opposite poles, pitting them against each other. He took Thoreau to task for sticking too close to the cabin. The Abbey dream was never about home and hearth. It was about breaking away from the domestic constraints of normal life.

I understand this. But it seems an adolescent way to divvy up the world. For me, any definition of wildness has to include my family. And, thinking of Terry Tempest Williams's koan, I wonder: does it qualify as radical in our times to make a promise to one person and keep it for a lifetime?

I need to believe that the domestic and the wild can coexist. This idea, this possibility, seems more complicated, messier, more true to life. I think again of the final scene of *The Spectator Bird*. Where a married couple, in their seventies, meet under a moon on a wind-blown midsummer's night. With a husband crying over a forbidden kiss twenty years before, and a hurt wife finally forgiving. It is a drama of hard-won fidelity, and at the risk of overstating, there is something primal about it too. Something visceral, something pagan, something real. Mate staying loyal to mate. Two decided people deciding. Could there be something wild about commitment? Could there be a wildness of union?

As it turned out, Nina and I had a practical matter of domestic wildness to hash out on our drive back to the Denver airport. Nina had bought round-trip tickets from our home in Wilmington to Denver for both Hadley and herself, but she had done so with the knowledge that Hadley might not use hers.

Nina is a writer and she had a book due by the end of summer. So our question today was: did Hadley fly home and go to camp while Nina tried to write, or did she stay with me as I continued my adventures in the West? Nina trusted me with our offspring, to some extent, but she had never been away from Hadley for more than a couple of days. She also knew that I tended to push things on these trips. While I doubt she thought I'd pull an Abbey and go wandering off into the desert without my child, she still had memories of a younger, less responsible me.

We remained undecided until the very last moment. Then, at the airport, both Hadley and I kissed Nina good-bye.

My daughter and I became a team, Lewis and Clark, or maybe closer to Moze and Addie of *Paper Moon*, with Hadley jammed in the back of the Scion, surrounded by her handy books and electronic screens, and me driving, yelling back to her over my shoulder, both of us giddy for a while with the idea of being on an adventure together.

Our first stop was in Fort Collins at the home of my old friends Emily Hammond and Steven Schwartz. When Nina and I had last visited them in Fort Collins, Hadley was not yet born and their daughter, Elena, was Hadley's age. Now Elena was in college, though, lucky for us, home on break. Both Hadley and Elena were dog lovers and soon they were next door playing with Canyon, the neighbor's collie. The girls also took a trip up to the nearby prairie-dog town, and later over dinner Hadley regaled Emily and Steven with tales of using the Groover, which in the end turned out to be the most fascinating aspect of the river trip for her.

We were there to visit friends, but also because Steven had been a student in the very first writing class Ed Abbey taught at the University of Arizona.

"Man, was he tough on us," he said after dinner.

He told me that, as a teacher, Abbey was not a performer or praiser. Not a nervous void-filler, as both Steven and I admitted to being, but quiet and spare with words. With a deep, deadpan voice.

"He was very intimidating. Not big on meting out kind words."

What did he think? the students naturally wondered. There was no telling.

It occurred to me that for prolific, word-loving men, both Abbey and Stegner could be surprisingly taciturn.

"Abbey didn't care what people thought of him," Steven said.

And he also did something that is inherently appalling to any graduate student: he actually gave grades less than A's.

In Tucson, I'd studied the notes Abbey made for his syllabus and it contained the names Montaigne, Emerson, Orwell, Edmund Wilson, Joseph Wood Krutch, Wendell Berry, Tom Wolfe (he meant Thomas), Annie Dillard, Joan Didion, and Edward Hoagland. The assignments he gave his class were creative enough that I scribbled down a couple of them for use in my own classes. In one he asked students to visit with "transient or homeless types," or go to a biker's bar, some "sleazy strip joint" or other example of, as he delicately put it, "Tucson lowlife," and then write about it. Another exercise was simpler: "A walk in the desert."

At his worst, according to Steven, Abbey displayed "a combination of seeming apathy and vulturish criticism." But he was quick to add that the class that he took was Abbey's very first, and it was "entirely possible that Ed got better at teaching."

After getting a B on his first story and not hearing even a faint word of praise, Steven decided he'd had enough. Abbey was hunched over a little school desk in his office when Steven went in to quit. Abbey looked up at him, suddenly engaged.

"You are one of the best writers in the class," he said.

Usually a sentence like that would be followed by something like "You should stick it out."

Not with Abbey. He just let it sit there.

"That was it," Steven said. "He shut down. His eyes went cold. He went back to work."

But looking back, Steven felt that he had learned something valuable. Abbey was a model in one important way.

"He used his non-writing energy sparingly," he told me. "He cared about writing more than anything else."

AFTER WE CLEARED the plates, Elena volunteered her babysitting services, and Emily and I drove up into the foothills above Fort Collins to see the scars from the recent fires. The fires had just died down, after raging for a month, and would have ended up being the most costly fires in the state's history were it not for the almost simultaneous conflagration down in Colorado Springs. It was a summer for the history books with the Front Range ablaze and often blanketed in smoke.

We drove following the river up into the hills, the river so dry it seemed no more than a red stain of itself. Soon we were staring up at miles of charred ridgeline. In Soldier Canyon we saw an entire charcoal hillside of blackened trees, the spindly remains looking like black skeletons. Emily told me that the high winds had caused the fire to jump from tree to tree, at one point actually jumping the river. She related the story of an acquaintance who was carefully evacuating, knowing the fire was miles away, when suddenly his house was aflame.

We drove past the Rist Canyon Volunteer Fire Department and to another charred ridge of forest. Dark, gnarled hands grasped at the sky. About 70 percent of the homes in the area had burned.

I asked Emily if I could get out of the car and walk up the ridge a bit. The land smelled of ash, the trees blackened. My footfalls made a sibilant hiss as I moved through the crisp, ashen landscape. The ridge above looked like a porcupine's back, the spikes consisting of black trees with only the slightest color from dead yellow foliage.

I knew that as historic and tragic as that summer's fires were, there was a very good chance they were just a preview. I thought of the way that the fight to tell the truth, and to get westerners to see the facts about their land, ultimately wore Wallace Stegner down. It isn't hard to see why. Stegner understood the necessity of hope, but in the end the facts painted a less than hopeful picture.

The facts have grown still more depressing. Over the last decade the cost of fighting fires has gone from making up 14 percent to 50 percent of the Forest Service's budget, and both firefighters and scientists tell us that we have entered a new era of fire in the American West. These recent fires, called "megafires" by some, are certainly exacerbated by climate change, but they are also aided by historic factors apart from rising temperatures and increased aridity. Primary among these is the long history of fire suppression in the West.

Fire suppression, of course, was supposed to be a good thing. Like the introduction of erosion-aiding tamarisk on the banks of western rivers, it was meant to help with an existing problem. In this case the problem was the "Big Blowup" fires that ravaged the West in 1910 and that gave weight to Bernard DeVoto's idea that in the West catastrophe might destroy half a region. During that historic summer millions of acres were burned and the flames eventually ignited not just forests but the country's imagination. Firefighters became

national heroes, and fighting fires, all fires, became the driving purpose, the idée fixe, of the Forest Service. But as often happens when
we intrude on natural processes, this created a problem. It turned
out that by suppressing fires, we stamped out even the smaller fires
that had beneficially rid forests of excess fuel in the form of scrub
growth, deadfall, and other organic debris. The end result, after
many years of suppression, was as if a giant had come along and
arranged things perfectly in the fireplace of our forests, with plenty
of kindling and paper below the big logs.

The trees have changed in another way. The altered climate is
effectively turning the West into a powder keg by reducing snowpack and lifting temperatures, with temperatures effectively sucking the moisture out of trunks and branches. This means that the
trees are perfectly built for ignition, the wood so dry that they are
always a spark away from burning. The result has been that in recent
years we have had our own Big Blowups, and have witnessed the
largest and hottest fires that have ever been recorded in the West.

Over the last few decades the Forest Service and other organizations have begun to understand the combination of factors that
aid these fires, and have tried to reduce the fuels that feed them by
clearing the forests of excessive deadfall. Policies of fire suppression
have also loosened, though in the current climate of understandable
fear, there have been renewed cries for the old ways of stamping out
every spark. Of course, in places like this hillside the houses themselves help provide the fuel, going up like torches.

Wendell Berry had urged me to consider land use as I explored
the West. This meant understanding which places are fit for farming, for building homes, for mining, for recreation. To begin, we
must question some basic assumptions. In this summer of fires,
one of those questions is simple enough: is it wise to build wooden
homes, or any homes, near national forests or in the fire-prone foothills above mountain towns? Then there is a larger question of land
use, one unique, in our country at least, to the West. When you build
a house in the western wilderness you are not building a cabin in the

Berkshires. You are laying claim to land that is at once vulnerable to human incursion and often inherently risky to settle.

Homeowners will soon be rebuilding in these burnt hills, but, while they don't want to hear it, there is little question that the land would be better off left alone. When people do build near forest land, they wisely fear the slightest sign of fire. Which means that they have little tolerance for even small fires, those beneficial blazes that have been a historic part of the cycles of western forests. And more people always means one more thing: a greater chance of sparking a fire.

Throughout the West, the human population will increase; that is a given. But even as it does we had better keep in mind the particulars of the place. There are landscapes in the West that are naturally ornery, that ask, in all but words, to be left alone. More specifically, what the land here asks for is a clustered population with large buffers where there are no humans at all. To our credit we have done just that, as a people, in establishing parks and national monuments and forests and other public lands. But as more of us crowd in and put more demands on this land and its water, and as more people attempt to pry away protected land and "put it to use," we had better remind ourselves of why large sections must remain free of human intrusion.

If parts of these western lands are really as vulnerable and difficult to inhabit as Stegner and others have suggested, as open to disaster, then perhaps to leave them alone is simply practical. We don't put land aside only because it makes for a pretty park. We put it aside because it makes sense. It is how it should be. Much of this land is properly wild.

IN THE MORNING, before we left Fort Collins, we made a quick stop at Wolverine Farm Bookstore to meet with Todd Simmons, whose Wolverine Farm Publishing had just put out a magazine anthology of all things Abbey. Todd testified as to Abbey's continued ability to create converts.

"A lot of people come here heading south to Moab," he said. "I ask them if they have read *Desert Solitaire*. If they say, 'Desert what?' I insist that they buy the book. If you don't like it, I tell them, I'll refund you double. So far no one has ever asked for their money back."

But Todd was recently back east and was shocked to find that no one in the group he was hanging with had ever heard of Abbey.

"It showed me what kind of bubble I live in," he said. "I just couldn't believe that no one had heard of him. At first I thought they were joking."

Hadley and I thanked him and pushed off for points north and west, driving out of Colorado and into Wyoming. We spent hours crossing southern Wyoming. In late afternoon we saw a herd of pronghorn antelopes gliding across the prairie. Pronghorns are the fastest land animals in the West, and the truth is it isn't even close. I told Hadley a fact I had learned from a friend: the reason pronghorns run so fast, much faster than any predator of theirs, is that they are outrunning a ghost—the long-extinct American cheetah, which centuries ago chased them across these grasslands.

To see a pronghorn run is to want to run yourself. A more graceful animal is hard to imagine. Delicate and gorgeously bedecked with rich brown-and-white patterns, with small horns and snow-white fur on their stomachs, they glide across the land. As we drove I was worried about all the barbed-wire fences that blocked their way as they roamed, at least until I saw one pronghorn fawn jump a fence like it was nothing, flowing over it like water.

But there are sterner obstacles to their migrations. Over the course of four recent seasons, a young journalist named Emilene Ostlind followed the migration of the pronghorns on one of their last remaining migratory routes through Wyoming, Idaho, and Montana. That 120-mile-long trip now includes "the Pinedale Anticline gas patch—an intensively drilled piece of public land in western Wyoming—a tricky highway crossing and a couple of subdivisions."

This migratory path is one of only two left since "residential and other development has stopped pronghorn from migrating through six of eight historic corridors." The trail consists of key stopover points and then corridors in between the stopover points. Ostlind compared the paths to a rosary, with "strings of beads with spaces in between, the bulbous stopover locations linked by narrow movement corridors."

One thing her trip taught, and that is apparent to scientists studying the pronghorn, is the vital importance of "connectivity." It is a lesson being learned, and preached, by innovative environmental thinkers all over the West, and it applies to many of the region's threatened species. It comes down to a simple point: wild animals need to roam. It's true that putting land aside for our national parks may be, to paraphrase Stegner paraphrasing Lord Bryce, the best idea our country ever had, and it's also true that at this point we have put aside more than 100 million acres of land, a tremendous accomplishment that we should be proud of. But what we are now learning is that parks are not enough. By themselves they are islands—particularly isolated and small islands—the sort of islands where many conservation biologists say species go to die.

That would change if the parks were connected, and connecting the parks, and other wild lands, is the mission of an old friend of Ed Abbey's, Dave Foreman. Foreman, one of the founders of Earth First!, eventually soured on the politics of the organization he helped create. In recent years he has focused his energy on his Wildlands Project, whose mission is the creation of a great wilderness corridor from Canada to Mexico, a corridor that takes into account the wider ranges of our larger predators. Parks alone can strand animals, and leave species vulnerable, unless connected by what Foreman calls "linkages." He believes that if we can connect the remaining wild scraps of land, we can return the West to being the home of a true wilderness. He calls the process "rewilding."

Why go to all this effort? Because dozens of so-called protected species, stranded on their eco-islands, are dying out. And because when they are gone they will not return. A few more shopping malls, another highway or gas patch, and there is no more path for the pronghorn. But there is an even more profound reason for trying to return wildness to the West. "We finally learned that wilderness is the arena of evolution," writes Foreman. Wilderness is where change happens. In other words, without wilderness we cut off not just species but the chance of animals adapting to changing conditions.

Nature, meanwhile, is already on the move, and as we try to aid species we are facing a moving target. Consider that the Audubon Society not long ago released a study that revealed that more than 305 species of North American birds were already spending their winters farther north, some more than three hundred miles north of their former range. Birds as varied as the golden-cheeked warbler (delicate, private, tiny) and the greater sage grouse (bulky, ground-dwelling, and famously flamboyant in courtship) face a problem that is both new and increasingly common: their futures are uncertain as climate change plays havoc with their habitats. For the sage grouse it means a big squeeze, as their sagebrush habitat, already threatened by development, faces transformation into woodland as the frost line shifts north. The warbler's troubles are even trickier, since they breed in only one place in the world, the Ashe juniper habitat near the Edwards Plateau of central Texas.

Which means that scientists now find themselves in the position of trying to predict the future movements of both animals and ecosystems. Habitat preservation, never easy, has become even more difficult. The new circumstances will require new science and a more active style of habitat management. It will no longer be enough to look back at what historically grew or lived in a place; now we will need to anticipate, through modeling, what will be there next. Sam Pearsall, who works with estuarine ecosystems back in North Carolina's Albemarle Sound, calls this "pre-storing" habitat—a kind of climate forecasting that will allow scientists to predict where different species, and different habitats, will be moving. In the case of North Carolina's coast, this can mean transporting oysters to areas where it is not presently salty enough, but will be, and doing something similar with bald cypress and salt-marsh grasses. In the West we can often anticipate a movement not just northward but upward in altitude.

In other words, to save remnant wildness we are going to have to be calculating, the opposite of wild. The problem is further complicated by the fact that phenology—nature's clock—is being thrown out of whack. A perfect example of this is the life of the lowly marmot. For millions of years marmots would crawl out of their dark winter dens to nibble on the green world outside. Their timing was exquisite, their internal clocks prodded by the warmth of spring.

"The salad bar was open," is how Anthony Barnosky, a University of California paleoecologist (and Allison Stegner's adviser), recently put it. "But now with warmer winters they wake early and stumble out into a still snow-covered world. They starve."

Many species will not have the luxury of simply migrating northward. In extreme cases, when species are stranded in patches of habitat, translocation—the actual moving of the threatened animals—will be necessary. There are many experts, Dr. Barnosky included, who are sensitive to the fact that this overly managed world might seem "unnatural," and he recommends that some wilderness lands simply be left as they are. But Barnosky also stresses something repeated by every scientist I have spoken to recently: this is a problem that we created and that we must help alleviate. This will require sharpening all of the tools we are already using, while at the same time creating new tools. In fact, in these uncertain times the art of preserving nature will have to become almost as adaptable as nature itself, as we, along with the golden-cheeked warbler and greater sage grouse, learn to move with a changing world.

To keep my own sense of hope, my own sense of wildness, alive, I like to return to imagining Foreman's vision of a rewilded West. After all, it isn't just pronghorns and wolves who evolved in nature.

The animal we are did too, and almost everything we learned as a species, and that remains alive in our genes, was learned in the wilderness. It is both where we were built and what we were built for. Which invites the question: could it be possible that it is not wise to destroy the place where we were first created? If the answer is yes, then we must resist the desire to tear apart and develop our last wild lands.

Rewilding is a radical idea, but so was saving parkland when it was first proposed. With the creation of the parks we did something that no one expected, something no one had ever done. Now imagine if parks became not just museums of remnant ecosystems but beads on a much larger rosary, stopover points in a migratory corridor that runs up and down the continent's spine. Anyone who looks too long at the environmental problems facing us can become overwhelmed and dispirited. But the thought of rewilding gives me hope. It is big. It is bold. It excites imaginations. And, as ideas go, it is wild.

AFTER SUNSET HADLEY spotted an osprey nest in a tree above a river. When we climbed out of the car to look and take pictures, we realized just how tired we were and decided it was time to grab a hotel for the night. The next morning we arrived in the Tetons, jagged and improbably high. I know that these mountains derive their name from the word for breasts, but they were too sharp for breasts, or rather the only breasts they resembled were Madonna's from her conical-bra period. We drove through Yellowstone like the tourists—the wheeled people—we were. Hadley spotted a buffalo and we pulled over and soon enough another dozen cars were parked behind us. This, it turns out, is the primary way of spotting wildlife in the park: not so much looking for animals as looking for cars full of people looking for animals. In fact, in Yellowstone we hit the worst traffic we had encountered since Denver.

The reason we were hurtling through the park, barely stopping to take in the famous geysers, is that we had a date with the man who had lived with bears. Not the over-the-top, aspiring actor from L.A., Timothy Treadwell, who was the subject of the Werner Herzog documentary *Grizzly Man*, and who was eventually killed with his girlfriend when he got too close to the bears he claimed to love. No, we were going to meet the *real* grizzly man, Doug Peacock.

For most people, Peacock is best known as the character, or caricature, that Edward Abbey created out of the raw materials of the man's life. Peacock grew up in Alma, Michigan, but during his three tours as a Green Beret medic in Vietnam he dreamed of the American West, clinging to a map of Montana like a secret and a promise. When he finally got home, he headed out into the western backcountry to try to make something out of the remains of his life. Shaken by all he had seen, numb but at the same time full of unnamed rage, he turned to a new hobby, to monkeywrenching, and also met a new friend named Ed Abbey. Abbey would eventually transform Peacock into a fictional character, the heroic but primitive George Washington Hayduke, one of the central figures in *The Monkey Wrench Gang*. But Peacock's own life would take a turn that Hayduke's did not. He would come to spend time deep in the Wyoming and Montana wildernesses, passing months living with grizzly bears. He didn't study them so much at first as get to know them, learning their ways. Meanwhile his fictional alter ego was growing into a legend around the West. And it still grows. When Hones and I were driving back from the river trip we'd stopped at the Muley Point overlook, and saw, painted in big black letters on the concrete barrier, the words HAYDUKE LIVES!

When I told Hadley that the man we were visiting once lived with bears, she thought about it for minute.

"If I were going to live with an animal it would be wolves," she said.

For the last three years she had been wolf-obsessed, had had wolf-themed birthday parties, and three months before we had visited, and howled with, the last red wolves in the wild in North Carolina.

"That's not exactly breaking news," I told her.

I was nervous about meeting Doug Peacock. At that point in my life I was rarely star-struck, but Peacock was different. I didn't have many living heroes left; Peacock was one. It wasn't just his lofty place in the Abbey firmament. It was the fact that I was a great admirer of his book *Grizzly Years*, which was as packed full of wildness as any book I had ever read, *Desert Solitaire* included. Though Peacock was not primarily a writer, in some ways the disciple had outdone the master: there were scenes in *Grizzly Years* wilder than any Abbey ever wrote. In places it felt less like a literary work than the notes of a mountain man: Peacock almost freezing to death before dipping into one of Yellowstone's thermal pools, Peacock returning the skull of a bear he knew from its place as a trophy in a bar back to its den, Peacock out watching the bears during a blizzard. The writing sometimes jump-cuts from these wild scenes to terse and direct descriptions of Vietnam, and the relative awkwardness of the jumps back and forth between the war and the bears is, for me, part of the book's beauty. Peacock's felt like a book more lived than written, a book that made you want to put it down and get right out into what was left of the wilderness.

Peacock got to know *individual* bears, like the Pelican Creek bear or Happy bear (check him out on YouTube and you'll see the frolicking that gave him his name). He also spent countless hours observing and filming the bears, but it wasn't just natural history that he was after. In his brilliant essay "The Importance of Peacock," the writer and environmental thinker Jack Turner describes those years in the wilderness as something greater, no less than an "attempt to integrate the wild and self by myth."

One other thing was established during those years. Peacock was no armchair environmentalist. He was the real deal, a brave man who would get out into it. "Peacock makes other environmentalists look like they are playing in an upper-class bridge tournament," said the novelist Jim Harrison.

So you can see why I'd been nervous when I called him earlier that morning. All I had to go on at that point was a curt e-mail that read: "If you're around come on by." Well, I would be around, I'd make sure of it, even if it required driving eight hundred miles out of my way. He'd given me directions to his house in Emigrant, Montana, along the Yellowstone River about an hour north of the park, and we had agreed to meet at five. I looked at the map and figured the mileage, but what I hadn't counted on was winding our way through Yellowstone and stopping every mile or two for an elk or buffalo traffic jam. There was an irony, of course, in bombing through one of America's most beautiful parks to go and meet a wild man.

But it wasn't irony but anxiety that started to fill me as I realized just how late we were going to be. I called again, telling him where we were.

"All right, shit," he said, and then paused. At that time I still took his swearing personally, not yet aware that for him it was simply punctuation.

"Well, you can't come up here then," he continued. "Andrea will be just home from work."

I'd blown it, I thought. His tone was curt, brusque, definitely irritated.

"Maybe we can meet at the bar. Yeah, let's do that. We'll meet at the bar."

He gave minimalist directions to the bar: you get into the town of Emigrant, cross the river, and you'll see it, it's called River's Edge.

"Sounds good," I said.

But by the time we crawled through Mammoth Hot Springs and escaped the park to the north we were even later, and Hadley sensed my uneasiness. She had been focusing on the checklist of animals she was given when we entered the park—buffalo, check, elk, check, no wolves yet—but now she turned her attention to me.

"What's wrong?"

"I'm worried about seeing this guy," I said.

"Is he famous?" she asked.

"Pretty famous."

Then I heard myself saying something my mother used to say to me but that I don't think I'd ever said before in my nine years as a parent: "We have to make a good impression."

"Okay," she said.

Make a good impression. What exactly did that mean when you were talking about a man who had lived with bears?

I glanced down at my clothes, at my T-shirt and shorts and flip-flops.

"I can't wear this," I said.

"You can't?" Hadley asked.

"I can't."

Even though we were late, I pulled over at a rest area and dug into my bag. I found some jeans and grabbed my hiking boots. I considered a flannel shirt but it was too hot so I opted for a rattier T-shirt than the one I had on. I felt a little better when I got back behind the wheel, costumed now more like someone who Doug Peacock might talk to.

"Why do we have to see this guy?" Hadley asked.

"Because we have to," I snapped, though I'm not a snapper.

"I hope he doesn't get angry like a bear."

Of course I got lost, crossing the river but not seeing the bar, at least not at first pass, driving three miles down the road before doubling back and finding it.

We walked out of the sunlight and into the dark of River's Edge, a plain, square room where the walls were decorated with antlers and the heads of animals. In the middle of the room sat Doug Peacock and a woman I assumed was Andrea. He was wearing a baseball cap, a gray sleeveless shirt that revealed muscled, freckled arms, and he squinted up at us. Andrea wore glasses and was younger than he was, prettier too, and she smiled kindly. I pushed Hadley in front of me like an offering. Then I began to babble about the traffic. I noticed a stuffed mountain lion nearby, and the skins of two baby bears on the wall.

Two things saved the day.

Before I'd visited Wendell Berry, a friend had told me that Wendell liked Maker's Mark, so I'd brought a bottle of whiskey as a gift.

That was the trip's first interview, and since this would be the last there was some symmetry in presenting the same gift.

The bottle made Peacock smile, and he wasted no time popping it open, right there in the bar.

He took a slug.

"Good stuff," he said. "Thanks."

He handed it to me and I followed suit.

The second thing that saved us were the dogs. River's Edge allowed canine as well as human customers, and dogs roamed all over both the bar and the outdoor dining area, where we soon moved to. Hadley was ecstatic, chasing and hugging the slobbery Saint Bernard and cuddling the shy Doberman. Her delight seemed to delight Peacock, and certainly delighted Andrea, who followed Hadley around the grounds on a dog tour.

I drink fast when nervous and both Peacock and I were doing double duty, drinking our beers while sipping the whiskey from paper cups I had picked up at the bar on our way outside. I stared across the picnic table at him. He must have been close to seventy, but still looked strong. The squinting I noticed was apparently habitual, and he had more than a few other tics. I also noted that he said the word "fuck" a lot, and when I asked if I could use the tape recorder he said, simply, "No." He didn't say it in an unfriendly way, but he was the first person on the whole trip to refuse.

I asked him how he felt when *The Monkey Wrench Gang* came out.

"I was fucking furious," he said. "Abbey's publisher made him write me a letter. Assuring me that only the good parts of Hayduke were based on me."

He laughed.

I understood why the character Abbey portrayed would have bothered Peacock, despite the fame it brought him. Hayduke was both a caricature and a caveman.

Then I told him about my project and about Terry Tempest Williams's koan.

He said he loved Terry, but didn't care for Stegner.

"He never wrote anything close to *Desert Solitaire*."

He was opinionated; of course he was, he was Doug Peacock. But the conversation seemed to be going well, maybe due to the alcohol but maybe because we were actually somewhat hitting it off. He knew I had grown up in Massachusetts and suddenly we were talking about Cape Cod of all places. It turned out he had lived in the town of Brewster for a while, after chasing a woman to Boston. I was amused by the idea of Doug Peacock in Massachusetts, but of course he did it his way, living by hunting and scavenging, eating mostly quahogs, clams, and oysters.

"If you like, you can come up to the house and have a beer," he said after a while. "And you could sleep in the trailer out behind the house."

Hadley was about fifty yards away, shooting baskets on a court with a girl around her age. Three dogs chased the two girls as they played. When I gathered her up I saw her face was covered with dirt. It occurred to me, as we drove the mile or two across the river and up the hill, that this was exactly what her mother was worried about, and maybe expected, when she left her with me.

We pulled up at the house and headed inside. But first I noticed the doormat.

COME BACK WITH A WARRANT, it read.

Once inside, Doug and Hadley talked wolves for a while. Then he showed her his grizzly bear skull collection. Hadley asked what the bears up here ate and he said mostly grass, and ants. To demonstrate, Doug did a fine impression of a bear turning over a rock with its paw.

Andrea was tired and said good night, and we set Hadley up in the living room with a Disney DVD. Once she was settled, we sat at the kitchen table and drank beer and talked about Abbey for a while. They were friends, yes, but there was always a father-son thing going on. Peacock had written about the "patriarchal haze" that "sometimes clouded the friendship." Though they camped, drank, and monkeywrenched together, Peacock was almost twenty years younger, and wrote that "there was a touch of old school paternalism to our brotherhood." Abbey's death in 1989 had rocked him.

Doug told me about Ed's last hours, being with him as he died. In turn I told him about holding my father's hand while he was dying, feeling the last pulsings of life, the final shallow breaths.

Hadley was happily absorbed in her movie, but her head popped up over the couch like a prairie dog whenever she heard Doug say the word *fuck*. Which meant her head popped up a lot.

He said it had been the same with his own kids. He had never been able to restrain himself when it came to that particular word. I mentioned that Abbey picked up on this in his portrait of Hayduke, and Peacock conceded that although Abbey exaggerated a lot, he had gotten that part right.

We talked for a while about the difficulty he and others had had trying to make a movie of *The Monkey Wrench Gang*. Part of the difficulty was that while Hollywood is fine with violence toward people and cars and buildings, they don't want to make a movie where the principal and intended victims are private or industrial property. Peacock cursed the various producers and directors. He had written several drafts of scripts for the movie and even had one in his room at that moment. The movie had almost been made a dozen times, with actors from Jack Nicholson to Matthew McConaughey cast as Hayduke.

We talked about various things until, at one point, I asked, "Why grizzlies?"

He explained that after returning from the war he began doing a lot of camping in wild places. One of the those places was the backcountry of Yellowstone and it was there that he started finding himself in the company of bears. During one of his very first encounters he had been soaking in a thermal pool, where he was startled by a sow and her cub. The bear had treed him and Peacock had ended up naked and shivering up in the tree for more than an hour.

Gradually, grizzlies became not the natural by-product of his trips into the backcountry but the purpose. He loved guns and owned

DOUG PEACOCK'S DOORMAT.

many, but he refused to bring them along when he knew he would encounter the bears.

"That would defeat the purpose," he said.

And what was the purpose? The purpose was to feel real humility, to be taken off the usual human pedestal. Which was easy enough when you were in the presence of an animal that might suddenly decide to eat you. Humility, Peacock came to believe, was the proper emotional backdrop for *reason*, and in the wilderness he became at once more reasonable and more wild. He was always amazed at the way his senses grew sharper after only a few days out in it, the way he could see better and smell other animals. It was as if he clicked into being an older, more primal self.

The purpose was also spiritual, and he believed that many of our basic spiritual archetypes grew out of observing bears. After all, what better animal to embody resurrection, the death of a winter's hibernation followed by the rebirth of spring's emergence from the den?

Before he was done talking bears, I remembered to ask him something for Hones.

"My friend wants to know what you really thought of Timothy Treadwell."

I expected outrage, since Treadwell, the subject of Herzog's documentary, seemed like such a phony to me. But Peacock's reply was calm and considered.

"He came to me after one summer of living with the bears. But I don't think he really wanted any advice. By then he had his own ideas about how to do it."

He took a sip of his beer.

"The thing about Tim is that he had a big personality." He paused before adding, "You really don't want to have a big personality around grizzly bears."

I was reminded of something that Jack Turner had said about Peacock in his essay. He wrote: "His manners, as a guest in the wild, are impeccable." That too would be a result of the necessary humility of living near bears. It struck me as funny that Hayduke, one of the most famously rude of fictional characters, had learned his manners in the wild.

When we finally said good night, Hadley and I made our way through the starry night out to the trailer. It was cramped inside but we each had beds built into the walls and Andrea had made them with sheets and blankets. Hadley was so excited about the accommodations that it took a while for her to calm down, despite the late hour. Eventually I heard her breathing slow, and then I followed her, drifting off into a deep sleep.

The next morning I got up early and, remembering the story of Susie Abbey, left Hadley a big note before going on a bike ride down the hill. Hadley was up when I got back, but Doug and Andrea were not. We decided to leave them a note, thanking them. We tucked it under the "Come Back with a Warrant" doormat.

We drove back into Yellowstone and went for a hike in the woods. Hadley pointed out the signs warning of bears, but we saw only elk and a gray jay, who was interested in our trail mix. When I'd complained to Doug about the touristy traffic jams in the park, he said that that was true, but then added: "Just go a hundred feet off the road and it's all still there." After our hike, we explored the unearthly hot springs of Mammoth. I told Hadley the story of how Peacock once was lost and frozen and had saved his life by stripping off his clothes and soaking in one of the steaming pools in the backcountry.

We were already back on the road, heading north, when I realized I had forgotten my binoculars at Peacock's house. We called and he said come by and before I knew it we were back in the house and then, before long, were back at the kitchen table cracking beers.

He told me that he had always been a migrant, never a settler.

"I have no homing instinct," he said.

I talked for a minute about my own troubles with finding a home, my sense of geographic uncertainty, how strange it was living in the South.

"We all need different-size territories," he said. "For some it might just be their backyard. For me I require a slightly bigger backyard."

Of course. That made perfect sense. Most of us are content with our little plots. But for Peacock, the backcountry of Yellowstone had served as his territory. As had, to some extent, the whole American West.

"One thing I know is that the inward way is not the way," he said. "That's a trap. Anything that gets you outside of yourself is good. Don't look inside for salvation. Go spend a little time alone in the wilderness."

High-flown talk, and inspiring, but Hadley was bored—as she had every right to be. At our next stop, the home of a friend of a friend in Big Sky, there would be kids. She tugged at my shirt.

Hadley and Doug hugged good-bye and I walked over to shake his hand. But he moved in for another hug instead, one that squeezed the air out of me.

I DON'T KNOW why, exactly, and I don't know how to describe it, but sleeping in an old trailer behind Doug Peacock's house, with my daughter in the other bunk, did me a world of good. Better than good. I felt great.

My life, like almost anyone's, is tame compared to Peacock's. I once spent a year or two observing ospreys on Cape Cod, but they weren't grizzlies and, despite their impressive talons, I never had to worry too much about the birds suddenly turning on and devouring me. Back at home in North Carolina, my relatively domestic wildness consisted of daily walks in the woods, bird-watching, kayaking, and two or three beers out in my writing shack in the evenings. Peacock said that we all have different-size territories and I would argue that one of the more important things that he and Abbey offer is that they make us uncomfortable with the size of the plots we have settled on. They push us, and inspire us to move beyond our comfortable cells. "It depends on how you are yarded," wrote Thoreau. In an age of cell phones and computers and little contact with the elemental earth, most of us are yarded pretty tightly.

It isn't just pronghorns who live in a diminished territory. Most modern humans know exactly how those ungulates feel. With each generation we settle for less wildness, less freedom, less space. We begin to accept things we would have previously deemed unacceptable. That our e-mails will be read, that we will stare down at screens for hours, that it's okay for drones to look down on us, that only crazy or dangerous individuals seek solace by going alone into the wilderness. We shrug, half-accepting our limited lives and damaged land. What can we do about it after all?

Abbey wrote of the way that the dogs in Tucson react with both fear and a kind of primal jealousy when they hear coyotes howling on the edge of town:

> They yip, yap, yelp, howl, and holler, teasing the dogs, taunting them, enticing them with the old-time call of the wild. And the dogs stand and tremble, shaking with indecision, furious, hating themselves. Tempted to join the coyotes, run off with them to the hills, but—afraid. Afraid to give up the comfort, security, and safety of their housebound existence. Afraid of the unknown and dangerous.

This quotation is from "Down the River with Henry Thoreau," and Abbey goes on to compare Thoreau to a coyote. Thoreau's job, like Abbey's and Peacock's, is to howl wildly and make the rest of us uneasy. And to maybe stir in us the desire to push outward. To make our lives wilder. To enlarge our turf and territory.

Abbey and Peacock demonstrate through their wilder existences just how tame our own lives are. And make no bones about it, our lives *are* tame. Just seven years before my western trip I had followed some radio-collared ospreys down through Cuba. It was the first time in my life I was carrying a cell phone as I traveled, and I soon realized that my location could be tracked almost as easily as the birds'. Now we all carry our own personal tracking devices. We are, most of us, town dogs, leashed by our daily obligations, the things to check off our lists and the many oh-so-urgent e-mails to answer.

What does it really mean to live a wilder life? And what does it mean to lead that life now, at a time when our virtual lives seem to have taken over our actual?

One thing I think it means, simply put, is getting into the wilderness, or what wilderness is left.

"We need wilderness because we are wild animals," Ed Abbey said.

But it is more than that. For me being wild doesn't mean being savage or extreme. It certainly doesn't mean being frat-boy wild. And it isn't just vague nature-writing shorthand for occasional spasms of Whitmanesque ecstasy, either. It is more complicated.

For me there is no wild life without a moral life. But we also have to be careful with a word like *goodness*. "If I repent anything it is my good behavior," said Thoreau, a thought that Abbey would have seconded. Neither of them had much use for do-gooders, and neither were joiners, despite the fact that their work stirred armies of followers and started many a cause. Part of this was having particular and individualistic notions of what being good meant. Emerson understood this when he wrote: "Your goodness must have some edge to it,—else it is none."

The question I now ask myself is whether it is possible to live responsibly, to have a Stegnerian commitment to wife and child, family and friends, while still having real wildness in my life. Is it possible to be properly wild?

It would be easy to say that we all outgrow our inner Abbeys. But growing up can also mean hiding out. Work and responsibility can swallow everything else like the incoming tide. We become so absorbed in our own lives that we can't see beyond them. In his essay on Peacock, Jack Turner writes of "our fundamentally Puritan focus on work and family at the expense of all else." One of the pleasures of workaholism is, as Donald Hall reminds us in his book *Life Work*, the sense of being a good boy or girl, of pleasing one's parents, of getting a gold star. Making work and career our supreme virtues, as many of us have these days, neatens up our lives, gives us a simple narrative, offers us a sense of control. And of course our effort is often rewarded by the work-driven society we just happen to live in.

What Abbey offers complicates this simple formula. He helps to pull our heads out of the sand and shows us, through his life and work, that a counterlife is still possible. A life against the prevailing current. He believed that so much of what we think right is emphatically wrong and that therefore we must live according to our own dictates. And just as important: he believed that a life with some sort of freedom from the usual dictates *can* still be lived. As Thoreau said: "The life that men praise and call successful is but one kind." Abbey showed us another kind. A life that doesn't value fame, efficiency, money, safety, success. A life where freedom, wildness, wilderness, and independence remain the truer priorities.

One of the pleasures of Abbey's work, particularly *Desert Solitaire* and the best essays, is that he shows us just what a counterlife might look like, what it means to live a life apart from "the cultural apparatus." He understands that it isn't only wilderness that is being threatened but human wildness. Without models for a wilder life, the sort of models that Abbey and Peacock can help provide, we forget that certain possibilities exist. But they still do. If you read Abbey carefully, you can see that he shows, very practically, what one might do if one held values contrary to the society one lived in. For one thing, you might care for and about the natural world while also getting out into it, watching the birds and beasts. For another, go down the river with others but also spend more time alone. Walk alone in the desert for ten days or go live on a barrier island for a while or even camp in the backcountry with bears. Not because you are going to film it or make a YouTube video about it but because of the experience itself. It goes without saying that bravery, at the expense of personal safety and career advancement, is also part of Abbey's wilder life, as are sex and comedy.

Finally, Abbey tells us that we can't expect to be rewarded, let alone celebrated, by a society we are acting in opposition to. In other words, if you choose to go against the world, you can't expect the world to heap praise on you. Choosing to go against will not make you comfortable. It will not make you rich. It will not make you famous (usually). And you might just go to jail.

To be truly countercultural, then, is difficult. It requires boldness and belief. It requires commitment. And it requires accepting consequences.

Let's be honest, though. Some of Abbey's bad personal behavior was brave. But some was simply bad. Stegner, meanwhile, is miscast in the role of company man; to lead a life like he did, of reading and writing and teaching, is hardly a conformist's life; it is in fact the opposite in a country that hardly celebrates its intellectuals. But as poles in our thinking, Stegner and Abbey work well enough. Read their lives deeply and they point as surely as road signs, even if they occasionally point in different directions. What they point to for me, and for anyone else who cares to look closely, are creative possibilities for living a life both good and wild.

GOING HOME AGAIN

"This is lonely country," Hadley said.

We were driving out of southern Alberta into southern Saskatchewan, the place that young Wally Stegner—just about Hadley's age at the time he moved here, come to think of it—first called home. We hadn't passed any other cars as we drove up through the endless albino wheat fields into Canada, and when we turned east on a dirt and gravel road toward Saskatchewan, rocks started kicking up under the car. It had been already almost six by the time we crossed the border, and by the time we were ten minutes down the dirt road I started feeling uneasy. As the road went on and on, I began to worry we wouldn't get to a town until after dark. And uglier worries: what if the car broke down out here? We were far out of cell-phone range. I had the bike on the back, but how far could I ride, my daughter jiggling on the handlebars or perched on the seat behind me?

"No wonder he became a writer," the border officer said when I told him that Stegner grew up on a farm in Saskatchewan. You could see why Salt Lake City would later seem such a place of thrills and novelty. Being a boy here you would long for civilization, for other people. You didn't need to long for wide-open spaces, that was for sure. Over the next forty miles we passed only one sign with a name on it. Ravenscrag Road. We saw no houses. I was also surprised by how relatively birdless the country seemed, though we did see a big, black Swainson's hawk lifting off through the wheat, and some swallows carving the air after insects.

My mood rose when I spotted a sign for Eastend. But the next two small towns we passed through did not have hotels. At last we curved down with the cleave of a hill, and saw the trees that meant we had finally come to Stegner's river, the Frenchman (or, as he called it in his fiction, and sometimes in his nonfiction, the Whitemud). Lights, too, which were a good sign. We pulled into the lot of the Riverside Hotel, a rambling one-story affair, and relief turned to unease when I noted all the large white trucks parked in front of the rooms.

"We only have one room," said Wendy, who stood behind the reception desk. "And it's smoking."

"We'll take it," I said.

Then I asked her if they were always this busy.

"My husband talked me into coming up here to retire," she said. "'It'll be only a few tourists now and then,' he told me. And then the drilling started."

I asked what kind of drilling.

"Horizontal fracturing," she said. "For oil."

Perfect. If George Stegner were alive he would no longer have to run elsewhere to find a boom. This time it would have come to him. The Big Rock Candy Mountain, right here in Eastend.

HADLEY AND I planned on touring the Stegner house first thing in the morning. But before we left for the house, the hotel's self-described "laundry lady," a woman named Bryson LaBoissiere, gave us her two cents about the Stegners. She told us she had a friend who used to play in the Stegner house as a child in the '50s, and that the house had trapdoors leading down to where George Stegner stashed his rum. Another friend told her that her father had been buddies with George Stegner and had seen the bullet holes in George's car. This didn't bother Bryson, not a bit. She was impressed by George's energy, his chutzpah, by the fact that he smuggled booze from Canada into the United States and then, when the laws reversed, simply carried on the same business in the opposite direction. She felt that most people didn't understand that the son had more than a little of the father in him.

"Wallace was a bit of a gay blade too," she said.

According to Bryson, George was not such a bad husband and father after all. Exhibit A, she explained, was the Stegner house itself, which George had built with his own hands in the summer of 1917.

"It was the only four-gabled house in town," she said. "There were a couple other gabled houses, but they were made from kits. I haven't seen a house anywhere hereabouts that had gables and was brand-new built."

"So he was trying to do the right thing?" I asked.

"More than the right thing. You don't build a house like that if you don't love your family."

When Hadley and I toured it later we didn't see any trapdoors, but we agreed that it was a fine house, and must have been hard for the family to leave behind. The rooms were small but comfortable and the boys' bedroom faced out back toward the Frenchman River, which took a sinuous turn right behind the house. After the tour we walked out back to the river and Hadley threw sticks into the current while I tried to imagine it as Stegner saw it. He would often say of Eastend that while it was a hard place to be a man, it was a great place to be a boy. He loved swimming in and skating on the river and building forts and roaming with a pack of boys, led by Cecil, his strong, athletic brother. He also loved starting mudfights and throwing rocks and causing mischief. He later described it as a Huckleberry Finn existence.

"Eastend was a failure place, ultimately," he wrote in his autobiography, but "it imprinted me, indelibly, with the perceptions, images, memories, behavior codes, and attitudes that have controlled my life and writing ever since." While the Stegners lived here their lives turned in seasonal cycles, from winter in town in the house along the river to isolated summers when the family farmed their wheat fields to the south, down by the US border, where Wallace lived the life of a "sensuous little savage."

But Stegner wasn't merely a little savage. It was here he learned to love books, too. "If you have only three books, books mean a good deal to you," he once said. For most of the other boys the imprisonment of school, from eight in the morning until four in the afternoon, was pure misery, but Wally gobbled up any news he could get from the outer world. He quickly discovered that most of what the children studied seemed to have nothing to do with their lives, imported as it was from Europe, which meant they suffered "not only from the rawest forms of deculturation but the most slavish respect for borrowed elegances." But that didn't stop Wally. He was hungry to learn and he was good at it, a natural, just the way Cecil was with sports. He had his father's appetite for huge, challenging work but he found that this applied to the life of the mind as well as it did to clearing fields.

It was in Eastend that Stegner's ideas about the frontier developed by living a life about as close to frontier life as you still could in 1912. Stegner wrote: "The exacerbated personal freedom of the frontier left us with myths, a folklore, a set of illusions, that are often comically at odds with the facts of life." This was where he saw the way the "folklore of hope" led people to plant crops in a dry land, and the way the land itself, through drought and winters filled with blizzards, seemed to try to shed people off it, like a dog shaking off fleas. He watched as his father threw himself into taming the land, trying to make it yield its fruits up to him, and in George Stegner's failure in Saskatchewan, the son saw that an individual, no matter how energetic or determined, could only do so much against the vast land and extreme climate of the West. In the end the true result of George's heroic efforts was to help create a dustbowl. In *Wolf Willow*, his son wrote: "How does one know what wilderness has meant to Americans unless he has shared in the guilt of wastefully and ignorantly tampering with it in the name of progress?" And: "The vein of melancholy in the North American mind may be owing to many causes, but it is surely not weakened by the perception that the fulfillment of the American Dream means inevitably the death of the noble savagery and freedom of the wild."

We now dream of a wilder time, while those living then dreamed of a tamer one. We secretly worship the mountain men because they were so wild, but the end result of their labors was the extinction of the beaver and the taming of the West. We love the frontiersmen who finished off the frontier. Huge expenditures of energy are required to tame a place, to make it even marginally profitable. But what does one do with that energy, those habits learned, once the place is tamed? Can we just turn these things off? Of course not. We have never been content to merely marvel at these lands and live with them in sustainable and moderate ways. We need to get something out of them. Put them to use. We turn to them with our usual chronic restlessness and rapacity.

YESTERDAY I HAD thought this place birdless, but Stegner's river proved me wrong. In the course of Hadley's twenty-minute bout of stick throwing, I saw a yellow warbler, a mountain bluebird, and some chickadees and mourning doves. Up above us spread the gentle yellow-domed hills of the old Whitemud Mine where George Stegner had sometimes worked. You could see how the mine got its name: pale streaks slanted through the green-and-yellow color scheme of the surrounding hills.

The trees that we stood among, and that clustered along the river, were not here when Stegner was growing up. That was the thing he'd noticed most when he returned as an adult. That the landscape that he'd used as material for his whole career no longer matched the actual landscape. "This is all very strange," he wrote to his good friends the Grays, "because I've written about this town until I think I've imagined it. Now I have to imagine it all over."

This morning, when Bryson had mentioned Stegner's return, she also said it had become something of a town myth.

"He stayed at our campground and didn't tell anyone who he was until he left," she said. "He was embarrassed to admit he was a Stegner due to his father, who still owed money in town."

It was June of 1953 when Wallace and Mary parked their trailer in the Eastend campground. Wallace went by the name of "Mr. Page" as he walked around town. He visited his old gabled house but refused to try to find the homestead on the border: he didn't like to imagine the place, with all its associated memories of work and family, swallowed up by the grasslands as if it had never existed.

When the woman who supplied the Stegners' trailer with electricity found out that they wanted to learn more about the town's history, she gave them some advice. She told them they should read a book by a local writer. The book was called *The Big Rock Candy Mountain*.

Maybe Bryson was right. Maybe the reason Stegner was nervous about returning was that his father owed money. But if he was, Wallace himself never mentioned it. Taking the alias was partly about a more general embarrassment over being a Stegner, over the ne'er-do-well father who supplemented his income with bootlegging. And it was partly about something else: as a writer, Stegner was there as a spy, coming back to gather materials and make something out of them.

Wolf Willow, the book that grew out of the visit, is extraordinary. Radical, even. Read it and you can laugh at the way we seem to think that our current debates about forms in creative nonfiction, about the mixing of fiction and nonfiction, are somehow new. In the pages of *Wolf Willow* you find memoir, history, social theory, and then, plop in the middle, you come upon a two-part short story. Perhaps after the arduous work of building *Beyond the Hundredth Meridian*, Stegner was ready to *play*. There is an easy freedom to the book, as if its author were at once a great, respected scholar and a kid throwing mud balls along the Frenchman. Partly a simple autobiographical story of Stegner coming home again to Eastend, it is also a history of the frontier. As for the fiction dropped in the middle of the nonfiction narrative, these were stories that had appeared elsewhere and would appear again in a couple of books, including Stegner's *Collected Short Stories*. But Stegner made no apologies for reusing material. It was another lesson the frontier (and his mother) had taught him: reuse everything. Recycle, re-can, use every scrap.

In *Wolf Willow*, Stegner manipulates time as he never had before. Later, in his biography of DeVoto, he would remark upon DeVoto's use of simultaneous chronology in his histories—that is, of the way he could write of a mountain man heading up the Missouri and then of James Polk addressing Congress, and it all seemed to be going on at once. DeVoto wrote somewhat in the manner of our contemporary narrative television, with jump cuts and threading plots. Stegner would master something similar that he would put to use not just in his nonfiction but in the later fiction, often establishing a present-moment through-line and a separate but connected past-tense narrative. Time on the move, back and forth and sideways. Stegner learned to play with time like clay, and one of the pleasures of reading a novel like *Angle of Repose* is that the narrative present and the past are at once fused and distinct. But it all started with *Wolf Willow*. With walking down the Eastend streets in 1953 while his mind traveled back to those same streets in 1910 or back further to when there were no streets at all and the Blackfeet Indians roamed the Cypress Hills.

THE HORSEHEAD PUMPS are everywhere in southern Saskatche-wan. What was once farmland is now oil land. As Hadley and I drove east to Shaunavon (the town that Stegner's Eastend hometown team played baseball against) and north to Gull Lake, then west to Moose Jaw and southeast to Weyburn, weaving through southern Sas-katchewan, we barely went a minute without seeing an oil pump. They bobbed like crazy rocking horses, *thirsty* horses that dipped, drank, and rose; dipped, drank, and rose. They had invaded those farmlands like equine aliens, and we saw them next to barns, next to silos, in the fields. Dipping and sipping. It was as bad as Vernal—worse, really—or maybe just easier to see from the road. The whole countryside appeared to be involved in a mass slurping, sucking up what was left of the land's blood. An occasional well rose like a rocket launch among the smaller pumps.

We passed a billboard that read, TEACH YOUR CHILDREN TO PRAY. IT PAYS. The sign provided a new image. Looking out at the pumps I now saw a great communal prayer service. A thousand machines bowing down and lifting up again and again, praising Allah or Jesus or whomever. Maybe it is the simplest and truest thing to say they were bowing down to the great modern god of Oil.

I remembered that Stegner had ended *Wolf Willow* optimistically, thinking the town of Eastend safe from future booms: "It has had its land rush and recovered." Less than a decade before Hadley's and my visit, Stegner's biographer Philip Fradkin made a trip up here and found the region's "relative lack of change" reassuring. That has all gone out the window now. This is the new boom, the fracking boom, son, and you had better get on board or get out of the way. Wendell Berry had told me to notice land use, and here it wasn't too hard to see how the land was being used. This was the densest con-centration of drilling I had yet seen on my trip.

By late afternoon Hadley and I were exhausted, but while the hotel signs said Welcome, we clearly were not. We stopped a half dozen times with no luck. It wasn't fathers and daughters—it wasn't tourists of any stripe—who were filling these hotels these days. It was this generation's George Stegners—young men come to make their fortune. This new society was a male society, a smoky society, a slightly scary society. These were men who would come here, change these towns, and then leave.

Near Weyburn we finally found a hotel with a single room left. There was a sign on the door that read: $200 FINE FOR SMOKING. We barricaded ourselves in, ordered room service, and called it an early night.

THREE DAYS LATER we had left Stegner's childhood home long behind and were awakening in a hotel in Beckley, West Virginia, to a landscape like the one Ed Abbey knew as a child. Stegner had called his home "the bald-assed prairie," but there was nothing bald about this shaggy, bearded place. The mountains, while beautiful, gave none of the lift I always felt upon seeing the Rockies. This was the land of hills and hollers, the landscape Ed Abbey knew in his bones.

Three years before his death, in April of 1986, Edward Abbey went home again, embarking on a road trip back east to the hills of Home, where his parents, Paul and Mildred, still lived. Even in her eighties, Mildred was a dynamo, basically running the local church and taking night classes at the nearby college. Over the years Paul had visited Ed at many of his fire-lookout and national-park jobs, and though the father drove the son a little nuts, they remained close. Ed admired his father as a man from another time, a jack-of-all-trades who was immensely capable with tools and animals and who was, like George Stegner, a crack shot. Ed had gone back east to visit the family a few times over the years, but this trip was different. His goal was to research the novel that would become *The Fool's Progress*, in which the Abbey-based protagonist, Henry Lightcap, is a hillbilly Ulysses, and his final destination is Stump Creek, West Virginia.

While his friend Dick Kirkpatrick drove, Abbey took notes and recorded his impressions on a tape recorder.

"The longer we drove, the sicker he got," Kirkpatrick said later. "We had planned on seeing Wendell Berry in Kentucky, but he didn't feel up to it."

Abbey had great ambitions for the story of Henry Lightcap. "A Fat Masterpiece," he'd hopefully called it. Henry, living in the West, had led a life of divorce, dissolution, and drinking, and the book opens with his final breakup with his wife, culminating in the shooting of their TV. It is one of the funniest set pieces that Abbey ever wrote, and one of the few times in his fiction that Abbey was able to re-create the drama of his own troubled mind in a way that he did so easily in his nonfiction. The book employs an alternating chronology, with present-tense scenes detailing the narrator's long journey from west to east, and past-tense scenes basically telling the story of his life. Unfortunately, the book grows clunkier as it proceeds, and many of the characters that Lightcap meets on the road are little more than cartoons.

One of the best characters in the book is Henry's brother, Will. While Henry Lightcap had spent his life as Abbey had, roaming the West, moving from place to place, brother Will's path was different. He had taken over the old family farm and settled there, never moving. Jim Cahalan, Abbey's biographer, notes that Will is at least partly based on Wendell Berry and his reclaiming of his own family farm in Kentucky. I find this fascinating. Both Abbey and Berry were students of Stegner's, of course, but only Berry truly saw Stegner as a model. Abbey understood the appeal of the return to home, of rooting down in a place, but also finally came to understand that for him this was not the way. Longing for home might be part of his makeup, but actually building one and staying put was not. Like George Stegner, he was always looking hopefully (and lustfully) around the next corner. Abbey was not one for waxing poetic about his home, unless you defined that home as the greater West, and perhaps one reason that Abbey, while caring deeply about his region, did not preach the gospel of home is that it has always had a hint of piousness to it. That hint was there at the very beginning, with Thoreau at Walden looking down on his neighbors, and it remains there still. Look at me, it says, this is where I *belong*. This is the only place on Earth for me. You poor placeless suckers don't know what it's like! The idea of commitment to home has in fact become a kind of gospel of the nature writing world, and it should be no surprise that Abbey responded to it as he did to any other piety: by thumbing his nose at it.

As for Paul Abbey, he for one wasn't too pleased with how the family was portrayed in the novel.

When Ed went home again after the publication of *The Fool's Progress*, father greeted son in the front yard waving the book in his hand.

"*Why? Why?*" he yelled.

TEACHERS

During the fall, between the cracks of my teaching schedule, I continued to try to read everything that Abbey and Stegner had written. Then, at the end of the fall term, I headed back out west.

On a sunny December morning I met Lynn Stegner and her daughter, Allison, at the Main Quad of Stanford. They were happy to see me, which made me happy. They would be heading back later in the day for Christmas in Vermont, so our meeting would have to be relatively quick. Allison had graduated from Stanford and Lynn still taught there, so I was in good hands. We parked in front of the quad and walked back to the classrooms where Wally had taught. (I still couldn't bring myself to say "Wally" out loud without cringing, but Wallace sounded too stiff in Lynn's company and Mr. Stegner too formal, so I tried.) We walked through the golden Mediterranean campus with its red roofs, Allison pointing to the palm trees where the woodpeckers kept their caches of stored acorns. She had spent the summer working as a paleoecologist in canyonlands in Utah, following, in her own way, in her grandfather's footsteps.

We pushed through some bushes at the corner of a yellow building and peeked in the windows.

"This was his office," Lynn said.

The view inside was not particularly exciting—the room was now a classroom—but the view out back from the office was of a beautiful shaded garden and a gnarled live oak, which, Lynn told me, had been alive when Wally was there. Was this the office he shared with Ed McClanahan? Lynn wasn't sure.

I wandered the garden for a minute and took it all in. This was where Wallace Stegner had spent his *other* working life, his life outside of writing. I knew he took his job seriously. He had little patience with the never-ending question that nonwriters seem to love, that of whether writing could be taught. "Nobody asks that question about painting or architecture or music," he said, and nobody "questions the neighborhood piano teacher." Of course it could be taught, and he had done so for forty years. A big part of the job was simply recognizing talent, and then nudging without pushing. If you didn't have talent, it made no sense to go into the field, and Stegner was impatient with indulgent teachers who found everything they read wonderful. Writing was hard work, and laziness was unacceptable. On the other hand, he understood that there were things he didn't understand, and was open to innovation to a degree. He wrote: "Tension, dynamic equilibrium between innovation and tradition, liberty and restraint, is what seems to me to make a writing class worthy of its possibilities."

His method was Socratic. For those who have never experienced a creative-writing workshop, they usually go a little like this: For homework the class reads a piece of creative writing composed by one or more of their classmates. In class the group sits around and discusses the writing without the participation of the writers themselves. In most classes, and certainly in Stegner's classes, the instructor listens more than lectures, facilitating a conversation that usually begins with positive remarks and moves toward the more critical. It is a delicate business, with student feelings always easily bruised, and there are many ways it can go badly. But one of the ways it can go well is if students start to focus less obsessively on their own work and start to see in the work of others—in ways they can't quite yet see in their own—mistakes made, possibilities to explore, techniques that might be tried.

As much as Wallace Stegner was a lifelong writer and environmentalist, he was also a lifelong teacher. His own academic life grew right alongside the growth of the modern creative-writing workshop method, beginning at Iowa, where he was in the first class to submit a creative thesis, to the early days of the Bread Loaf Writers' Conference, and then as one of the first group of Briggs-Copeland lecturers at Harvard. He took what he learned in these places and applied them to the program he founded at Stanford in 1946. In keeping with the philosophies of the places where he had taught, his approach was both artistic and practical. He believed that the first goal of becoming a writer was to make something fine, but once that happened he was not so highbrow as to ignore the fact that the fine thing had to be sold.

Stegner was also a member of the first generation to experience the tension that can rise between writing and teaching, but at times

STEGNER IN THE LOS ALTOS HILLS NEAR HIS HOME.

he pooh-poohed the whole idea that there even was a conflict. A product of the Depression, he had solved the great and ever-pressing economic question of the writing life with a simple answer: he got a job. Though he wasn't above griping (and Stegner admitted that griping was one of the pleasures of being a workaholic), the job, in his eyes, was a good one, allowing him to support a family while cranking out a steady stream of novels, stories, essays, and histories. Stegner wrote fast and he wrote well, with a journalist's facility and toughness. When faced with the problem of completing long books while also teaching, he always replied briskly with some variant of "That's what summers are for."

If Stegner was the model writer-teacher, then Abbey, at first glance, was anything but. In fact, with the possible exception of Hunter Thompson, Ed Abbey might have been voted least likely among his kind to ever wear academic robes. No one expected the wild man to be domesticated by the academy, but he was in the end. In January of 1981 he was hired by the poet and nonfiction writer Dick Shelton, who once said to me, "Everybody told me I was crazy when I hired him." He was quick to add that Abbey surprised a lot of people: he was strict in class—"a real schoolmarm"—and shy and quiet with his colleagues. He taught on and off over the next seven years, right up until the year before his death, and, with the help of support letters from Wendell Berry and Wallace Stegner, was appointed a full professor in 1988.

After we had finished exploring the school, Lynn, Allison, and I climbed into the car and took the winding road up into the Los Altos Hills to the old house. This had been a beautiful, undeveloped landscape that Wallace and Mary Stegner once rode horses through. But the fields were now clotted with houses, suburbia imprinted on the hills. It wasn't just his region that Stegner had watched be despoiled, but his neighborhood. He had seen those fields become suburbs, and bore witness as his peaceful valley became the Silicon Valley, trophy houses sprouting up everywhere.

Wally and Mary's retreat, where they had built their modest ranch-style house, now sat amid the second wealthiest zip code in the United States. As we curled up the driveway, through a tunnel of live and scrub oaks, Lynn pointed out the new neighbor's house, recently built, and, through the trees, I noticed a putting green near the driveway. Forty years earlier the Stegners had organized a neighborhood conservation group here, and Wallace had written that open space was the local equivalent of wilderness. It was a lost cause now. I knew the sadness of living in a beautiful place and watching it become less beautiful, and then, ruined. It is an experience that most of us have had at this stage in the country's "development."

Allison told me that the new owner of the Stegner house had grown weary of unexpected visitors, specifically Stegner fans who wanted a peek at the house. Lynn said her palms were sweating as we pulled in the driveway. The plan was to sneak in, get a good look, and sneak out. But the owner, an older Asian man, happened to be piddling around in his garage and saw us coming. We parked in the driveway, behind his car, and Allison, thinking quickly, got out and walked over to ask the man for directions. Meanwhile Lynn pointed out some details of the plain, one-story ranch house, and described how the studio was out back, by the swimming pool.

If I couldn't see it, I could picture it. I knew that often at the beginning of the year, and sometimes during the year, Stegner would have the students up to the house on the then-secluded hilltop. When I'd visited Ed McClanahan in Kentucky, he told me about a particularly stunning afternoon up at the Stegners'. McClanahan and the other members of one of the workshop groups were having drinks out on the back patio in the late afternoon when someone looked up and noticed that there was a hawk circling above with a big rattlesnake in its talons. While not every day could be that dramatic, those visits to the house must have been as stimulating for the students as the classes themselves. They got to see a working writer's home with a studio out back and a book-lined living room, a place of the sort they could perhaps one day inhabit, and a writer's life they could imagine themselves one day leading.

The studio was still there, but when I mentioned this to Lynn she said, "Not for long."

She explained that there had been a recent uproar. The new owner wanted to tear down Wally's study.

While we were talking, Allison hurried back to the car. She climbed in and closed the door.

"Let's go," she said.

Mission somewhat accomplished, we made our getaway.

STEGNER WAS, BY almost all accounts, a great teacher. But even he showed some cracks. He worried about serving two masters and, for all his renown as a professor, said this upon his retirement from Stanford in 1971: "I am never going to miss teaching. . . . I never gave it more than half my heart, the ventricle, say." Once he quit he felt that for the first time in his life he was able to concentrate fully on individual projects. Over the next twenty-two years, until his death at eighty-four, he produced six books of nonfiction, including his underrated biography of DeVoto, and three of his best novels: *Crossing to Safety*, the National Book Award–winning *The Spectator Bird*, and the Pulitzer Prize–winning *Angle of Repose*. It is true that *Angle of Repose*, the most ambitious of those books, was composed while he still had one foot in the classroom, but during those last two decades there is a sense of almost crystallized concentration, all the energy that had sprayed off in so many directions suddenly lasered in on the work.

I am fascinated by this late-life kick, by how Stegner grew as a writer as he got older. Something happened to the man's work just about the time he retired from Stanford, and that something enlivened his books over the next twenty years. The first hints of where things would go showed as far back as 1952 with the creation of Joe

Allston, the narrator of the short story "A Field Guide to Western Birds." Joe is a literary agent who has retired to his home in the California hills, where he lives with his wife, Ruth. More important, he is the prototype of the classic first-person old-man Stegnerian doppelgänger, what I have come to call the "grumbling grandpa" narrators who are crucial to the later work. Through his use of these exaggerated fictional stand-ins, he created some of his best, and certainly most readable, fiction. Joe Allston came back for the novels *All the Little Live Things* (1967) and *The Spectator Bird* (1976), and a similar, if less jokey, narrator named Larry Morgan would take over for Stegner's last novel, *Crossing to Safety* (1987). Both of these men are opinionated, gruff, and none too happy about the way the world has been hijacked by its at once soft-headed and dogmatic young people. To the contemporary ear, there is a sometimes aw-shucks manner that takes some getting used to, particularly with Joe Allston, who has a little dash of by-golly Ronald Reagan jargon in his vocabulary (if not his politics). But all Stegner's older protagonists have a barely disguised, old-fashioned agenda. They embody "continuance, rootedness," though they are not mere symbols of those qualities. These are novels, after all, not sermons, and the beauty of the books is that the old "decided" men who narrate them are actually full of uncertainty, anxiety, and questioning. Luckily these men are also sharp, smart, and articulate, and it is the articulation of that uncertainty that brings the books alive.

Lyman Ward, the narrator of *Angle of Repose*, is a darker version of Joe Allston and Larry Morgan. He has reason to be dark: he is literally truncated, his legs amputated by the same doctor who has since run off with his wife. Meanwhile, his radical son doesn't think his father can take care of himself and hopes to put him in a nursing home. Stegner wrote this book at the height of his troubles with the young radicals who had "ruined" Stanford, and there is both some serious venting about the state of the rootless young and something close to conscious self-parody in the hippie-hating Ward. Tired of the shallow present, the narrator, a historian by trade, tunnels into the past, specifically into the lives of his pioneering western grandparents, Oliver and Susan Ward. In the book itself, these excursions into the past are first presented as artifacts, mostly as the transcripts of letters. But they soon segue into a third-person re-creation of the past, dramatizing the lives and many moves of Susan and Oliver. In the course of empathizing with his grandparents and imagining their lives, the historian-narrator becomes something else, something very close to a writer of fiction.

The book proceeds in two simultaneous narratives, Lyman's present and his grandparents' past. Stegner had always been an admirer of DeVoto's use of simultaneous chronology, of having many things happening at once. He had already learned much about moving in time by writing his own nonfiction, and it is in *Angle of Repose* that he most clearly plays with time like an accordion, squeezing it tight then letting it spread out.

Angle of Repose was also Stegner's most criticized book. The criticism stems from the fact that the life of Susan Ward was based heavily on the life of Mary Hallock Foote, and that Stegner used some of Foote's letters to create the words of Ward. My first instinct was to dismiss this criticism, since I so admired the book. But while in Salt Lake, I read through the original Foote letters and saw that some sections were lifted whole-cloth and plopped down into the book. In short, I saw what all the fuss was about. This was a new Wallace Stegner to me: Wally the rapper, sampling earlier work. It is a silly image but somewhat apt, too. Artists are a tribe of borrowers, which is why I have a hard time getting too worked up about Stegner's crime. While I would have preferred it if he had reworded the sections of the original letters that he used, as the book progresses he begins to do just that, taking the same language and making it his and Susan's (and Lyman's) own. What begins as borrowing ends as ventriloquism, the character and her voice coming alive apart from its model. The letters prove a jumping-off point into voice. Perhaps it would have been better if Stegner had at least scumbled the sentences from the original letters, but what he ultimately does with them is pure fiction. He uses a life to create a myth.

The myth he creates is the forever Stegner myth, the myth not just of Oliver and Susan Ward but of George and Hilda Stegner, and of Bo and Elsa Mason. It is the myth of the nester, always trying to create community, continuity, and culture in a wild land that rejects it, and of a boomer who sees that same land as his big chance. Oliver is a more subtle and reluctant boomer than either George or Bo, moving for his job and often against his will, but he is a boomer still, a member of the tribe of wheeled people. The book ends when the couple finally makes a "permanent" home in Grass Valley, California, but it is a bitter sort of settling, the result of betrayal and compromise. Stegner, writing in the notebook I found in Salt Lake, said of Lyman Ward: "One of the reasons for stubbornly writing his grandparents' lives is to save them from neglect, reassert them. As to using historical people for a partly fictional purpose, so did Hawthorne, and for the same reason: *the search for a usable past.*"

AFTER STANFORD, I drove out to Half-Moon Bay, where Abbey had lived during his time at the school. From there I'd planned on a pilgrimage up to Lassen Volcanic National Park, where I had first read *Desert Solitaire* and where, prompted by that book, I spent my first night alone in the backcountry. But a summer fire that spread over 15,000 acres, or 15 percent of the park, had turned the wilderness to ash.

The truth was that, after two years immersed in his words and life, there were times when I had grown a little weary of Cactus Ed Abbey. For instance, I'd spent a good part of the fall with his novels and, honestly, rereading his fiction had been, at times, a task. *The Monkey Wrench Gang* is an important book and a book with historic interest. It is also a very silly and dated book. Not just silly-funny, either, but silly-sloppy. Take the character of Bonnie Abzug, for instance. The novel is told through a series of jumps into different characters' points of view. When we are in Hayduke's point of view, for example, we experience the world through the eyes of the passionate, deranged, scatological primitive that Abbey created out of the raw material of poor Doug Peacock: *It was fucking good. He would blow it the fuck up.* The writer maintains some distance from these characters and allows himself to comment on them, but the perspective is colored by the viewpoint character so that, when we shift to the more refined Doc Sarvis's point of view, the language becomes philosophical and pompous, like Doc himself.

Not so with Bonnie. When we are in her point of view the main thing we hear about are her own curves. She is Jessica Rabbit, a lascivious cartoon, a Playboy bunny sketched by a horny adolescent. It is as if all *she* spends her time thinking about are her own breasts, legs, and ass. There is plenty more of this sloppiness and outright sexist language, like Doc spouting crude metaphors as he plunges down the lever to the TNT to blow up the bridge, and at times the book shares a sensibility with recent movie comedies of the *Dumb & Dumber* school. Or, as Abbey wrote in the pages of the book itself: "Pleistocene humor—the best kind." What is bad in *Monkey Wrench* is worse in *Hayduke Lives*, an uninspired bit of hackwork that is told in cartoon strokes, rarely funny in the way Abbey was at his best.

The way Abbey was funny at his best, I think, was when the serious sat right next to the scatological, the ridiculous next to the sublime, the high next to the low. Abbey has moments like these in *The Monkey Wrench Gang*, and even more in *The Fool's Progress*, but nowhere in the fiction do these moments rise to the level and frequency that they do in his nonfiction. This is a verdict others have pronounced about his work before, a verdict Abbey himself hated, but a verdict that in the end seems to me unavoidable. The times his Pleistocene humor really catches us by surprise are when it comes out of the mouth of the nonfiction character named Ed Abbey. Wendell Berry wrote of Abbey that there is more movement, from subject to subject, on his page than on almost any page of any other writer, and it is this movement, not just from subject to subject but from mood to mood, that makes those marks on the page seem to represent an actual man.

Abbey would not want to hear it, but I would say that the work that is most alive and that most keeps Abbey alive today, outside of *Desert Solitaire*, are the individual essays. It is in these that we still hear the voice and sense the man. I earlier called the late essays "slapdash" and they were in the way the collections were thrown together. But in each of those essays, no matter how quickly written, you can hear the Abbey voice: the rumbles, the jokes, the profundities, the love and the hate.

It is not fashionable to use a term like "literary immortality." On a finite planet with a possible expiration date, it seems both anthropocentric and pompous to talk in terms of "forever." But if we are to take seriously the fact that some writers last, then we need to think about the different ways in which they do. The most obvious way to do this is to look at writers from long ago who are still read. The two handiest, and best for the comparison I want to make, are writers who wrote more than four centuries ago but who overlapped in their own times. Most people would consider both Montaigne and Shakespeare "immortal writers." And most would consider Shakespeare more so in the traditional sense: his plays are still frequently performed, his work taught in schools, his name bandied about in learned society, his reputation unparalleled. All true, but I would contend that in a different, less-traditional sense Montaigne is more "immortal." How so? Because he is still alive to us through his book, since, as he said, his book is himself. Thanks to the marks he made on a page four hundred and fifty years ago, we feel we have a very real sense of the man, of who he was, of what it felt like to be him. We feel we know his personality, its quirks.

This, at his very best, is what Edward Paul Abbey offers. Read him and you will know him. More than almost any writer I've read he remains alive on the page. You may not like him very much, but there he is. Opinionated, moody, troubled, confident, angry, compassionate, smart, kind of stupid. If this character was, as Abbey says it was, "a fictional creation," then it was a brilliant one.

GETTING AT ABBEY and Stegner requires not just imagining but re-imagining, freeing them, to the extent that seems accurate and not reactionary, from their hardened images. Both men have clearly been mummified by their reputations: Saint Wallace the Good and Randy Ed, Wild Man. Abbey may get it worse but Stegner risks being purified beyond interest. From some of the tributes and testimonials I've read, you would have thought it surprising that he kept writing and fighting for the land and instead didn't just give it all up to teach Sunday school.

But of course anyone who is lifted up so high is in danger of being toppled over, especially in our contentious times. The Stegner of the '60s risks looking not like Terry Tempest Williams's "radical," but like a caricature of the grumpy old conservative telling the damn kids to get off his lawn. Ken Kesey went as far as once suggesting that opposition to Stegner was part of the unifying force that brought the Merry Pranksters together and led to their LSD-fueled bus trip: "I have felt impelled into the future by Wally, by his dislike of what I was doing, of what we were doing. That was the kiss of approval in some way."

There are those who have gone even further, suggesting that Kesey based Nurse Ratched—one of if not the most notorious authority figures in all of American literature—at least partly on the man running the particular institution Kesey was part of: the Stanford Creative Writing Program. Stanford professor and literary scholar Mark McGurl, whose book *The Program Era: Postwar Fiction and the*

Rise of Creative Writing is a brilliant treatment of the rise of creative writing programs and their impact on postwar literature, writes: "It is hard to read about the bad behavior of McMurphy in the Group Meeting, his all-too-evident disrespect for Nurse Ratched, without connecting it to Kesey's well-documented antagonism toward his teacher Wallace Stegner, whom, as John Daniel reports, Kesey saw as the 'epitome of academic staidness and convention' even as Stegner found Kesey irritatingly 'half-baked.' "

Try as I might, I can't quite picture Stegner in a nurse's uniform and little hat, enforcing order on a group of patients in a psych ward. But there are those who see in the Stegner of the '60s a less than noble figure, one whose striving for largeness couldn't overcome the old angry smallness.

Perhaps there are books to come that will focus on this aspect of the man, knocking him off his pedestal. Perhaps they will attempt to expose Wallace Stegner. But that is not what I'm after.

What *am* I after?

It certainly is not my goal to maintain a false-front image of the man. "Biography cannot reform the truth," Stegner himself wrote in his little orange notebook. When I e-mailed a writer friend of Abbey's early in the research for this project, he wrote back, "I'm not much into hero worship." We are all wary of this, having seen too many of our idols fall. Ours is an age of building up, and pulling down. We overcelebrate and then overexpose.

But there is another use for biography. One that involves, in Stegner's own words, "a search for a usable past." In this use, it is not the subject's toilet training that matters but the ways in which what they achieved and how they lived can be helpful in the life of a reader. Can be, in Samuel Johnson's words, "put to use" in our own lives. The goal here is not to make false heroes, but it is perhaps to look for the better self, the effort as well as the failures. To approach with sympathy not cynicism.

I know that Wallace Stegner the man had fears, flaws, prejudices.

But what I will not believe is that he was unaware of these and that he didn't make an effort to overcome them. Largeness was a lifelong effort, and if he sometimes failed in this effort this did not discount the trying. He never resorted to the artist's usual trick of indulging his own bad behavior, of passing it off in the name of his great art. He adamantly disagreed with the Oscar Wilde statement that the fact that a man is a poisoner has nothing to do with his prose. "It does have something to do with his prose," he wrote. "A poisoner will write poisoner's prose, however beautiful. Even if it has nothing to do with private life, personal morality, or his general ethical character, being a poisoner suggests some flaw somewhere—in the sensibility or humanity or compassion or the largeness of mind—that is going to reflect itself in the prose."

Stegner's life embodied Hawthorne's notion that an ideal artist must be both hard and sensitive, combining an outer toughness and competence with an artistic sensibility. Stegner lived in the world, fighting for the environment (even when this meant sitting in on boring meetings), teaching (even when he'd rather be writing), and caring for family and friends—these were priorities not to be entirely swamped by the attempt to make great art. And he went further, seeing a kind of morality in efficacy, sharing the practical person's belief that there is something *good* about doing a job well. He believed it was possible to be both a great writer and a good human being. Perhaps his stubbornness sometimes got in his own way and perhaps he could be rigid. But he was also a model for those who have come after him, a model that of course even he sometimes fell short of.

My abbey and Stegner books sat stacked on a table, warped by another year of humidity, as summer came around again down in my writing shack. In the weeks around solstice the weather was perfect: breezes blew the glistening saw grass and the birds filled the marsh with song. Soon Hadley and I would be heading west again while Nina worked on another book. We were looking forward to seeing the mountains.

If mine was an adventure in geography, it was just as much an adventure in reading. The type of reading I like best is the kind Montaigne described in an essay called "Of Books": "I seek only the learning that treats of the knowledge of myself and instructs me how to die well and live well." The strange thing is that writers long dead can grow and change and live in the minds of those of us who are still alive. And if you believe as I do that these voices can have an influence on our daily lives, that we take from them and use them during our time on Earth, then you also believe that they are not just models but companions, members of a larger community. For my part, I've always liked the idea of talking to ghosts.

"You need the way lighted," Wendell Berry had said.

At this point I feel like I know what Edward Abbey and Wallace Stegner have to offer me, but that doesn't mean, as Wendell added, that I really know what I get from them. Nor do I know, as a member of the community, exactly what I offer to others. If we are lucky, our reading and influences are like a vast underground root system, and about as easily deciphered.

"He provided me in that moment with a way of thinking about the American West," former secretary of the Interior Bruce Babbitt wrote of Stegner. It is a phrase that has stayed with me, since I know I wouldn't even be able to think of the West, or my home in the East, for that matter, in the same terms and language if Wallace Stegner had not written his books. The beautiful thing is that the same basic set of tools for thinking can extend far beyond the American West. Wendell Berry had said he wanted to take Stegner's ideas and try them out in his own "neck of the woods," and in similar ways many others have transplanted Stegnerian ideas to their own backyards. When I first moved back from the West to Cape Cod, for instance, I transplanted some of my new western tools and used them to think about my new-old region. I considered the sandy soil, the rising sea, the lack of groundwater, the fact that the place I loved was essentially a vacation destination with a seasonal economy. I'm not sure I'd ever thought about the place that way before. The questions I was asking were my own, but the habit and way of asking had been learned somewhere, and I wasn't foolish enough to forget where they had been learned.

It isn't specifics we take from our predecessors, but the spirit and the tools. And each of us uses the old tools in new ways. The same set of tools helps me see how fracking in Utah connects to rising seas and how rising seas connect to western drought and to oil spills in the Gulf of Mexico. In fact, you could make an argument that not just Wallace Stegner's ideas but his habits of thought have never been more relevant than they are today. Making connections has always been the naturalist's job, but it is also, like it or not, the job that has fallen to all modern thinkers and writers in a time when global systems of weather, climate, and migration are being affected by man's

WALLACE STEGNER IN THE 1960S.

actions. Stegner was a master of the old children's game of connecting the dots, and ours is a time for connecting the dots like none other. He handed down to us a way to talk and think about resources and jobs and land, and to consider the larger connections between economics, diverse cultures, geographies, industries, and peoples.

Of course, Stegner never would have claimed to have invented these ideas whole-cloth. Those who lighted his way included DeVoto and Powell, and he leaned on them just as those who have come after have leaned on him. His books helped spread a new vocabulary of the West as a home of aridity, vast spaces, and government subsidization, and his ideas were extended, altered, and complicated by the next generation of alternative western thinkers, turned to the field of law, for instance, by Charles Wilkinson, and toward history by Patricia Limerick, and toward memoir and fiction by William Kittredge, and toward journalism by Marc Reisner, whose book *Cadillac Desert* is a brilliant exposé of the history of dams in the West. Even many of today's western economists look back to Stegner. It is hard to exaggerate the spreading web of this basic construct of ideas, and how much intellectual influence it has had in the West.

It is not ideas that we remember Edward Abbey for. Nor does he share with Stegner the burden of living up to some paragon of moral virtue. He is a man known as much for his faults as his virtues. If ever a writer had feet of clay, here he is. Abbey suffers from both excessive criticism—from those who see him as sexist, racist, xenophobic—and excessive love, from those members of what Luis Urrea called "the Abbeyite Order," those who revere the externals: the flannel shirts, the trucks, the beer-swilling, the monkeywrenching. But while we are swinging between the extremes of love and hate, we might remember that this was a writer who created at least one great book. And here was a man who, for all his flaws, showed through his example what it meant to live a counterlife, a life where the love of wildness really mattered and where one's priorities grew out of that love. He shared with Thoreau the conviction that our society is full of dry rot, and a belief that much of what the world considers good is truly bad. If you really believe this, it is not just foolish but immoral to live in the way that a rotten society tells you to live. And how did society tell you to live? A successful life, a prosperous life, a life of progress, of achievement, of getting bigger. It took a strong person to say, *Hey, wait a minute.* Abbey agreed with Thoreau that there were good lives other than those that most of us call success-ful. Some might see something adolescent in this rebellion against the way things are. But going against and staying against requires a deep bravery, a ballsiness, a commitment.

Finally, there is this: I can't think of a better antidote to our vir-tual age than a strong dose of Edward Abbey. He is a writer who speaks of things that are now in short supply. In an age of security and surveillance, he speaks of independence and freedom. In an age of ever-increasing computerization and industrialization, he speaks of the world and the Earth. In an age of the tame and the virtual, he speaks of the wild and the real. He loved life—this comes right through the page—and he loved the physical world. And he is still alive to us. Take October 5, 1962, for instance, just yesterday it seems, when he wrote in his journal:

> Early morning snow falling in the desert—the bright vast land—coffee and hotcakes on the stove—all around golden silence spangled by bird cries—the feeling of something splen-did about to occur—a setting for visions, pageants, dreams, cavalry battles—Balanced Rock at Arches, snow covered moun-tains beyond me and me squatting on sandstone in the clean chill air, coffee cup in hand, sun blazing down on snow already beginning to melt from juniper, cliffrose, dead pine, pinnacle, ramada—brief bliss.

Is this mere romanticism? Something we have grown out of? Have we no use for this, and no use either for Whitman, Dickinson, and Thoreau? Have we grown past them, too? I don't believe it works that way. Perhaps in other professions we can buy the illusion that things are always getting better, sharper, cleaner—the central illusion of progress. But you cannot believe that in literature. Literature reminds us that, no matter how we would like to think otherwise, the essential human animal has not changed. We are still and always hungry for words that remind us how to live.

We are also hungry, Abbey reminds us, for wilderness. Wilderness is our first home, the laboratory where human beings were created,

EDWARD ABBEY IN THE DESERT IN SOUTHEAST UTAH.

where the human genome was hammered out over millennia, and that essence does not suddenly change in a hundred years because someone invented a car or computer. Our needs are still the same.

The spirit of the fight, the thrill of the physical. If we go in search of Abbey, we find he can still offer us these. But there is something else, too, that makes Abbey relevant today. This is his willingness to tell the truth. It is a handy tool, and a lot more. Readers enjoy the thrill of transgression when he blurts something out about lust, hypocrisy, or the idiots who rankle him.

He makes bluntness a high art. For instance, here is what Abbey wrote to the poet Gary Snyder: "I like your work except for all the Zen bullshit."

But there is a deeper honesty too. A willingness to say exactly what you feel no matter the consequences, to serve the truth even if the truth you serve promises to make you unpopular in your time. The great biographer Walter Jackson Bate wrote that one reason writers need to have recourse to writers from other times is that they help us stand firm against the fickle mores of the time in which we live. Abbey served a larger truth, and wasn't willing to budge an inch to please those who wished his truth was more appealing. It is in this tough, independent way, always insisting that we shouldn't follow him, that he still serves as a model, a teacher.

By all accounts, dying was the bravest thing that Ed Abbey ever did. The first of what would be his multiple death sentences came in the form of a false diagnosis: he was told he had pancreatic cancer and had only a few months to live. His early novels tended to feature men making stands against the modern world, and men dying brave deaths. He vowed to do the same, claiming that he wouldn't succumb to the usual modern end of a long and miserable hospital stay. He stuck to his insistence on dying well through the first long false death, and then again through his longer, more drawn-out decline

from esophageal varices. Before he died he managed to complete
Hayduke Lives!, the sequel to *The Monkey Wrench Gang.* It was written
under a true deadline, mostly to provide for his family, and finished
less than a week before his life ended.

When the real end came he was ready. He vowed not to die in a
hospital and he didn't.

He had been hospitalized for two days already when, according to Doug Peacock: "Finally, he pulled out all the tubes and
announced, with the clearest eyes I have ever seen, that it was time
to go." His wife Clarke, Peacock, Jack Loeffler, and another friend,
Steve Prescott, hustled him out of the hospital and took him into
the hills near Tucson, granting his request to die in the wilderness.
The problem was that once he was out in nature he didn't die, but
recovered. The morning passed and it grew hot and Abbey said he
wanted to go home to die in his writing cabin. Abbey survived the
night and the next day, buoyed by blood taken from the hospital,
blood that his friends used to "top him off." He was surprisingly
upbeat during his last day, but the night was full of pain and cough-
ing fits, fits that only quieted after Peacock injected him with a mix
of Demerol and Compazine. Just before dawn, with his family gathered around him, Abbey's breathing slowed, became deep and gut-
tural, and finally stopped.

For me, Abbey's death reinforces a lesson my own father first
taught me. That death can be one of life's most elemental and visceral experiences. I had the good fortune of being there with my
father, gripping his hand, as his breath slowed and his pulse faded.
If there is one thing that all of Abbey's friends agree on, it is that his
death was a brave one. And as I look ahead to the coming years, I
think that this example might just come in handy.

Stegner's death was not as dramatic as Abbey's. How could it be?
Ironically, while Abbey died at home, Stegner died on the road. He
was in Santa Fe for a reading and was pulling his car out onto a highway on-ramp when he was hit by another car. Mary was with him but

unhurt. "I'm sorry it was my fault," he whispered to her in the hospital, taking responsibility to the end. He was eighty-four years old.

His death saddens me, but what I am really haunted by is what Mary Stegner found when she got home. On his desk in his study was an unfinished to-do list.

I think of that list now and remind myself that there are still many items that have not been checked off.

That, for all of us, there is still much work to do.

ACKNOWLEDGMENTS

The seeds of this book were planted long ago during my years in Colorado, when I first began to study Edward Abbey and Wallace Stegner. It's true that *Desert Solitaire* was already among my books when I landed in the West, but it would take Rob Bleiberg, Ultimate Frisbee teammate, western convert, and roommate, to open up a larger world to me with the books he brought into our house. Meanwhile, at the University of Colorado, Reg Saner showed me, through words and example, how thinking about the land and the humans and other animals who live on it could be transformed into art. A class with Linda Hogan nudged me toward writing about nature and helped deepen my love of birds, and an academic paper on Abbey for Marty Bickman led to an early essay (and accompanying cartoons) about Abbey and Stegner that would eventually find its way, with the help of Betsy Marston, into *High Country News*. For companionship and inspiration during those early years in the West I need to thank my classmates and friends Mark Spitzer, Mark Karger, Karen Auvinen, Jim Campbell, and Heidi Krauth. I also need to thank Heidi's dad, Lee Krauth, whose underlined and annotated copy of *Abbey's Road* I borrowed and still have (sorry, Lee). I could also thank almost every one of my Ultimate teammates in Boulder, who were always pushing me toward adventure, particularly Chris "Captain" Brooks, in whose VW van many of those adventures took place.

Back here in my adopted hometown of Wilmington, North Carolina, where my trip began in the summer of 2012, I had the support of the University of North Carolina Wilmington and my colleagues in the Creative Writing Department. David Webster and Philip Gerard were great early supporters of the project and helped me find the time and funding to make it happen. Bekki Lee, Clyde Edgerton, Mike White, and the rest of the writers who populate our hallway were supportive and inspiring, and Megan Hubbard was, as usual, my go-to person for all things practical. My long trip west was preceded by a few shorter journeys, one of them to Tucson, where I relied on Alison Hawthorne Deming, Simmons Bunting, and Chris Cokinos to help me learn the lay of the land. Also Richard Shelton, who has always been a supporter of my work and who talked to me about his decision to hire Ed Abbey at the University of Arizona. Curator Roger Meyers and the other members of the staff at the University of Arizona Special Collections helped me find my way around Abbey's papers.

In Pennsylvania, I was helped by Ian Marshall and Bob Burkholder, and, thanks to them and to Mark McLaughlin, the director of the Shaver's Creek Environmental Center, I was allowed to spend a week in a cabin in the woods. As for Jim Cahalan, author of *Edward Abbey: A Life*, both the text and my notes must make it clear how indispensable and generous he was during this entire project. If you have enjoyed my book and find yourself still hungry for more Abbey, I enthusiastically recommend that you read his.

Perhaps the most important thank-yous, apart from the final ones, need to go to Page, Lynn, and Allison Stegner, who let me visit their home in Greensboro, Vermont, and freely shared their insights about their famous relative, and who later read an earlier draft of the book. They were the definition of generous. Also thanks to Jen Sahn of *Orion* magazine, who has always supported me in my work and who accompanied me on a walk to the top of Barr Hill above the Stegners' home, the setting of the last scene in *Crossing to Safety*.

Before I headed west I received the e-mail—my "koan"—from Terry Tempest Williams that kicked off the trip. Once I pushed off, my first stop was in Port Royal, Kentucky, at the home of Wendell and Tanya Berry, who graciously made time to talk to me, with Wendell later reading some of the early pages. Thanks also to Erik Reece in Lexington for giving me a couch to sleep on and for introducing me to the inimitable Ed McClanahan, who shared his thoughts on Abbey and Stegner.

My next stop was in St. Louis, where I stayed at the home of Tom Beattie, who took me down to the Missouri River, bought me drinks, and set me up with contacts for the rest of my trip out west. In Denver, I stayed with Randy Ricks, who has always been a great friend and a big supporter of my work, and in Paonia I spent two nights in the cabin of Adam Petry, writer, scientist, former student, present friend. During my time in that delightful mountain town, I also attended a party at the home of the brilliant environmental writer Michelle Nijhuis, and it was there that Cally Carswell, a contributing editor at *High Country News*, pointed me toward Vernal, Utah.

In Moab, Andy Nettell of Back of Beyond Books took time out to speak to me about his encounters with Abbey, and Ken Sleight invited me up to his bunker of an office, where we picked up a conversation from four years before. That earlier trip to Ken's Pack Creek was made possible by Susan Zakin and made more fun by Dave Smith, who let me try to keep up with him on the Slickrock trail. During that trip, Jane Sleight was a generous hostess, cooking us dinner and refereeing as Ken, Susan, and I yelled at the TV during the first Sarah Palin–Joe Biden debate. During my more recent trip to Pack Creek, Bob and Cady Aspinwall were kind enough to show me the small cabin where Abbey wrote.

My thinking about the economies of western towns owes much to Thomas Michael Power, a professor in the economics department at the University of Montana, and to Ben Alexander of Headwaters Economics, who was always ready to answer my questions. I also need to thank Dave Earley, Liz Thomas of the Southern Utah Wilderness Alliance, and Bill Hedden, executive director of the Grand Canyon Trust, all of whom I interviewed on my earlier trip.

In Vernal, Utah, I relied on the guidance of legendary river runner and provocateur Herm Hoops. Bruce and Jane Gordon of EcoFlight, a nonprofit organization that sponsors flights all over the western landscape, helped me see with my own eyes what all that drilling was doing to the land, and during our flight, Ray Bloxham and Steve Bloch of the Southern Utah Wilderness Alliance provided commentary as I took notes. In addition, Bloxham and Bloch were extremely helpful in the months after our flight, and I owe them many thanks for allowing me to pester them with e-mails. The filmmaker John McChesney also added insightful comments during the flight.

I need to pause here and thank the writer and editor George Black for putting me in touch with the Gordons and EcoFlight, and for six years ago first nudging me toward and then guiding me into what was then the unfamiliar world of environmental journalism. If not for George and the magazine he edited, *OnEarth*, I would not have been in Vernal in the first place, and I owe him and his colleagues at *OnEarth*, Scott Dodd and Douglas Barasch, a world of thanks.

From Vernal I traveled to Salt Lake City, where Stephen Trimble, who served as the 2008–2009 Wallace Stegner Centennial Fellow at the University of Utah, took time out to talk and to bring me up to the cemetery where Wallace's brother and parents are buried. He also reminded me of the key scenes in Stegner's novel *Recapitulation*, scenes that provide a structure for the Salt Lake chapter. I am equally indebted to Ken Sanders of Ken Sanders Rare Books, who regaled me with stories of Abbey and Stegner, providing some of the smartest and sharpest commentary I heard during my travels. From Salt Lake I pushed off to points south, eventually stopping at the Santa Fe airport to pick up my old traveling companion and friend, Mark Honerkamp, who now has taken to describing himself as a "professional literary sidekick." Together we drove to Jack Loeffler's home in the hills outside Santa Fe. Jack made us feel as if we were at home and treated us like old friends, generously sitting down for a taped conversation that lasted over two hours.

Next I headed to the San Juan River, where we were in the more than capable hands of Kristen McKinnon and Wild River Expeditions, which, for my money (or in this case, thanks to Kristen, nonmoney) is the best rafting company in the West. Many thanks to Greg Lameman and all the other guides. I am also thankful to Luis Urrea, whose musings about Ed Abbey I reread on the trip and who helped me think about what we might call, perhaps too politely, Abbey's "warts."

Thanks to Jane Quimby in Grand Junction for her honesty and insights. And thanks to Tim DeChristopher, whom I interviewed in the fall of 2013 in Cambridge, Massachusetts, where he was attending Harvard Divinity School after his release from prison.

From Grand Junction I headed to Denver and then to Fort Collins, where Todd Simmons of Wolverine Farm Bookstore and Publishing took time to talk with me about Abbey and his power to convert. Many thanks are owed to Emily Hammond, Steven Schwartz, and Elena Schwartz for their great generosity in hosting my daughter, Hadley, and me, giving us a tour of the fire damage, offering insights into Abbey's first term teaching, and finally slipping me the envelope with a hundred bucks in it to keep us going. That money helped us make it all the way to Montana, where Doug and Andrea Peacock generously gave of their time and their trailer. I had always regarded Doug as an environmental hero but was not aware that he is also, no matter his wild reputation, a very nice guy. And thanks to David Quammen for putting me in touch with him. After we left the Peacocks we spent two nights at the beautiful river home of Karen and Scott Amero, who, along with their sons, Xander and Jake, treated us like visiting royalty. From there it was north into Alberta and Saskatchewan, where thanks are due to Wendy at Riverside Motel in Eastend and Bryson LaBoissiere, for her insights into the Stegner family.

It was a long way home from there, and here I must give my

heartfelt thanks to my intrepid traveling companion Hadley Gessner and to Joss Wheedon, whose CD of the Buffy musical episode helped us make it home. We stopped in Minnesota for dinner with Patrick Thomas, a good friend whose initial enthusiasm for the project is part of why it came to life in the first place. Our next stop was in Wisconsin, where Jim and Elizabeth Campbell and their beautiful girls, Aiden, Rachel, and Willa, gave us a place to rest, play, eat, and drink before pushing on for the next thousand miles.

The trip over, it was time to write the book. Two students aided me with the logistics of bookmaking, Carson Vaughan in the early stages and Liz Granger, who later helped with permissions. Doug Diesenhaus was, as usual, invaluable, this time under tough circumstances as no one seemed to be replying to our queries for photographic permissions. My colleague Emily Smith, the publisher of Lookout Books, helped by chiming in on design choices. Then, in the late stages of pulling the book together I received invaluable help from Eric Temple, Jim Hepworth, and Dick Kirkpatrick. Clarke Abbey also came through in a big way, granting permission for the use of quotes and photos and waiving any fee.

Thanks to my agent Russ Galen for swinging the deal. At Norton, Remy Cawley and Anna Mageras brilliantly shepherded the book toward reality. Meanwhile Rachelle Mandik as a copyeditor was a dream come true—with a great ear and keen eye.

As for my editor, Alane Salierno Mason, this wouldn't have been close to the book it has become without her. She pushed me in some ways that I didn't always want to go at first, but that were always in the direction of expansion, that is toward what Stegner called "largeness," and which were, I can see now, just what I, and the book, needed. My gratitude is deep to her for having the initial vision to see what the book could be and for nudging me out of my comfort zone and toward something more.

Finally, as always, it comes back to family. My mother Barbara and sister Heidi have been forever supporters, and my second parents, George and Carol de Gramont, never waver in their interest and seeming pleasure in my work. They also happened to have produced a daughter who is my best friend in the world and who, as my fellow writer, keeps me from getting lost in the hall of mirrors that the writing life can become. Which means once again that my final and deepest thanks go to my wife, Nina de Gramont.

This book, as I said in the text, was an adventure in reading. The main task was reacquainting myself with the words that Wallace Stegner and Edward Abbey put on the page, to try to read all, or almost all, that they had written, and to see if those words still held the power to unlock potentials and energies in myself that they had twenty years before. While I admit that I grumbled occasionally about rereading some of Abbey's fiction and was completely stymied by Stegner's *Discovery! The Search for Arabian Oil*, I am happy to report that for the most part the experience was not just pleasurable but stirring. Later, studying Stegner's papers in the special collections room at the University of Utah, I came across a small journal of his that held these words about writing biography: "If one has known his biographee personally, he is lucky. If he has to get him from reading, he has an act of imagination to perform—he has to bring paper to life."

As I suggest in the text, both men have been mummified by their reputations, almost to the point where we can imagine tiny versions of the two sitting on our shoulders, giving conflicting advice on most matters not environmental. But if Abbey's stereotyped role was as the devil, he was a devil who inspired emulation that often danced close to pure hero worship, and that emulation extended not just to people's lives but to the pages many young writers wrote as they tried on the Wild Ed style. While this sometimes made it hard for me to cut through to the actual man, I insist, as I do in the book, that while hero worship might be a little embarrassing it is not all bad.

In some ways it is, if we clean it up and call it "finding a model," at the heart of much of biography's appeal. Clearly there is something about Abbey's words that strikes a chord, and that makes readers see new possibilities, in much the way Thoreau's sentences did in *Walden*.

Since I did not define the book as pure biography but as a hybrid animal—part dueling biography, part travel narrative, part meditation, part criticism, part nature writing—I can admit more freely than most biographers of my reliance on the biographies that came before, which I often read alongside the authors' works, a happy combination that sparked many ideas. These books included, among others, James M. Cahalan's *Edward Abbey: A Life*, Jackson J. Benson's *Wallace Stegner: His Life and Work*, and Philip L. Fradkin's *Wallace Stegner and the American West*. Also vital were Jack Loeffler's *Adventures with Ed: A Portrait of Abbey* and all of Doug Peacock's work, most relevantly *Walking It Off: A Veteran's Chronicle of War and Wilderness*, as well as Richard W. Etulain's wonderful interviews in *Conversations with Wallace Stegner on Western History and Literature*.

But while the book was not a biography per se, I was determined to do a biographer's work. In the late spring of 2012 I took a series of trips that started to help me see Stegner and Abbey more fully. The first of these trips was in May to Tucson, Arizona, where Abbey had lived on and off and where the University of Arizona and curator Roger Myers housed the Edward Abbey papers in their special collections. The experience of spending days with Abbey's journal notes and drafts and letters let me see just how smart and how deadly serious a writer Abbey was. Then I took the notes, or photocopies of them, on the road, down into Havasu Canyon for a camping trip. It was the right way, and the right place, to immerse myself in all things Abbey, and the cellulitus I contracted in the canyon from a cut on my leg gave the right air of intensity to reading the young Abbey's often melancholic sentences. Poring over the words in my tent, my mind slightly warped by fever, I saw that this man who often celebrated animal moments free of thought was in fact a nearly constant thinker. In those journals I heard the voice that later found its way into the books.

The next journey was in June to Pennsylvania, to the Shaver's Creek Environmental Center in Petersburg, in the hills outside of State College. Through the generosity of the center's director, Mark McLaughlin, and professors Ian Marshall and Bob Burkholder, I was allowed to spend a week in a cabin in the woods around Shaver's Creek. The dilapidated stone walls and thick woods helped me get a sense of the landscape Abbey grew up in, a sense that was crystallized at the week's end when I drove an hour west to Home, Pennsylvania, and was given a tour of young Abbey's stomping grounds by his biographer, the generous James Cahalan. Jim brought me to the homesite that Abbey called the Old Lonesome Briar Patch, and then on to the cemetery and to the other homes where various Abbeys had lived at various times. Finally, he invited me back to his house and, putting the lie to the cliché of scholarly competition, shared Abbey photos and stories as well as tips for Abbey contacts.

Only a week after my Pennsylvania trip I was scheduled to teach at the Wildbranch Writing Workshop, sponsored by *Orion* magazine, in Craftsbury Common, Vermont. By good luck the conference was only ten minutes down the road from the town of Greensboro, where Wallace and Mary Stegner had spent their summers for over four decades, and where their only child, Page, and his wife, Lynn, still had a summer home. After a few e-mails, the Stegners invited me to visit, but when I showed up one evening, a six-pack of beer in hand, I had no idea what to expect. What I got was a combination of graciousness and good humor, shot through with a dose of honesty about their famous relative who, lo and behold, turned out to be a flawed human being like the rest of us. But this honesty was not of the "tear down" variety, and it gave me a larger sense of what the man (whom I couldn't quite bring myself to call Wally despite their insistence) was battling against in his efforts to attain "largeness." We spent three hours talking that night, joined by their daughter, Allison, and the next day they invited me back, showing me the house where Wallace and Mary had lived and the small cabin that was Wallace's study, and pointing the way to the path up to the mountaintop overlook where *Crossing to Safety* ended, a path that I hiked up with a friend later that day.

I consciously held off on some of my research for the book until the larger trip itself. My working method over the last seven years or so has been to throw myself into situations, to not overplan my itineraries and let coincidence and chance have their way. I knew I wanted to wait to read certain things until I got to the places that inspired them, and so, for instance, I read the letters that George Stegner wrote his son, begging for money before he committed suicide, in Salt Lake City, only a couple of miles from where that fateful event occurred. Though I will mostly mention books and people in the notes that follow, spending time in the places themselves meant just as much, and helped me in perhaps unnameable ways in my job of bringing paper to life.

CHAPTER 1: GOING WEST

The information on the population increase in the West came from the 2010 census.

Edward Abbey more than once joked about being called Edward Albee, including a reference to a letter written to him under that name in the introduction to his essay collection *Abbey's Road*. People I talked to made this same mistake at least a half dozen times, and though the number of times "Stevens" replaced "Stegner" was fewer than that, it was once made, remarkably, by a curator at a California mine-turned-museum. In general, it continues to astound me how two writers so well known in the West can be so relatively obscure in the East, as if we were talking about the literatures of two different countries, not just two different regions.

Wallace Stegner's ideas about aridity and the need for community in the West permeate almost all of his nonfiction and a good deal of his fiction, and my synthesis of those ideas is drawn from many different books and interviews. But if you want to get a sense of his big-picture view of the West, the later essay collections, notably *Where the Bluebird Sings to the Lemonade Springs: Living and Writing in the West*, are a good place to start. Reading both the Benson and Fradkin biographies was helpful in laying out a basic timeline of Stegner's life, and the author's own work, often autobiographical, helped too, though, as Stegner himself cautioned, one shouldn't read too much fact into the fiction. Luckily Stegner wrote a short and, for me, indispensable autobiography, never published, which is housed in the Special Collections Department of the J. Willard Marriott Library at the University of Utah.

Abbey's comments about New York City come from his journal. I found many of the journal passages in the Abbey papers in the Special Collections Library at the University of Arizona, but others were taken directly from *Confessions of a Barbarian*, a great collection of selections from Abbey's journals edited by David Petersen.

There are many records of Abbey's influence on monkeywrenching, but the best is Susan Zakin's *Coyotes and Town Dogs: Earth First! and the Environmental Movement*, which describes the birth, rise, and fall of Earth First! Wendell Berry's essay "A Few Words in Favor of Edward Abbey," in his collection *What Are People For?*, is must-reading for those who want to understand Abbey's appeal. As is Abbey's own "A Walk in the Desert Hills" in *Beyond the Wall*, which is where I pulled the "cocky as a rooster" quotation from. This essay provides a fine example of the Abbey style, as we follow him out into the wilderness, and up and down with his moods, from somber to raucous to desperate to joyful, while he spends a week hiking through the desert. If you haven't read Abbey before, it's a fine place to start.

David Quammen's eulogy, "Bagpipes for Ed," appeared in the April

1989 issue of *Outside* magazine and gives a real sense of Abbey's power
to inspire and convert.

The letter in which Stegner reflects on Abbey's time at Stanford
was mailed to Eric Temple, in response to an interview request. Here
is the letter in its entirety:

Los Altos Hills, CA 94022
Feb. 23, 1992

Dear Mr. Temple:

*I'm afraid an interview, at least for the next while, is out. I seem
to be both overloaded with obligations and under-supplied with
health. But I can tell you all I know about Ed Abbey in a half page
letter.*

*He came here as a Stegner Fellow sometime in the late fifties or
early sixties (before the publication of DESERT SOLITAIRE, in
any case), and was here for two quarters before he got lonesome for
the desert and went back. He tried to get me to continue his fellowship for the quarter he missed, but I couldn't do that. While he was
here he was working on what later became The Monkey Wrench
Gang, though it didn't then have a title, as far as I remember. He
was quiet, reclusive, clean shaven, watchful. He lived over in Half
Moon Bay, so that we saw him only at class time twice a week.
He attended faithfully, made great sense in class, had all his later
attitudes well in place but did not express them quite so forcibly as
he did later. The only other person in the workshop who was anywhere near in his class as a writer was Don Moser, now the editor
of SMITHSONIAN MAGAZINE. I don't think he was particularly happy at Stanford—indeed he barely broke the surface—and
the reason was the reason for his later great success: he yearned to
be back in the sagebrush and not hanging around in classrooms. I
respected him greatly, both for his environmental views and for his
often manic writing ability, and I think he respected me; but the*

circumstances were not the kind that permitted the growth of real acquaintance.

One thing he did more responsibly than almost any Fellow I remember. We had a practice then of having the current Fellows act as preliminary readers on the applications of people wanting to come the next year. Among the manuscripts that he got to read was one by Ken Kesey, then still at Oregon. The manuscript was a football novel all about homosexual quarterbacks and corrupt coaches. Ed's comment (we asked only for a rating: Good, possible, or impossible) was one sentence: "Football has found its James Jones."

And that's about all I know. I never saw Ed Abbey after he left here, though I read his books with pleasure and we had some correspondence, reviewed each other, wrote blurbs for each other's books. I couldn't attend his funeral service in Moab; all I could do was send a letter that Wendell Berry read for me at the "ceremony."

I hope this helps a comma's worth. And I'm sorry I'm not up to an interview.

Sincerely,
Wallace Stegner

The "ideology of a cancer cell" quote comes from Abbey's essay "Arizona: How Big Is Big Enough?" in *One Life at a Time, Please.*

CHAPTER 2: FIRST SIGHT

Abbey's comparison of seeing the West to being like seeing a naked girl for the first time is on page 2 of "Hallelujah on the Bum" in the essay collection *The Journey Home.* The poetic quotations from his first hitchhiking trip west also come from this essay.

As I mentioned above, James Cahalan was more than generous during my trip to Home, Pennsylvania, showing me the cemetery where earlier Abbeys were buried and the Washington Presbyterian Church that Mildred Abbey "ran."

The description of Stegner's childhood and first return west is taken from several sources, including interviews (Etulain's *Conversations with Wallace Stegner on Western History and Literature* was a big help) and his own unpublished autobiography, from which the "savage innocence" sentences were lifted. The description of the fictional return of Bruce Mason occurs at the conclusion of the major novel of Stegner's early years, *The Big Rock Candy Mountain*. The comments on scale and color in the West come from "Thoughts in a Dry Land" in Stegner's *Where the Bluebird Sings to the Lemonade Springs*.

Maybe nobody better exemplifies the myth of the effete easterner who goes west and is transformed than our twenty-sixth president, and I took a brief break from Stegner and Abbey to reread *The Rise of Theodore Roosevelt* and *Theodore Rex* by Edmund Morris. I first wrote of my own move west after an operation for testicular cancer in a book called *Under the Devil's Thumb*. I was twenty-eight years old when I first read *Desert Solitaire* in Lassen Volcanic National Park in 1988, the same year that Abbey died.

Nobody does a better job of smashing apart western myths, and revealing the sheer silliness of ideas like "rain follows the plow," than Stegner himself in *Beyond the Hundredth Meridian*, which seems to me a must-read for westerners. But Bernard DeVoto's words are equally important and the articles he wrote from the 1930s through the '50s, when he was fighting against the boomers as the "Lone Ranger," remain relevant and still make for bracing reading. We are lucky they have been collected in a book called *The Western Paradox: A Conservation Reader*, edited by Douglas Brinkley and Patricia Nelson Limerick, which is where most of the DeVoto quotes in this chapter are taken from.

I write regularly for *OnEarth* and OnEarth.org, the publications of the Natural Resources Defense Council, and for my updating of the big-picture ideas about the aridity of the West I relied on the up-to-the-minute reporting of my colleagues at that magazine, particularly that of Michael Kodas on the western fires. For a larger synthesis of current and coming climate changes I looked toward Fred Pearce's *When the Rivers Run Dry: Water—the Defining Crisis of the Twenty-First Century* and, especially, *A Great Aridness: Climate Change and the Future of the American Southwest* by William deBuys, a writer who calmly but convincingly presents a terrifying picture of the current and future West.

Reg Saner's nonfiction books, which record his explorations of southwestern history and nature, and of course his ruminations on these, include *The Four-Cornered Falcon: Essays on the Interior West and the Natural Scene, Reaching Keet Seel: Ruin's Echo & the Anasazi,* and *The Dawn Collector: On My Way to the Natural World.*

CHAPTER 3: LIGHTING THE WAY

You can hear Wallace Stegner speak on this interview from the old TV show *Day at Night*: http://www.youtube.com/watch?v=CFj2EID6u4w.

The primary source for the first part of this chapter is a long conversation I had with Wendell and Tanya Berry at their dining-room table at their home in Port Royal, Kentucky. With Wendell's permission, I taped the conversation, but due to the needs of the book only a small part of it made it into the pages. "I loved him but never felt equal to him," Wendell said of his old teacher. We talked for a long while about Ken Kesey and his relationship with Wallace Stegner. Wendell told a story about a poetry reading he had given at Stanford where one of the poems he read was about Kesey. Afterward Stegner said of the poems, "I liked them all except one."

My description of the myth of Berry's return to Kentucky is based on the essays "The Long-Legged House" and "A Native Hill" in his book *The Long-Legged House.*

Wendell Berry's notion of "lighting the way" corresponded almost exactly to the ideas that my former teacher Walter Jackson Bate put forth in his biographies and in his book *The Burden of the Past and the English Poet.* Bate's ideas, it should be noted, permeate the whole project, and it was his books and lectures that made me first love the art of biography, and come to see that part of its greatness was that we could apply it to our own lives.

My sense of what Stegner was like during the late 1950s and early '60s was greatly enhanced by another interview, in Lexington, Kentucky, with Ed McClanahan, Stegner's old officemate at Stanford. McClanahan was generous, having to nearly shout stories into my tape recorder over the din of a loud bar, and inviting me over to see his home the next day. The meeting was facilitated by the writer Erik Reece.

For a great discussion of the relationship of Stegner and Kesey, their similarities and differences, and the way they both chafed at and influenced each other, take a look at pages 199–212 of Mark McGurl's *The Program Era: Postwar Fiction and the Rise of Creative Writing.* Interestingly, both men would be criticized for the creation of domineering fictional women, Kesey's Nurse Ratched and Stegner's Charity of *Crossing to Safety.* When I brought up the latter character with Page and Lynn Stegner, they suggested that Peg Gray, the model for Charity, was actually much *more* domineering than the character she inspired, insisting, for instance, that Mary be called "Molly" around her because she liked the name. Oddly, the name stuck, at least in the Gray family circle.

The quote from Reg Saner about geological time is taken from the essay "Desert River/Different River" in *The Dawn Collector.* The paragraphs on beetles in the West come from several sources, including the work of Jeffrey Lockwood at the University of Wyoming, *Empire of the Beetle: How Human Folly and a Tiny Bug Are Killing North America's Great Forests* by Andrew Nikiforuk, and deBuy's *A Great Aridness.*

The summary of the fight to save Dinosaur came from several sources, including Stegner's autobiography and "A Capsule History of Conservation" in *Where the Bluebird Sings to the Lemonade Springs.*

Terry Tempest Williams's koan came to me in an e-mail, which reads: "I loved both these men. I still feel their hands on my shoulder, wondering what they would be saying, writing, now. In so many ways, Ed was the conservative, Wally, forever the radical."

The story about Ken Kesey, Dolly Kringle, and the apple comes from my interview with Ed McClanahan.

CHAPTER 4: PARADISE, LOST AND FOUND

For the geology of the Utah canyons I was greatly helped by a little book I bought twenty years ago, *Canyonlands Country: Geology of Canyonlands and Arches National Parks* by Donald L. Baars. *Brave New West: Morphing Moab at the Speed of Greed* by Jim Stiles does a fine job of portraying, in cartoon form, the madness of Moab.

Robinson Jeffers was clearly a writer whom Abbey admired, and the two shared an uncompromising attitude and a gift for bluntness. The quotation about the spoiler is from the poem "Carmel Point" in *Selected Poems*.

The student who asked Abbey if he wrote every day was the writer Steven Schwartz, who took Abbey's very first class at the University of Arizona.

Abbey's journals were my main source for his state of mind as a young writer. The movie version of *The Brave Cowboy* is called *Lonely Are the Brave* and stars not just Kirk Douglas but Carroll O'Connor and Walter Matthau.

Much of the research on economics and off-road vehicles was done originally for an article for *OnEarth* magazine called "Loving the West to Death," published on December 1, 2008. For that article I read all of the books of Thomas Michael Power, a professor of economics at the Economics Department at the University of Montana. I also corresponded with Ben Alexander of Headwaters Economics and interviewed Liz Thomas of the Southern Utah Wilderness Alliance and Bill Hedden, executive director of the Grand Canyon Trust.

During that earlier trip I also interviewed Ken Sleight and had dinner with Ken and his wife, Jane Sleight. Four years later I sat down with Ken again, and he was as generous and forthcoming as ever.

Most of my thoughts on *Desert Solitaire* come directly from my own rereadings of that strange, often-unwieldy but wonder-filled book. But some of the ideas were sparked by reading *Henry David Thoreau* by Joseph Wood Krutch, a book that I initially encountered in the back of a Toyota Tercel during the return trip of my first drive west in 1983. Krutch himself was "reborn" as a westerner when he moved from New York City, where he was a professor at Columbia, to Arizona, where his work turned away from biography and toward natural history. I remember Walter Jackson Bate saying that Krutch had been a fine scholar and biographer until he went west and began writing about "cacti." One of the last interviews that Krutch gave was to Edward Abbey, who would eventually write it up as "Mr. Krutch," which he would publish both in magazine form and in *One Life at a Time, Please.*

CHAPTER 5: OIL AND WATER

Government records provided many of the stats on Vernal, with the Utah Department of Health providing the statistics behind my statements about the incidence of rape. For descriptions of the boom I relied on several articles in the *Salt Lake Tribune, High Country News,* and on interviews in town. Steve Bloch of the Southern Utah Wilderness Alliance (SUWA) patiently explained to me the various ways that towns benefit from the taxes and other less-direct monies from the oil companies. For the economic breakdown of boom towns I turned to Ben Alexander of Headwaters Economics. Alexander also pointed me toward Headwaters's recent "West Is Best: Protected Lands Promote Jobs and Higher Incomes" report on how protected public lands positively affect a town's economy: http://headwaterseconomics.org/land/west-is-best-value-of-public-lands.

In Vernal I interviewed George Burnett of "I ♥ Drilling" fame and the river runner and provocateur Herm Hoops. I also recorded my conversations with dozens of other people in town, including an oil worker named Rich who insisted that I not use his last name but took me out on the first ORV ride of my life outside of town.

In several interviews, Rob Bleiberg, executive director of the Mesa Land Trust, described the impact of booms and busts on his adopted hometown of Grand Junction. I learned about the new computers in the classrooms of Pinedale, Wyoming, from "Gold from the Gas Fields," an article by Ray Ring that appeared in the November 28, 2005, edition of *High Country News*.

Bruce Gordon of EcoFlight, a nonprofit organization that sponsors flights all over the western landscape, helped me see with my own eyes what all that drilling was doing to the land. During our flight, Ray Bloxham and Steve Bloch of the Southern Utah Wilderness Alliance provided commentary as I took notes.

CHAPTER 6: MAKING A NAME

Terry Tempest Williams's *Refuge: An Unnatural History of Family and Place* was my literary introduction to Salt Lake City and its environs, and I read that beautiful book again before writing the material for this chapter.

I am also indebted to Stephen Trimble, who served as the 2008–09 Wallace Stegner Centennial Fellow at the University of Utah, for taking time out to talk to me and giving me the lay of the land in Salt Lake City. Stephen reminded me of the key scenes in Stegner's novel *Recapitulation*, which provide a structure for this chapter. I am equally indebted to Ken Sanders for taking the time to talk about Abbey and Stegner, and for teaching me how to do a great Abbey impression (the trick is to not move your lips).

Here is the complete text of the letter that Wallace Stegner wrote and that Wendell Berry read at Abbey's wake:

> *I regret that I am unable to be in Moab on the day when Ed Abbey's friends gather to see him off. The best I can do is send a hail and farewell note and ask Wendell Berry to deliver it.*
>
> *By an unfortunate alignment of chance and circumstance, I never saw Ed in the flesh after he left Stanford where, for a while, he was my student. But I have never been far from the sound of his name and never for a moment out of reach of the waves he caused and the influence he radiated.*
>
> *He squatted in country that I had known and loved since my boyhood, and made it singularly and importantly his own, as Robert Frost made New England his own, and Muir and Ansel Adams made Yosemite [theirs].*
>
> *His books were burrs under the saddle blanket of complacency. His urgency was a lever under inertia. He had the zeal of a true believer and a stinger like a scorpion when defending the natural, free, unmanaged, unmanhandled wilderness of his chosen country. He was a red hot moment in the conscience of the country. And I suspect that the half-life of his intransigence will turn out to be comparable to that of uranium.*
>
> *We will miss him. The comfort is that when we need him, he will still be there.*
>
> Signed, Wallace Stegner

Stegner wrote the line about "a neat and workmanlike job of murder and suicide" on page 124 of his unpublished autobiography. Page Stegner's comments about the lack of skeletons in the family closet and his father speaking the "King's English" occurred during a taped interview in Greensboro, Vermont.

The letter from Wallace to Page Stegner in 1979 is on pages 213–14 of *The Selected Letters of Wallace Stegner*, edited by Page Stegner.

I found the letters from George Stegner to his son in the Special Collections Department of the J. Willard Marriott Library at the University of Utah, curated by Liz Rogers. The same collection contains young Allison Stegner's book report and Wallace Stegner's small notebook, which I quote from extensively at chapter's end.

CHAPTER 7: HOW TO FIGHT

Marc Reisner's *Cadillac Desert: The American West and Its Disappearing Water* is a classic of environmental writing. It was revised in 1993 and still makes for bracing reading, the best overview of the damming of the West. James Lawrence Powell's *Dead Pool: Lake Powell, Global Warming, and the Future of Water in the West* and Fred Pearce's *When the Rivers Run Dry* helped me understand how climate change will worsen the already perilous water situation.

Ed Abbey tells us that Powell's *The Exploration of the Colorado River and Its Canyons* is his favorite western book in *The Journey Home*, in the essay "Down the River with Major Powell." The sign warning boaters to leave the river is described in the "Down the River" chapter of *Desert Solitaire*. "Canyonlands did have a heart," "grottoes," "decomposing water-skiers," and "wheelchair ethos" are quotations from "The Damnation of a Canyon" in *Beyond the Wall*. "Fueled in equal parts by anger and love" is from the preface of *The Best of Edward Abbey*. "Bashing their way" is from the short essay "Eco-Defense," in *One Life at a Time, Please*.

The story of how Wallace Stegner began to write environmental articles comes from his unpublished autobiography. Stegner's "A Capsule History of Conservation" describes the same period in a less personal manner. The fascinating exchange of letters between Gary Snyder and Wallace Stegner can be found in the Special Collections Department of the J. Willard Marriott Library at the University of Utah.

Abbey's description of the "small and imperfect sampling" of the remnant Glen Canyon comes from "The Damnation of a Canyon" in *Beyond the Wall*. Once again Reisner's *Cadillac Desert*, Fred Pearce's *When the Rivers Run Dry*, and deBuys's *A Great Aridness* proved invaluable in giving me a big-picture sense of the water crisis in the West. This was supplemented by regular reading of *High Country News*, which consistently puts out the West's best eco-journalism.

The "I grew up in a cowboy culture" quotation also comes from Stegner's letter to Gary Snyder. The description of my meeting with Jack Loeffler is of necessity condensed. He sat down for a taped conversation that lasted more than two hours. The quoted Abbey phrase—"democracy taken seriously"—comes from "Theory of Anarchy" in *One Life at a Time, Please*.

CHAPTER 8: DOWN THE RIVER WITH ED AND WALLY

Abbey's line about "sitting out back on my 33,000 acre terrace" comes from *Desert Solitaire*. Stegner's sentence about "the primary unity of the West is the shortage of water" comes from "Thoughts in a Dry Land" in *Where the Bluebird Sings to the Lemonade Springs*.

Most of the quotations spoken by people in this book were taped, but in this chapter, with water all around, I resorted instead to scribbling down what I heard in my journal as soon as I could. This is also the only chapter where I have chosen to replace a person's real name with a fictitious one. I did not think it fair for "Ralph," lead guide on his very first trip, to be singled out, but on the other hand, it was important to include his story to get across the tension between him and Jordan, and, to a lesser extent, him and me. I'm sure that Ralph has already developed into a fine guide, with that amazing river runner's combination of easy-goingness and the toughness to shoulder life-or-death responsibility, but beginning is always hard.

The many quotations from the story of how Abbey almost died come from the "Havasu" chapter of *Desert Solitaire*, which I think is one of that book's high points. I hope that the field notes from my own trip into the canyon enhance my descriptions of the place.

The controversial essay "Immigration and Liberal Taboos" appears in the essay collection *One Life at a Time, Please*. Luis Urrea's essay in response is in the collection of pieces about Abbey, *Resist Much, Obey Little: Remembering Ed Abbey*, edited by James R. Hepworth and Gregory McNamee. Wendell Berry wrestles with the topic, too, in "A Few Words in Favor of Edward Abbey," in his collection *What Are People For?*

Though Abbey is more of a lightning rod for criticism, Stegner has not escape unscathed. Perhaps the most well-known example is *Why I Can't Read Wallace Stegner and Other Essays: A Tribal Voice* by Elizabeth Cook-Lynn, a Native American feminist intellectual. While it is easy enough to see how Stegner could be painted as patriarchal or even colonial, many of his ideas about cooperation and knowledge of place—and his holding up the example of how native people interacted with the land—can just as easily be taken in the opposite direction. I mention Patricia Nelson Limerick, who in her work, and especially in her great book *The Legacy of Conquest*, seems influenced in this more positive way.

CHAPTER 9: THE DEATH AND LIFE OF MONKEYWRENCHING

The majority of the material in this chapter comes from a taped interview on July 31, 2012, with Jane Quimby, who was an FBI agent in the Grand Junction, Colorado, office for twenty-five years.

It is supplemented by a taped interview with Tim DeChristopher that I conducted on September 29, 2013, in Cambridge, Massachusetts, where Tim was attending Harvard Divinity School after being released from prison. I also draw from my aforementioned interviews with Page Stegner.

Copies of Edward Abbey's FBI files can be found in the special collections at the University of Arizona.

CHAPTER 10: PROPERLY WILD

The letters from Abbey's sons, Josh and Aaron, are in the special collections of Abbey's papers at the University of Arizona.

The quotations from Page Stegner came from our interviews in Greensboro, Vermont, in June 2012.

The quotations about Astrid and Joe and Ruth Allston all come from Stegner's *The Spectator Bird*.

Emily Hammond gave me a long guided tour of the fire damage in the hills above Fort Collins, and her husband, Steven Schwartz, sat down for a taped interview about his time in Abbey's first graduate class. Some of Abbey's syllabi for his writing classes are in the special collections at the University of Arizona.

A *New York Times* article, "Experts See New Normal as a Hotter, Drier West Faces More Huge Fires" by Felicity Barringer and Kenneth Chang, not only helped me organize my thoughts on fires but pointed me toward the work of two University of Arizona professors, Gregg Garfin and Stephen J. Pyne.

The friend from whom I learned about pronghorns was the writer and eco-critic Michael Branch, who wrote a beautiful essay, "Ghosts Chasing Ghosts: Pronghorn and the Long Shadow of Evolution," for the magazine I founded, *Ecotone*. Obviously, the rest of my writing on pronghorns leans heavily on Emilene Ostlind's wonderful article "The Perilous Journey of Wyoming's Migrating Pronghorn," which was published on December 26, 2011, in *High Country News*.

Dave Foreman's *Rewilding North America: A Vision for Conservation in the 21st Century* was my main source for the section on connectivity between parks. The sections about anticipating climate change and "pre-storing" habitat grew out of an article I wrote for the Environmental Defense Fund that included interviews with Sam Pearsall and other EDF scientists.

For the history of Yellowstone I read George Black's comprehensive *Empire of Shadows: The Epic Story of Yellowstone*.

Doug Peacock was the only person I encountered who wouldn't let me tape-record our conversation, so whenever one of us went to the bathroom I did a lot of furious scribbling in my journal. If you want a quick immersion course in all things Peacock, you can do worse than to watch a video from the classic TV series from the 1960s and '70s *The American Sportsman*. The episode chronicles a week that Peacock spent in the backcountry of Yellowstone looking for grizzly bears with none other than Arnold Schwarzenegger. This is a younger, more innocent Arnold, pre-superstardom and politics and scandal, fresh off his early *Pumping Iron* and *Conan* fame, and one of the pleasures of the clip is the odd-couple factor. There is Peacock in archetypal wild-man mode, spouting his radical enviro-philosophy—including some great lines about his goal of "preserving an element of risk in wilderness" by spending time around an animal that can kill humans—and there is Arnold, kind of stiff and silly at first, but gradually getting more and more into it. To add yet another surreal element to the video, you slowly notice that the show is being narrated by a voice you have known forever: Curt Gowdy's. Arnold and Doug see no bears, only tracks, on the first day, but that evening they stand in the smoke of the fire to disguise what Peacock calls their "foul human scent," after which Arnold says: "I hope the whole week is going to be as strange as the first night." The next day Peacock pontificates while Arnold trots behind, wearing a camo jacket and chewing gum. When they finally do see grizzlies, a sow and its yearling, Arnold's whole face lights up with a goofy enthusiasm and he begins to mutter things— in an accent you can likely imitate—like "This is fantastic" and "This is unbelievable, Doug." Peacock is clearly pleased, though he tries not to show it. In a way the not-yet Terminator perfectly embodies Peacock's main point: that we feel more alive when the threat of death is near.

This confluence of wildness and celebrity has few matches in our country's history, topped perhaps only by the three nights that another toothy political megastar, Teddy Roosevelt, spent camping in the Yosemite backcountry (while in office!) with that most arch of druids, John Muir. It reminds us of the truly wild streak that has always, until recently at least, been such a part of this country's character.

CHAPTER 11: GOING HOME AGAIN

Stegner's memories of Eastend, and his return there, are drawn primarily from his unpublished autobiography and *Wolf Willow*. My interview with Bryson LaBoissiere of Eastend was a great help in getting a local perspective.

The letter to the Grays that I quote from is in the Special Collections Department of the J. Willard Marriott Library at the University of Utah.

The trip that Philip Fradkin made to Eastend is reported near the end of his biography of Stegner, *Wallace Stegner and the American West*.

My summary of Abbey's trip back home with Dick Kirkpatrick comes from a telephone interview with Dick but also from James Cahalan's *Edward Abbey: A Life*. In fact, much of my knowledge of Home, Pennsylvania, and its environs comes from Cahalan, either in person or on his pages.

CHAPTER 12: TEACHERS

Lynn and Allison Stegner were kind enough to give me a tour of the Stanford campus and to drive me up to the home where the Stegners had lived for most of their lives, all the while sharing stories about the family.

For my impressions of Stegner as a teacher I drew on my interviews with Wendell Berry and Ed McClanahan, and for his teaching philosophy I focused on his book *On Teaching and Writing Fiction*. Some of the material on the tension Stegner felt between teaching and writing originally appeared in an essay I wrote, "Those Who Write, Teach," for the September 19, 2008, issue of the *New York Times Magazine*.

My interview with Steven Schwartz helped me get a sense of Abbey the teacher. I conducted a phone interview, and had a subsequent e-mail exchange, with the teacher and writer Dick Shelton, who recruited Abbey to teach at the University of Arizona.

The analysis of Stegner's evolving use of chronology comes from a close rereading of *All the Little Live Things, Wolf Willow, The Spectator Bird, Angle of Repose,* and *Crossing to Safety,* but also relies on Stegner's own analysis of DeVoto's writing in *The Uneasy Chair: A Biography of Bernard DeVoto.* To see DeVoto's own dazzling use of time and synecdoche, you can turn to his prize-winning and ground-breaking histories *Across the Wide Missouri, The Course of Empire* and *The Year of Decision: 1846.*

Stegner's correspondence with the family of Mary Hallock Foote can be found at the Special Collections Library at the University of Utah, as can his quotes about "the search for a usable past" and "Biography cannot reform the truth," both appearing in the small notebook mentioned in the text. For a much fuller discussion of the controversy surrounding *Angle of Repose,* see Philip Fradkin's *Wallace Stegner and the American West.*

The writer who responded to my queries about Abbey with "I'm not much into hero worship" was Gary Nabhan in a personal e-mail dated May 28, 2012.

Walter Jackson Bate, in his biography of Samuel Johnson, emphasizes the importance of material that can be "put to use." Once again, Bate's ideas about biography were formative for me and no doubt permeate this final chapter.

Stegner's comments on a "poisoner's prose" are taken from *On Teaching and Writing Fiction.*

I found Abbey's long journal quote about "early morning snow" in *Confessions of a Barbarian* and his "Zen bullshit" line in *Postcards from Ed: Dispatches and Salvos from an American Iconoclast,* both books edited by David Petersen.

My account of Abbey's death draws on interviews with Doug Peacock and Jack Loeffler, as well as Loeffler's written account in *Adventures with Ed* and Peacock's in *Walking It Off.* Doug Peacock read through an earlier draft of this scene and made corrections.

Wallace Stegner's final to-do list appears on page 420 of *Wallace Stegner: His Life and Work* by Jackson J. Benson, and was provided to Mr. Benson by Mary Stegner.

IMAGE CREDITS

Page 167: The Glen Canyon Dam. Photograph by David Gessner.

Page 171: Abbey in a characteristic pose. Photograph by Dick Kirkpatrick.

Page 210: The datura ceremony. Photograph by David Gessner.

Page 229: Wallace and Mary Stegner. Photograph by Jenna Calk, courtesy of *The Los Altos Town Crier.*

Page 250: Doug Peacock's doormat. Photograph by David Gessner.

Page 270: Stegner in the Los Altos hills near his home. Chuck Painter / Stanford News Service.

Page 283: Wallace Stegner in the 1960s. Jose Mercado / Stanford News Service.

Page 286: Edward Abbey in the desert in Southeast Utah. Photograph courtesy of Ed Marston and *High Country News.*

INDEX

Page numbers in *italics* refer to illustrations.
Page numbers starting at 299 refer to source notes.